Polish Detroit
and the
Kolasiński Affair

Fr. Dominik H. Kolasiński.
Courtesy of St. Albertus's Parish and Allan R. Treppa.

Polish Detroit
— and the —
Kolasiński Affair

Lawrence D. Orton, *Oakland University*

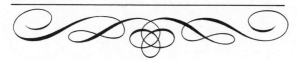

Wayne State University Press, Detroit, 1981

Library of Congress Cataloging in Publication Data
Orton, Lawrence D
   Polish Detroit and the Kolasiński affair.

   Bibliography: p.
   Includes index.
   1. Kolasiński, Dominic Hippolytus, 1838–1898.
2. Catholic Church—Clergy—Biography. 3. Clergy—
Michigan—Detroit—Biography. 4. Detroit—Biography.
5. Polish American—Michigan—Detroit—History—
19th century. I. Title
BX4705.K624077   282'.092'4 [B]   80–25290
ISBN 0–8143–1671–9

FOR MAGDA

CONTENTS

ILLUSTRATIONS

PREFACE

"A priest conscious of his charms" and "an unholy usurper" are but two of the epithets contemporaries used to describe the Reverend Dominik Kolasiński, whose turbulent career rocked Detroit and its Polish immigrant community in the last two decades of the nineteenth century. Perhaps no religious figure in Detroit, with the notable exception of Fr. Charles Coughlin, ever received more attention and notoriety in the local press than Kolasiński. His funeral in 1898 was said to be the largest ever seen in the city, with nearly 15 percent of the populace in attendance. Yet today few Detroiters, even Polish Detroiters, know anything of the immigrant Galician pastor from partitioned Poland and his activities. The meager literature on Polish Detroit is largely silent on this man, whom some later writers called a "flawed priest" who brought disrepute on himself and the Polish community.

Believing himself unjustly suspended as pastor of St. Albertus's Church, Father Kolasiński struggled for almost a decade, against seemingly insurmountable odds and the avowed opposition of two Detroit bishops, to attain vindication and reinstatement as a priest in the diocese of Detroit. The 1880s and 1890s were years of almost constant turmoil in the Polish community, and the figure of Father Kolasiński, even during a two-and-a-half-year period of ecclesiastical banishment from the city, loomed over Detroit's east-side Polish neighborhood. Father Kolasiński not only was directly responsible for the creation of the city's two most magnificent Polish churches, but also—and more importantly—he instilled confidence in peasant immigrants bewildered by life in urban Detroit. In return, they idolized him.

Although Kolasiński is of course the focus of this study, I have tried as well to provide a broad portrait of the beginnings, expansion, and consolidation of Detroit's Polish community in the late nineteenth century. Particular attention is paid to the perceptions and attitudes of native Detroiters toward the immigrants' ways. The opening chapter traces the beginning of Polish settlement in Detroit and Kolasiński's three-and-a-half-year pastorate at St. Albertus's before the crisis erupted. Chapters 2 through 5 provide a narrative of the so-called Kolasiński Affair from the priest's suspension in November 1885 to his death in April 1898. The concluding chapter draws together material that does not bear directly on Kolasiński, but that is necessary to understanding the nature and growth of the city's Polish community. Here the reader will find a discussion of living and working conditions among the immigrants. Special attention is devoted to the impact of economic depression on the mostly unskilled Polish laborers and their involvement in labor clashes, notably the celebrated Connor's Creek incident of April 1894. Also depicted are the immigrants' involvement in the city's political life and the institutions they formed to enhance their mutual well-being and which ultimately facilitated their adjustment to a new life in the city of the strait.

I am grateful to Professor Jerzy W. Borejsza of Warsaw, Poland, who first suggested that I explore the history of Detroit's Polish community. Little did I realize then the excitement and fascination his proposal would bring me. I wish also to thank Professor Stanislaus A. Blejwas of New Britain, Connecticut, for his friendly encouragement and advice. My greatest debt is to the late Marian Wilson, editorial assistant to the College of Arts and Sciences, Oakland University, who died as this book went to press. Her friendship and support have meant very much to me.

This book is dedicated to my wife.

CHAPTER 1
THE BEGINNINGS OF
DETROIT'S POLISH COMMUNITY

Popular legend attributes the starting point of a Polish community on Detroit's near east side to the arrival in the city in 1859 of Jan Lemke, accompanied by his wife, three sons, sister-in-law, and two cousins. The Lemkes were headed for Milwaukee but, according to one of the first chroniclers of Polish settlement in America, Fr. Wacław Kruszka, were persuaded to remain in Detroit by a Jew who "promised them [that] mountains of gold" could be made in the city of the strait. This same Jew, Kruszka continues, "told them also about the Poles already settled in Detroit; he indicated the street they lived on, and the whole Lemke family set out in search of them. On Clinton Street, between Hastings and Antoine, they met a stranger whom they asked in German where the Poles lived. The stranger asked why they wanted to know, and when they told him that they too were Poles, his joy was boundless." The stranger whom the Lemkes had encountered by chance was Jakób Mindak, who had come to Detroit from Bydgoszcz (Bromberg) in Prussian Poland a year earlier with his brother-in-law Franciszek Melin to join Melin's cousin Stanisław, who had arrived in August 1857. Mindak took the newcomers to the "abode" he shared with the Melins. All three men were tailors, which happened to be Jan Lemke's trade. The Polish bachelors quickly took a fancy to Mrs. Lemke's sister, Augusta Rohr. Stanisław Melin won her favor, and they were married in September 1860.[1]

This small group, the nucleus of what in the next decade would become an expanding Polish neighborhood, had emigrated from Prussian-held former Polish territories. The Melins, like Mindak, were natives of the province of Poznania; Jan Lemke's hometown was Berent (Kościerzyna), in the region of Pomerelia or West Prussia, about thirty miles southwest of Gdańsk (Danzig). It has been suggested that the Melins (and possibly Mindak and the Lemkes) were not Poles per se but Kashubs, a closely related Slavic ethnic group. The language of the Kashubs, who were concentrated in the left bank region of the lower Vistula River, remains a matter of dispute among linguists. Some regard it as a Polish dialect; others consider it a separate West Slavic language. In the decade after 1848, in a concerted attempt to settle German colonists on ancient Kashubian soil, the Maritime Navigation Company of Hamburg had been offering free passage to America to Kashubs who would sell their land to the company.[2]

The first Poles and Kashubs to settle in Detroit from Prussian-ruled lands generally arrived with a modest capital acquired from the sale of their property in the old country, which they used to build homes.[3] And although many were from rural areas, they had a rudimentary education and had often learned a trade in addition to farming. Lemke, with a German partner, continued his trade as a tailor in Detroit. He bought a "neat new cottage" on Antoine Street, close to St. Mary's Church, because, it was said, "no Pole would care to live where he could not see the spire of the church, or at least hear the Angelus." In the 1870s, after the Poles had established their own parish, he bought property near their church, where he built a grocery store to which he eventually added hardware. The store prospered and Lemke was able to invest in real estate, buying unimproved land which he subdivided and sold to later Polish immigrants. By the end of the nineteenth century he owned four stores, which his sons operated.[4] For several years after his marriage to Augusta Rohr, Stanisław Melin worked in the Wyandotte iron mills. Later he returned to Detroit, where he too acquired considerable wealth and raised a family of twelve children.[5]

The Prussian Polish immigrants of the late 1850s and the 1860s were not the first Poles in Detroit, but they did represent the first who came primarily for economic betterment and who eventually united to establish a cohesive ethnic community. Their settling in Detroit had postdated by only a few years the establishment of the earliest permanent Polish settlement in America in 1854 in Panna Maria, Texas (named for the Virgin Mary, so revered in Polish religious tradition), by a sizable group of Polish farmers from Prussian Silesia. Other settlements were founded in the upper Midwestern states—one in Polonia, Wisconsin, in 1856, and another a year later which was called Paris (later Parisville) in the so-called thumb region of Huron County, Michigan.

The midcentury Polish immigrants differed in several ways from the adventurers and stateless Polish soldiers who had found their way to America since the seventeenth century. The latter, usually men of education and gentry status, had come as individuals to offer their military skills to the new republic. Such names as Tadeusz Kościuszko and Kazimierz Pułaski immediately come to mind. With the defeat in 1831 of the Polish insurrection against tsarist Russian domination, tens of thousands of Poles departed from their homeland, especially for political exile in France and England. A small number—only a few hundred—had come to America.

The first Polish settler in Detroit about whom we possess at least a little information was Andrzej Kamiński, one of the hapless veterans of the abortive November 1830 uprising in Russian Poland. (The registers of St. Anne's Church, the city's oldest Catholic parish, reveal names dating as far back as 1762 which might be Polish, but there is no additional information about them.)[6] Kamiński arrived in New York on 15 April 1837, aboard the *Talisman* from the Austrian-held Adriatic port of Trieste. Though several of his companions—fellow Polish exiles and veterans of the 1830–31 war—enlisted immediately in the United States army, Kamiński tried his fortune in the new country for two years before joining the army in Albany on 6 May 1839. His enlistment papers recorded his birthplace as "Cracow, Poland," and gave his age as forty, although he was certainly much younger. Five years later to the day, Kamiński was discharged at the Detroit military barracks.[7] He decided to remain in Detroit, and in 1845, perhaps with money saved from his military service, he purchased several lots on Mullett and Hastings streets. On 13 July 1846 he married Christine Gibels in St. Mary's Church, where two years later the baptismal register notes the christening of their twin sons, Andrew and Stephen. Meantime, Kamiński had become a United States citizen. Despite having a family, when war came with Mexico he reenlisted and fought in Mexico under the command of Col. Andrew T. McReynolds of Detroit. Kamiński survived the rigors of that conflict, and a decade later when the Civil War broke out he enlisted in the Union army.[8]

Even less is known of other early settlers. Another veteran of the 1830 uprising was Filip Jasnowski. He arrived in Detroit around

The original St. Albertus's Church as it appeared in Missye Katolickie, *August 1884. Courtesy of Jagiellonian University, Kraków.*

Fr. Kazimierz Gutowski.
Reproduced by permission from the
Detroit Free Press, *20 November 1893.*

Fr. Józef Dąbrowski.
Courtesy of the Archives of the
Orchard Lake Schools.

Architect's sketch for the new St. Albertus's Church as it appeared in
Missye Katolickie, *August 1884. Courtesy of Jagiellonian University, Kraków.*

1849 with his wife and two sons, after spending eighteen years as an exile in England. A recruiting agent in England had very likely signed up Jasnowski for the Michigan Central Railway, for whom he worked as a carpenter in the company's west-side shop until his death in 1860.[9] In the 1850s two Polish priests, Frs. Julian Maciejewski and Leopold Pawłowski, were received into the diocese of Detroit. Although they were assigned by Acting Bishop Peter Paul Lefevere to mostly German parishes outside the city proper, it is probable that on visits to Detroit they came into contact with its handful of Polish inhabitants.[10] One other early Polish settler to the Detroit area on whom some information has survived is Antoni Leszczyński. He came around 1850 and later acquired a farm in Wyandotte. While a student he had fought in Galicia in the revolution of 1848–49 against the Austrians. After the revolution was suppressed, he and other Polish volunteers escaped from Hungary in 1849 and reached Constantinople. Leszczyński's companions, dreaming of a new day to fight for Poland's liberation, decided to remain in Constantinople, but he elected to try his fortune in America. In Wyandotte he was instrumental in organizing the Polish settlers in the St. Stanisław Society. In 1876, while battling a fire on his property, he died of smoke inhalation.[11]

During the 1860s Polish immigration to Detroit—almost exclusively at this time from Prussian Poland—mounted steadily. By 1870 there were close to three hundred families. The Prussian Poles, most of whom understood and spoke German, clustered in or near the east-side German neighborhood which was expanding along Gratiot Avenue toward Mt. Elliott, then Detroit's eastern boundary. They worshiped in the area's two German Catholic churches: St. Mary's (at Antoine and Croghan streets), built in 1843; and especially St. Joseph's (on Gratiot between Riopelle and Orleans streets), established in 1856.[12] The pace of German immigration to the city had not abated (though it would after 1870), and plans were made to build a new and larger St. Joseph's Church. Father Kruszka has alleged that when the Polish parishioners offered to help in the project the Germans informed them that "their pews in the new church would have to stand apart." Only then, according to Kruszka, did the Poles begin to think of building their own church.[13]

The story is probably apocryphal, the result of the deep-rooted mistrust of Germans growing out of the Germans' anti-Polish policies in Poznania. Besides, there is evidence that the Detroit Poles had already been thinking of starting their own parish. Early in 1870 Fr. Szymon Wieczorek, who had charge of the Polish congregation in outstate Parisville, had begun to visit the Detroit Poles and occasionally conducted services in St. Joseph's Church. Realizing that the expanding Detroit community was overtaking his rural parish in size, he probably encouraged a group of Poles who had already formed a lay St. Stanisław Kostka Society to petition the new bishop of Detroit, Caspar H. Borgess, for permission to organize a parish of their own.[14]

Wieczorek had come to minister to the Parisville Poles in 1868, at the invitation of Acting Bishop Lefevere. Founded in 1857 by Silesian and Poznanian Polish immigrant farmers, the rural community had grown to 127 families when Wieczorek took over the mission. Born in 1834 in Russian Poland, Wieczorek had seen his seminary and theological studies interrupted by renewed insurrection against tsarist rule in January 1863. After a brief imprisonment, he was allowed to leave Poland and finally was ordained in Rome in May 1868 at age thirty-four. The new pastor belonged to the missionary Resurrectionist order (Congregation of the Resurrection of Our Lord Jesus Christ [C.R.]), originally founded in France by Polish exiles. Later the order attracted French, German, and Italian priests as well. One of the founders, Hieronim Kajsiewicz, was general superior of the order and had made the arrangements with Bishop Lefevere, who paid the cost of the ocean voyage for Wieczorek and Fr. Jan Wołłowski. Wieczorek's pastorate in Parisville abruptly ended in October 1871, when a fire that raged across Huron County destroyed the church and the homes and crops of most of the Polish immigrants.[15]

Shortly before the tragic fire, Bishop Borgess, after temporizing for almost a year, granted the Detroit Poles' request for a parish of their own and requested Wieczorek to oversee the project. One factor that influenced his decision was the assurance from General Superior Kajsiewicz that two additional Resurrectionist priests would be sent to guide the new parish. Then a few weeks later Parisville burned, the settlers became scattered, and Wieczorek moved to Detroit. Not long after, Borgess gave him formal charge of the new parish.[16]

Probably at Wieczorek's suggestion, the new parish chose Saint Adalbert (Św. Wojciech) for its patron saint. This Bohemian-born, late-tenth-century missionary to Poland perished at the hands of pagan Prussian warriors near Gdańsk. His martyred remains were enshrined in Gniezno and, since much of his missionary work took place near Poznań, he was particularly revered by the Prussian Poles and Kashubs. For some reason, the English and Latin versions of the saint's name were recorded in the Detroit press and by Bishop Borgess as "Albert" or "Albertus." Actually, Albertus was an entirely different saint. To this day the error has not been corrected; the parish is known in English usage as St. Albertus and to the Poles as Św. Wojciech (or colloquially as "Wojciechowo").[17]

In granting his permission to the Poles to begin collecting funds to establish their parish, Borgess warned them not to exceed their resources. With some initial money on hand, a committee of four men—Jan Lemke, Jan Kołodziejczyk, Antoni Treppa, and Antoni Ostrowski—purchased a lot near the southwestern corner of Fremont (later Canfield) and St. Aubin, which had been part of the old French St. Aubin farm. The purchase price of $600 was paid to the owner, Phillis Beaubien, and the deed was executed in the name of Bishop Borgess (as was customary in recording diocesan property); the transaction was completed on 9 November 1871. The site chosen for the church building was on the northeastern fringe of the Polish neighborhood, but within a decade the Polish settlement would naturally concentrate more and more in the area immediately around and to the west of the church.[18] A month earlier a building contract had been concluded between the architect John Wiesenhoefer and the committee. The contract called for the construction of two frame buildings, a rectory and the church proper. The latter would be 130 feet long, 54 feet wide, and 30 feet high, with the bell tower reaching to 165 feet. Construction was to be completed by 15 June 1872. The congregation agreed to pay $8,860 in four equal installments. Father Wieczorek's surviving correspondence of 1872 indicates his satisfaction with the progress on the church and his missionary work with the Polish community. His greatest need, as he repeatedly emphasized, was for an assistant (as Father Kajsiewicz had promised Bishop Borgess) to work in the outlying Polish settlements, which would free the pastor to devote his full energy to the new parish.[19]

Notwithstanding delays, including a violent windstorm that destroyed the initial framework, the church was completed on schedule. The committee, however, withheld the last payment until some repairs were made, in particular to the laying of the roof. But these were minor matters. On 14 July 1872, the bishop and congregation proceeded with the formal dedication of St. Albertus's Church. Representatives of citywide Catholic lay and religious organizations—especially German—attended the opening of the thirteenth edifice of Catholic worship in Detroit. Two Polish Resurrectionist priests from the Chicago diocese took part in the ceremonies and remained briefly in the parish to conduct a mission.

Borgess preached a sermon in English in which he congratulated the parishioners for their hard work and sacrifice in making the church possible.[20]

Father Bakanowski, one of the Resurrectionists, noted that in private conversations the bishop reiterated his warning to the pastor that the parish must live within its own financial means. Bakanowski was already under the impression that the bishop was not satisfied with Wieczorek's handling of the new parish and intended to replace him at an opportune moment.[21] Within four months of the dedication, as a consequence of the unresolved dispute between the building committee and the architect, Bishop Borgess translated his warnings into a threat of severe sanctions against the congregation and its pastor for what he called financial recklessness and mismanagement. In November 1872 Wiesenhoefer had filed suit for nonfulfillment of contract. The parish refused to release the final installment of $2,096.63 on the grounds of shoddy workmanship and failure to make necessary repairs. The bishop's response to the court action was a stern rebuke to Father Wieczorek and the congregation without bothering to hear their side of the dispute. The bishop's letter to Wieczorek, dated 24 November 1872, closed with a threat.

> If therefore the committee and the whole community does not make any effort to avoid the court procedure and to pay the debts, and thus fulfill the promises given me, I shall be forced to punish all proportionately. Therefore, I ask you Rev. Father, to inform the committee and the community that if after two weeks the judicial procedure has not been revoked, and the matter has not been settled with the architect, that is, on the 8th of December, 1872, St. Albertus Church will be under interdict, and the community under excommunication, and your jurisdiction for the community will be revoked on that day.[22]

The bishop's threats were enough for this time. The parish obtained a loan to pay the final installment, and the architect put up a bond in that amount until the repairs were made. Not content, the bishop responded with another warning on 11 December, repeating his threat of sanctions if the parish failed again to heed his fiscal guidelines and caused him and the diocese further "inconvenience." He demanded that the parish liquidate all outstanding indebtedness before undertaking any new contractual obligation. All future undertakings would have to be cleared in advance, in writing, by the bishop.[23]

Despite the warnings, a few weeks after the dispute with the architect was settled, Wieczorek submitted to the bishop a petition, signed by 131 parishioners, requesting permission to erect a parish school. The bishop approved the idea in general but reiterated his demand that the parish be debt free at the outset and that a statement be submitted to him, before any contracts were signed, detailing all new financial obligations necessary for building the school. Until now the parish had been making do with a makeshift school in a house owned by Jan Lemke. Both pastor and congregation were strongly set on having a permanent school. Acting on the bishop's conditional permission, but paying little heed to his strictures, three parish trustees—Jan Lemke, Jakób Mindak, and Antoni Ostrowski —on 11 January 1873 bought from a Mary Moran another lot of the St. Aubin farm, located just north of the church at the southwest corner of St. Aubin and Fremont. The transaction stipulated a deadline for securing a mortgage and allowed for the outright return of the property to its original owner if the buyers failed to meet all obligations. The trustees submitted the real estate papers to the bishop and began contracting for the construction of the school. But once the bishop's attorney examined the land sale and discovered the indenture on the property, the bishop immediately ordered a halt to construction. In line with his orders that all old debts were to be retired before new obligations were undertaken, he demanded clear title to the land before building on it commenced. The parishioners, however, chose to ignore, or perhaps misunderstood, this latest episcopal directive, and the construction of the school continued.[24]

Then, on 6 June 1873, upon learning that Mary Moran was going to foreclose on the property the next day, the parish having failed to meet its obligation, Borgess made good his threats and directed that "insomuch as the Rev. Pastor, as well as the Church Committee, have shown an unpardonable disobedience, we declare herewith that St. Albertus Church in Detroit is closed for every Catholic divine service of any kind, and that every and all jurisdiction in this diocese has been taken away from the Rev. Simon Wieczorek."[25] This order of interdict and the summary dismissal of the pastor was only the first such action that the bishop would take against the city's first Polish parish. In fairness to the parish committee, it should be noted that the wave of bank failures in early 1873 had had an immediate depressing effect on economic conditions in the city, thereby hampering the committee's efforts to acquire a mortgage on the school property.[26]

After leaving Detroit, the founding pastor of St. Albertus's

Church continued to minister for twenty-eight years, mostly to Polish parishes in Ohio, Illinois, and Wisconsin, before his death in 1901. On at least two occasions Wieczorek returned to Detroit, first to take part in the opening of a Polish seminary in 1886, and later for the silver jubilee of St. Albertus's in 1897. The three pastors who followed Father Wieczorek at St. Albertus's Church in the next decade have been characterized by Fr. Joseph Swastek as "pastors in passage." Although their tenures did coincide with significant expansion and change in the growing Polish community, in retrospect their ministries have been overshadowed by the more colorful priests who preceded and followed them.[27]

The parish remained without a pastor for over three months and the church presumably was under interdict. But Bishop Borgess relented after the congregation sent him a contrite plea for forgiveness, explaining that they had been led into error by their former pastor. The bishop allowed two priests from nearby St. Joseph's Church to hold occasional services at St. Albertus's until a new pastor could be found. On 24 September 1873 the bishop appointed Fr. Teodor Gieryk, who had been in the United States about one year, to take charge of the troubled east-side parish. The new pastor, aged thirty-five when he arrived in Detroit, came from Prussian Poland and had been a chaplain in the Prussian army during the 1870–71 war with France.[28]

Although he managed to bring fiscal stability and to reestablish calm in the parish, Father Gieryk's pastorate lasted but a year and a half. Work on the school was allowed to resume, and with its opening in early 1874 the parish drew new members, especially among the Kashubs, many of whom had continued to worship at the neighboring St. Joseph's German parish. Early in his tenure at St. Albertus's, however, it became evident that Gieryk's overriding concern was to establish a countrywide umbrella organization to unite and work for the betterment of all Polish Catholics in America. In late 1873 he convened in Detroit the founding gathering of the Union of Polish Catholics. In Chicago a year later, at its first convention, Gieryk was chosen first president of the new organization, renamed the Polish Roman Catholic Union of America (PRCU). Accompanying him to Chicago were two of Polish Detroit's prominent pioneers, Jan Lemke and Julian Piotrowski. In order to publicize the views of the new organization, Gieryk, aided by a young journalist named Jan Barzyński, brought the Polish Resurrectionist newspaper *Pielgrzym* [Pilgrim] from Union, Missouri. Renamed *Gazeta Polska Katolicka* [Polish Catholic gazette], it became Detroit's first Polish paper, which was published weekly in Piotrowski's book-shop.[29]

Father Gieryk's efforts to organize the Poles nationally soon became a subject of concern to Bishop Borgess. In general, he preferred the priests of his diocese to confine themselves to orderly pastoral duties; besides, he had little understanding of the particular interests of Polish Catholics in America. Kruszka, though, perhaps exaggerates when he writes that Gieryk's national organization plan was "salt in the eye of Bishop Borgess," who now began to look for a justification to remove the pastor.[30] It is equally probable that Gieryk realized that he could not properly fulfill his pastoral duties and at the same time devote the necessary time and energy to the affairs of the new organization. In any case, voluntarily or not, Gieryk submitted his resignation in January 1875 and, after giving the bishop time to find a replacement, left for Chicago in April, taking with him the organization's Polish newspaper. In Chicago, however, perhaps because of intrigue or jealousy, Gieryk failed to gain formal admittance to the diocese, and in June 1875 was replaced as president of the PRCU. For the remaining three years of his life he ministered to small Polish parishes in rural Illinois and Wisconsin. For many years he was forgotten by the organization created largely by his efforts; only in 1937 did the PRCU officially recognize him as its founder. In recent years his remains have been transferred to the Polish-American shrine of Częstochowa in Doylestown, Pennsylvania.[31] The PRCU never flourished in nineteenth-century Detroit, which instead became a stronghold of the rival Polish National Alliance.

Little is known of the background of Gieryk's successor, who was a Franciscan. Fr. Alfons Dombrowski used the anglicized spelling of his name in preference to the Polish "Dąbrowski." He occasionally added a "von" before his surname and corresponded with Bishop Borgess in fluent German, which has led Swastek to speculate that "perhaps he was a Germanised Pole to whom the Polish heritage was secondary."[32] But whatever his national predilection, Dombrowski displayed considerable disdain for what he perceived to be the unhealthy moral condition of his Polish parish. Writing on his own initiative to Borgess several months after taking charge of St. Albertus's, Dombrowski described his congregation as "pious but superficially religious and inadequately cared for by former pastors, predominantly of working class background, rude, hypercritical, quarrelsome, disunited, and dissatisfied." Especially annoying was the congregation's desire, through its elected trustees, "to control the administration of parish properties and finances." No less troublesome for Father Dombrowski was his parishioners' propensity to burden their pastor "with their property and business problems," which they expected him to resolve. He was also expected to be "ultra Polish" and to fraternize, even to the extent of "drinking beer" with the laity. In concluding his report, he wrote: "I have good will toward the Poles, but I do not go blindly with them; I cannot procede [sic] without questioning their aims and plans. My ministry has resulted in some unpleasantness, but I cannot act against my principles."[33]

But as Dombrowski's pastorate wore on, the parishioners as well as the bishop came to discover an even more "unhealthy moral condition" in the pastor than he had discerned in the congregation. In 1879 complaints against the priest reached the bishop with mounting frequency. He was accused of denying confession and communion to impoverished members who had failed to pay their parish dues and of "drinking and playing cards" on Sunday evenings in public places.[34] Worse, on 8 September the *Evening News* disclosed a far more serious charge. It reported that an irate Pole had awakened Circuit Court Commissioner J. A. Randall in the middle of the night to press charges against Dombrowski for seducing his wife and being the father of her recently born child. Not only had the couple been married only six months, but just prior to the marriage the woman, identified as Jula Kuhla, had worked as a domestic in the priest's house. Kuhla swore out a warrant against Dombrowski, but when the priest agreed to pay $1,100 in damages, Kuhla dropped the suit. The scandal prompted Borgess to summon the accused priest to the episcopal residence the next day, 9 September. After a "summary trial" that apparently satisfied the bishop that the charges were based on fact, he removed Dombrowski as pastor of St. Albertus's Church. This was only the first of Dombrowski's troubles. When he failed to vacate the rectory immediately, a mob of Poles besieged him there on the evening of 10 September and attempted to evict him by force. The priest took refuge at a friend's house and, angered by the threat to his person, swore out a complaint against three of the trustees, whom he accused of being the ringleaders. Dombrowski remained in Detroit for several weeks and reportedly tried to bribe Mrs. Kuhla to sign a paper (in English, which she could not read) absolving him of the paternity claim. The ruse failed, and the unfortunate "von" Dombrowski left the city and, it is assumed, the priesthood as well.[35]

Father Dombrowski's four-year tenure at St. Albertus's coincided with the rapid recovery from the economic panic of 1873. The parish prospered, increasing between 1873 and 1879 from about five hundred to seven hundred and fifty families. During these years, the *Detroit Free Press* frequently noted in its front-page city chronicle the arrival in the city of contingents of Polish immigrants, who usually came in groups of several families, probably from a single town or band of neighboring villages. In March 1873 it reported that "within the next month it is expected that fifty Poles will arrive to increase the settlement on Russell street"; in December 1874 that "twenty-five Polish families, numbering about one hundred persons, arrived . . . yesterday morning and took up quarters in the Polish settlement"; and in March 1875 that "fifteen Polish families arrived . . . yesterday, direct from Poland. They were received at the depot by some of their countrymen here."[36] The newspaper found the newcomers among the "most frugal of any [nationality] which is thrown upon our shores by the tide of emigration." This was conspicuously evident in the Poles' predilection for keeping hogs and planting vegetable gardens on their small lots. The most popularly cultivated crop seemed to be string beans.[37] The city into which these immigrants were settling was described in 1876 in a report for a Warsaw newspaper by a Polish visitor (soon to become a celebrated novelist), Henryk Sienkiewicz, as "an enormous city, exceptionally clean and more attractive than any I had thus far seen in America."[38]

In 1877, midway in Dombrowski's pastorate, the parish received its first assistant priest, Fr. Jan Wołłowski, the Resurrectionist who had accompanied Father Wieczorek to the Parisville mission nine years earlier. Unfortunately, Wołłowski had a serious handicap which had limited his pastoral effectiveness among the sensitive Polish immigrants. While serving as a chaplain with the Polish insurrectionaries in 1863, he had lost his right arm. Most of his missions in America had been brief, and at one point he had returned to Europe. With the dismissal of Dombrowski, however, the bishop elevated the assistant of two years to the St. Albertus's pastorate. Even for a physically sound priest, care of the rapidly growing and still troubled parish would have been difficult. Though the bishop did not provide a new assistant, Wołłowski sought aid on his own within the diocese, often from the Czech Fr. Václav Tilek, who lived nearby. But among the parishioners the rumor persisted that Wołłowski, because of his disability, was not able to celebrate mass properly. Whatever his physical limitation, however, Wołłowski, unlike his predecessor, was never faulted for not being "ultra Polish," and during his pastorate he fostered numerous Polish religious traditions, notably the *pasterka*, or Christmas Eve midnight mass.[39]

In addition to recognizing the feelings of those parishioners who could not fully accept a handicapped priest, Bishop Borgess realized that the parish required a physically active leader who could command the entire respect of his large congregation and endure the physical strain of counseling so many of them.[40] When one parishioner wrote to Austrian Poland for a suitable replacement for Father Wołłowski, Borgess requested supporting testimony from the Kraków archdiocese. Apparently satisfied by what he learned, he invited Fr. Dominik Kolasiński to assume the pastoral duties at St. Albertus's. The initiative in proposing Kolasiński's candidacy may first have come from Józef Przybyłowski. It is known that Przybyłowski knew the Galician priest personally and urged his friend to accept the bishop's offer.[41] On 30 March 1882 Borgess wrote to Wołłowski: "This morning Rev. Dominic Kolasinski arrived here from Europe, and has been adopted. This enables us to relieve you of the pastoral charge of St. Albert's temporarily given you on the 20th of September 1879 which we hereby recall. . . . If you would wish it and it will be agreeable to you, you remain at St. Albert's for the present as the Rev. assistant." A disappointed and disheartened Father Wołłowski chose to leave Detroit.[42]

At age forty-three, the new pastor was at the peak of his pastoral powers when he arrived in Detroit. He had been born in the Galician town of Mielec on 13 August 1838, the oldest of four sons of a weaver.[43] Kolasiński's life prior to his coming to Detroit is shrouded in considerable uncertainty and controversy, especially since extravagant claims, such as his being of noble background, were frequently aired in the Detroit newspapers once he had become the object of intense public curiosity. Following his ordination in 1864, he served in various western Galician parishes before being appointed assistant pastor in 1875 in the town of Czernichów, near Kraków. There, according to Eduard A. Skendzel, who has investigated this early phase of Kolasiński's career, his behavior got him into "various difficulties," when "complaints" against him were lodged with the church authorities in Kraków. He was reassigned in 1879 to the neighboring village of Rybna, where seemingly these unidentified troubles pursued him. Thereupon, in late 1879, he requested and was granted a leave from pastoral duties to study philosophy in Vienna, but ended up instead at the university in Lwów (Lemberg). A canonical hearing of the allegations against him apparently was never held. To support himself Kolasiński worked as a chaplain and also hired out as a tutor for the children of a wealthy Galician nobleman.

Already by 1880, Kolasiński, to find a way out of his various ecclesiastical and financial difficulties, began to explore the possibility of obtaining a missionary post in America. On the basis of Bishop Borgess's invitation, he was granted an exeat (a form of priestly laissez-passer which enables a priest to leave one diocese and enter another) from the Kraków archdiocese to minister to the Polish immigrants in Detroit. Dated 22 January 1882, it stated:

> We dismiss you, the Reverend D. Kolasinski, a priest of our diocese to the Diocese of Detroit, with God's blessings, and we declare you to be free of all spiritual connection with us, testifying that you are not bound in our Curia by any censures, nor, as far as we know, held by any other canonical impediments.[44]

Later, when charges of malfeasance by Kolasiński would prompt Borgess to make further inquiry of the Kraków chancery, Archbishop Albin Dunajewski of Kraków confirmed that he had provided Kolasiński with these dismissal letters.[45]

Not long after he arrived in Detroit, the *Evening News* described the new Polish pastor as "a polished gentleman."

> His full ruddy features are well rounded. His hair of light auburn tinge rises from a forehead in curls. His light gray eyes are quick and active, and his lips seeming ever ready to part in a smile which breaks into dimples on either cheek. Brumel [George Bryan "Beau" Brummell?] would stop to admire his splendid white teeth. His manner is hardy and vigorous like his appearance, and his action is full of attitude and gestures which would be applauded in an actor. He dresses with the care and elegance of a man who is conscious of his charms and intends that they should be noted and admired.[46]

The new pastor certainly seemed to possess the commanding presence and energy that the bishop and many of the parishioners had found wanting in Father Wołłowski. By all accounts Kolasiński's early contacts with Bishop Borgess were cordial, and the same appeared to be so with his colleagues. He was affable, immediately popular with his congregation, and well received as a representative of the rapidly growing Polish community which, according to reports submitted for 1882 to the diocesan chancery, had risen to almost twelve hundred families. The times were good economically.

The American Car and Foundry Company, which had opened a couple of years earlier, was employing a large number of Poles, and Detroit-manufactured stoves were acquiring an international reputation.[47]

A good example of the new pastor's success among the Poles was his organization of a splendid public observance of the two-hundredth anniversary of the Battle of Vienna, at which Polish forces commanded by King Jan Sobieski routed the Turks and removed the Moslem threat to Christian Central Europe, initiating the decline from which the Ottoman empire never recovered. The English-language press described the events of 12 September 1883 as "the first celebration of its kind that has ever been held in Detroit by the Poles, . . . [and] the largest and most interesting in a historical sense ever seen in Detroit in which a single race has participated." The parade was complete with bands, floats, horsemen, carriages, and thousands of marchers. The climax of the day was a high mass celebrated by Father Kolasiński, in which an estimated fifteen thousand persons took part.[48]

Sometime after arriving in Detroit, Kolasiński began sending reports of his activities to the Kraków monthly *Missye Katolickie* [Catholic missions]. Whether it was the pastor's belief that these reports would induce the growing number of emigrants, largely peasants, to settle in Detroit is not known. The reports were likely read by some Galician priests to their rural parishioners and may have influenced their choice of destination.[49] To be sure, the newly arriving Galicians, or Austrian Poles, became Kolasiński's most ardent admirers, but the priest's reports to Poland are in many ways more interesting for what they reveal about the man himself. In his first letter, dated 14 March 1883—that is, almost a year after his arrival—Kolasiński described in colorful and melodramatic terms his harrowing voyage from Bremerhaven to New York. The ship, fittingly named the *Habsburg*, was constantly buffeted by storms, which delayed the crossing by six days. "Debarking on American soil, the first thing we did was to take ourselves to the nearest Irish church, not far from the docks, and thank God for our salvation." Kolasiński stayed thirty-six hours in New York, where he was deeply impressed by the number of inhabitants and their incessant movement, as well as by the city's partially constructed massive cathedral. He also gave his readers a glowing description of Niagara Falls as seen from his train.[50]

Another year passed before Kolasiński sent the follow-up report that he had promised would describe the Polish community in

Detroit. With scant concern for factual accuracy but displaying his ability to dramatize and embellish, he traced the history of Polish settlement in Detroit as the story of a people's determination, against great odds, to hold to their native traditions, build their own place of worship, and prosper in a strange land. Kolasiński attributed their achievements to their intense religious faith, "even more than at home," and to the immigrants' deep attachment to Polish traditions.

> Not comprehending English and unschooled in American customs and ways, they feel somewhat estranged in American churches and, therefore, they desire nothing more earnestly for themselves than their own church, in which the pastor could address them in their own tongue, in which they could sing the songs of their homeland, and in their own way take comfort from the Holy faith. No difficulties, no sacrifices are too great, where the gratification of this so natural and so important heartfelt need is involved.[51]

As we shall see, few immigrant pastors ever succeeded so well in filling these spiritual and emotional needs, particularly among the largely unsophisticated, village-oriented Polish congregations in nineteenth-century America. And in America Kolasiński commanded greater respect and devotion and exerted more influence over his parishioners than could have been possible in their homeland, where the local priest had to compete with the nobility and governmental officials in exercising authority over the peasant masses.

Because of the rapid growth of the east-side Polish community, and especially in the wake of the considerable attention given to the anniversary celebration of the defense of Vienna, native Detroiters began to show more interest in what the press was now terming "the Polack Quarter." In November 1883 the *Evening News* ran an article under that title, the first extensive description of the Polish community to appear in the city's English-language press.[52] The author found some Polish ways eccentric and incomprehensible by American standards, but he paid tribute to the immigrants' hard work and thrift. The article was a unique portrayal of the Polish community at the beginning of Kolasiński's pastorate. After noting that there were "over 20,000" Poles or persons of Polish descent in Detroit and neighboring Springwells (15,000 would be more accurate), the author began by describing these "curious people."

The Polanders are gregarious in their instincts, and when they settled down in such numbers in this neighborhood they merely obeyed a law of their nature which teaches them to herd together. It is not that this section of the city offers any special inducement to the Polish immigrant. Chance threw there some of his countrymen, and this fact drew the rest with the magnetic power affinities attract one another. At any rate, here they are, and here they live and retain their native customs to such an extent that the whole region more nearly resembles a fraction of Poland than part of a city in the heart of America.

The writer dealt with the puzzle to native Americans of the Poles' ability to become property owners so quickly.

How the Pole who comes here but a trifle above the degree of a pauper, rears a large family, and yet in a few years becomes the owner of a house and lot, is a matter of perpetual mystification. . . . A surface investigation alone would satisfy the average American that the Pole's rise from penury to independence is no mystery at all, but the legitimate fruit of a system of living which the American could not be induced to undergo at any price whatever.

What then constituted this Polish "system of living" that the typical American could not endure? First was the Pole's willingness to take any form of work, since he had been inured to dreary toil all his life.

He will, upon arrival here, work early and late for whatever wages he can get. . . . He will not only work and exercise a stern self-denial himself, but he exacts a maximum of labor from each individual member of his household, and compels them to measure their wants by his own standard of requirements. . . . The children of tender years even are not exempt from their share of toil. They are scarcely free from swaddling bands before they are compelled to contribute their moiety to the family sustenance. The supply of household fuel is dependent upon the labor of these infant gleaners, and so keen becomes their scent for refuse wood that the first blow of a hammer engaged in the destruction of a building is a tocsin which never fails to rally a small army of Polish children to the scene. The amount of fuel they can gather and take to their homes in a day is almost incredible. . . . Among the Poles early marriages are the rule, and there is consequently a never-failing supply of children to keep a woodpile sufficiently high-heaped to guard against possible contingencies, and its only cost is the labor expended in gathering it.[53]

With less sympathy, the author remarked that the Poles' simple tastes also contributed to their ability to make ends meet.

The Pole is not fastidious in his clothing, and is a stranger to epicurean fancies of the table. His dress is sufficient if it hides his nakedness, and he eats only to live. The entire wardrobe of an ordinary Polish family would hardly suffice to decently wad a gun, and the table is not the inviting banquet which would tempt an anchorite from his vows. . . . A Polish family will supply its table for a week with the amount of money an American enjoying the same income would consume in a single day. Tea, coffee or milk seldom appear upon the table, meat very rarely, and butter is an entire stranger. The principal food is a coarse black bread made of rye flour. It is very wholesome, but nauseating to the palate that has never been attuned to its flavor. Blood-sausages, potatoes, cabbage and kindred vegetables make up the daily fare of a Polish family. . . . But the great luxury of the Polander's table—the dish which crowns his board upon rare occasions—is a decoction with an unpronounceable name made by chopping a cabbage head fine, mixing it with cut meats and vegetables of various kinds, and then boiling it until the whole mass is reduced to about the consistency of paste. [The informed reader will recognize the recipe for bigos.] This preparation is about as objectionable to a sensitive olfactory nerve as Scotch haggis.

Having described the Poles' habits, the author suggested that it should be clear just how the Poles managed to save for the purchase of a home and maintain their lavish churches.

It will thus be seen that the actual cost of their maintenance is almost nothing, while every individual member of the household contributes according to his or her strength, to the family exchequer. . . . The account book of a Polish family of 10 might fairly be footed up in this manner: Wages of the father for one week, $10; wages of two boys, $10; wages of the mother, $2; wages of two girls, $2; contributions to the family supplies in garbage, fuel, etc., etc., by the four younger children, $4; total receipts, $28; expenses—meat, 75c; rye flour, 75c; barley, 20c; vegetables, 50c; rent (where the property is not owned), $3; schnapps and beer, $2; tobacco, 10c; incidentals, $1; total outlay, $8.30; clear profit, $19.70.

Nonetheless, the author concluded that the Pole compared well with other immigrants.

> In spite of the domestic penury which rules his life, however, the Pole averages up very well with the other European immigrants who come to America. It may be placed to his credit that he is invariably honest, and though he does not rapidly assimilate with the new life that surrounds him, manages to take care of his own and seldom leaves a tax upon public charity. Neither is he a frequent figure in the police court. When he is called to answer there it is for some of the minor charges, and rarely for any flagrant breach of law or morals. An occasional 'drunk and disorderly' comprises the sum of his sinning against the peace and dignity of the state.

It should be emphasized that the *Evening News* writer's description applied in particular to the lives of those who had arrived during the last half-dozen years. By the 1880s there were two discernible classes within the Polish community: a smaller number of reasonably well-off Prussian Polish and Kashubian community elders who had been settled in Detroit for over a decade and were engaged mostly in the trades (with a few entering the professions), and the large majority of Austrian or Russian Polish peasant background, poor and with little or no education, who struggled as day laborers, some in factories but many on construction or digging projects of various sorts.[54]

The same year—1882—that Father Kolasiński arrived in Detroit saw the admittance to the diocese of two other Polish priests, Frs. Paweł Gutowski and Józef Dąbrowski. Both were destined to play major roles over the next two decades in the Polish community and would align themselves, once the troubles developed, against St. Albertus's flamboyant pastor. By the early 1880s Detroit's Polish community had divided into two distinct geographical neighborhoods: the original and larger east-side quarter; and a smaller west-side one which extended from about Twentieth Street along both sides of Michigan Avenue beyond the city's borders at Twenty-fifth Street into Springwells. For many years the west-side Poles had been trekking several miles across the city to attend services at St. Albertus's. In March 1876, having collected approximately five hundred dollars, they asked Bishop Borgess to authorize the establishment of a new parish in their own neighborhood. The bishop refused[55]—perhaps his unpleasant memories of the difficulties that beset the founding of St. Albertus's were still too fresh. Six years passed. Not until November 1882 did he accede to a new petition from the west-side Poles for a separate parish. Although the new parish would absorb a number of families from St. Albertus's, Kolasiński aided in organizing the west-side Poles into a separate congregation until the bishop could find a suitable pastor for them. His choice, apparently supported by Kolasiński, was Fr. Paweł Gutowski, a refugee from Bismarck's anti-Polish and anti-Catholic Kulturkampf. A native of Prussian Poland, Gutowski had made his way to America without papers, stopping in Baltimore and then Shamokie, Pennsylvania, before coming to Detroit. The new parish took the name of St. Casimir (Św. Kazimierz), and the first wooden frame structure was dedicated and opened in April 1883. Later it would be replaced by a permanent stone and brick structure.[56]

In August 1882, shortly before the founding of St. Casimir's, Bishop Borgess had received Fr. Józef Dąbrowski into the diocese. Unlike Kolasiński and Gutowski, who had come to Detroit shortly after reaching this country, Dąbrowski had twelve years' previous experience ministering to Polish immigrants. A native of Russian Poland, Dąbrowski's studies in Warsaw had been interrupted by the Polish uprising of 1863; when the insurrection failed, he decided to go to Rome. There he attended the newly opened Pontifical Polish College and completed his studies at the Pontifical Gregorian University. In 1869 he was ordained a diocesan priest for missionary work in America and that same year was received into the diocese of Green Bay, Wisconsin. For twelve years he ministered to the Polish community in and around Polonia, Wisconsin. In 1874 he was instrumental in bringing the first Felician Sisters (a Polish order originally established in Warsaw) to America, and from then until his death in 1903 served as their chaplain and director, first in Polonia and later in Detroit. In 1879 he concluded arrangements with Bishop Borgess and Father Wołłowski—then pastor of St. Albertus's—for a group of five Felician Sisters to teach at the parish school. Shortly thereafter, with the approval of Bishop Borgess and Mother Monika, he decided to transfer the Felicians' permanent headquarters to Detroit.[57] With Dąbrowski's guidance, the order purchased a parcel of land across the street from St. Albertus's Church, where they built a new motherhouse. The structure included a chapel, convent, novitiate, and orphanage. The cornerstone was laid on 4 October 1880; then in 1882, when the building was completed, the sisters and Father Dąbrowski settled permanently in Detroit.[58]

Soon after moving to Detroit, though he continued to guide the Felicians, Dąbrowski began to devote his main attention to a project that he and the Polish pioneer in America, Fr. Leopold Moczygemba, had toyed with for several years—namely, the establishment of a seminary to train Polish-speaking priests in America. The shortage of priests in general to minister to the rapidly rising number of American Catholics was a serious concern of the Third Plenary Council of the American hierarchy in Baltimore in 1884, where it was noted that there was only about one priest for every thousand Catholics.[59] The lack was especially pronounced among immigrants from southern and eastern Europe, who were demanding pastors able to speak their language and observe their traditional religious practices. The difficulty Bishop Borgess had encountered over the years in obtaining from Poland "a sufficient number of good and zealous pastors" was one of the principal reasons he cited in his letter of 14 March 1884 approving Dąbrowski's request to proceed with the establishment of a Polish seminary in Detroit.[60] A week after receiving the bishop's approval, Dąbrowski sent a printed circular to all Catholic prelates in America who had Polish parishioners in their dioceses, announcing the seminary project and asking permission to solicit contributions. In April he bought for $5,000 two acres on the west side of St. Aubin Street, two blocks north of St. Albertus's Church and the Felician motherhouse. Some financial assistance came from the sale of property in Nebraska by Father Moczygemba. Until that property, originally intended for the seminary, could be sold, Moczygemba personally lent $4,000 to start construction. Dąbrowski obtained an assistant, Fr. Antoni Jaworski, who devoted much of his time to fund raising in distant Polish settlements in America.[61]

In early 1885, with sufficient funds on hand to begin construction, Dąbrowski concluded an agreement with an architect for a four-story brick building to cost $35,000. It was to be a three-wing, U-shaped structure, but to hold down costs initially only the front part was built. On 19 May 1885, ground was broken. Because 22 July 1885 marked the millennial anniversary of the first Christian mission to the Slavs of Saints Cyril and Methodius, that day was chosen to lay and bless the cornerstone. For this reason also, Cyril and Methodius were adopted as the patron saints of the institution. An elaborate ceremony was held, attended by Bishop Borgess, Bishop Stephen V. Ryan of Buffalo, and thirty-six priests, seventeen of them Polish.[62] Commenting on the dedication ceremonies, a *Free*

Press reporter described Dąbrowski as "a very modest and unassuming man [who] has gained the love and respect of his entire people by his unselfish efforts on their behalf." In an interview with the same reporter after the ceremonies, Dąbrowski remarked, "Heretofore we have been obliged to procure Polish priests from Europe, but they cannot do what a native American might." Then he added these pointed words: "I deem the erection of this seminary more necessary than the building of expensive churches."[63] As we shall see, these remarks were made eighteen days after Father Kolasiński had opened a new, massive, and expensive St. Albertus's Church. The rivalry between the two priests apparently existed well before the Polish church troubles came to a head in December of that year.

Although the establishment of St. Casimir's Parish on the west side had removed a hundred or so families from St. Albertus's Church, the east-side Polish community was growing rapidly in the early 1880s. The original frame church built in 1872, with a seating capacity of less than a thousand, was quite inadequate for a parish which, by some estimates, had grown to over fifteen thousand souls. Soon after taking charge of the parish, Kolasiński had begun to plan for a larger and more permanent edifice that could not only accommodate the expanding parish but also would stand as a symbol of pride and dignity for Detroit's Poles and, not incidentally, their pastor. From the outset, Kolasiński had in mind a massive edifice, and his ambitious plans soon were questioned by the more cautious Prussian-Polish elders who predominated on the building committee. On 6 February 1883 twenty-four of the thirty committee members set down their misgivings in a letter to Bishop Borgess. They questioned the great expense that Kolasiński's plans would entail (well beyond the parish's means, they argued); they also proposed that the new church be built several blocks west of the present church, on a site more central to the Polish neighborhood. Kolasiński proposed to build adjacent to the existing frame structure, which in time would be torn down.[64]

Several days later the pastor himself wrote to the bishop, decrying the interference by some members of the congregation. He denied that they represented majority opinion and refuted their arguments. Borgess, always inclined to frown on any form of "trusteeism" (the European tradition of according church donors a say in the property affairs of the parish), supported the pastor, and in May 1884 formally authorized Kolasiński to contract "for the early and immediate completion of St. Albert's new church." The bishop, who in January 1883 had granted tentative approval provided no debt was incurred, now authorized the pastor to borrow up to $25,000, which would have to be repaid within two years.[65]

Kolasiński had no intention of being bound by this limitation; in fact, even before getting the bishop's approval, he and twelve committeemen had signed contracts with the builders on 14 February 1884 which called for the church to be built within fifteen months at a cost of $61,000. It was to be in the red-brick, neo-Gothic style then prevalent in much of Central Europe, especially in the German- and Austrian-held portions of Poland. The plans called for a structure 208 feet long, 75 feet wide (104 feet at the transept), and stretching to 200 feet at the top of the cross on the spire. It was to be equipped with steam heating and incandescent electric lights (the first to be installed in a Detroit church). The seating capacity was nearly 2,500, with 2,078 on the main floor and 410 in the gallery.[66] Even before the laying of the cornerstone on 29 June 1884, Kolasiński sent press reports on the new church, a picture of the old church, and an architectural rendition of the new structure to the Kraków journal *Missye Katolickie*. In an accompanying letter the pastor noted that, while Catholic churches in Europe were being closed and subjected to tight governmental restrictions, in America no permission other than the bishop's approval and the congregation's willingness to make material sacrifices was necessary.[67]

Neither Kolasiński nor Dąbrowski could have foreseen, when they launched their respective building projects in 1883 and early 1884, the collapse of the New York Stock Exchange in May 1884, which quickly led to a countrywide panic and depression lasting over two years. The effect of the depression, with its bank failures and widespread unemployment, was vividly depicted in an *Evening News* report in December 1884 that described horrendous scenes of "squalid poverty" in the Polish quarter. "In the side streets dirty, ragged children, barefooted and bareheaded, play in the gutters; half-clothed women . . . sew coarse looking stuff as they sit in groups in doorways." (This was the newspaper that just a year earlier, in better economic times, had described the hard work and thrift of the Polish immigrants.) It claimed that "never in the history of Detroit has work been so scarce . . . ; thousands of men are searching vainly for employment." The impact was of course greater on the recent immigrants, who often held seasonal or day-laboring jobs and were the first to be let go, than on Detroit workers in general. The reporter encountered a number of Poles who said "they would gladly return to Poland" if they had the passage money.[68] The bad times not only made it impossible for the two Polish priests to raise the sums they had anticipated when they contracted for their respective projects, but the competition for the limited available funds was accentuated.

Notwithstanding the adverse economic conditions, the new St. Albertus's Church was completed on schedule and opened on 4 July 1885, with an impressive dedication ceremony presided over by Bishop Borgess and his former secretary, now Bishop Camillus P. Maes of Covington, Kentucky. Early that Saturday morning the members of the four parish lay societies of St. Stanisław Kostka, the Children of Mary, St. Albert, and St. Joseph—Kolasiński had overseen the founding of the latter two—led by the semimilitary Kościuszko Guard of laymen, escorted the bishops' party from the episcopal residence on Washington Avenue to the site of the old and new St. Albertus's churches. First the official party disinvested the old "wooden and barnlike" church of its ecclesiastical character; then the exterior and interior of the magnificent new church was blessed. Bishop Maes was the chief celebrant of the high mass, and the pastor's brother, Fr. Nikodem Kolasiński of Berea, Ohio, delivered the sermon.[69]

In marked contrast to the press reports thirteen years earlier, when the first St. Albertus's was built, the *Evening News* now wrote: "The magnitude of the task which the Polish catholics have accomplished in the erection of the new church becomes evident when the comparative poverty of the members of the congregation is considered." The newspaper also noted the remarks of a "gentleman" familiar with the Poles, who, though he would soon be proved wrong, believed he discerned a practical side effect stemming from the Poles' sacrifice. He had "no doubt that the new St. Albert's church represents the results of 100,000 days of labor on the part of individual members of the congregation. That is the best investment that could be made for contentment and a panacea against the evils of the laboring classes. . . . The Polish laborers, who rely on the judicious direction of their priest in almost every move, are the most contented in the city, poor though they be."[70]

Father Kolasiński, however, would remain the pastor of what the newspapers were already calling "the largest church in Michigan" and "the finest Polish Church in America" for less than five months. In the second half of 1885 increasing numbers of complaints about lax administration of parish finances and allegations of the pastor's moral turpitude came to Borgess's attention. Rumors of Kolasiński's failings had been circulating since soon after his arrival in 1882. According to Swastek, the bishop, who at first discounted the charges of immoral behavior as "hearsay" and "vindictive slander," "decided . . . upon a thorough investigation into Fr. Kolasinski's Galician background as well as his Detroit activities." Again according to Swastek, "after a two-year accumulation of records, statements, and affidavits, the bishop found himself with a file of data that presented an unflattering moral profile of Fr. Kolasinski—a record of moral turpitude that began in Galicia and continued in Detroit."[71] (Kolasiński steadfastly denied all such accusations, and neither Borgess nor his successor ever made public the supposedly incriminating evidence or, for that matter, conducted a properly constituted ecclesiastical hearing on the charges.)

Whatever the nature of the evidence of moral failing against Kolasiński, the bishop in late 1885 chose not to proceed on it but instead to bring the pastor to account for the purported mismanagement of parish financial matters. The complaints included charging excessive fees for performing funerals and marriages, exorbitant tithes (one day's income out of thirty working days), careless supervision of the Sunday collections, poor bookkeeping, and, even worse, involving the congregation in a debt at least double the $25,000 authorized by the bishop.[72] The bishop chose to concentrate on the last two items when, in October 1885, he directed Kolasiński to make a full accounting of the building fund and the parish's financial affairs by the end of the year. Then, in late November, perhaps because of further complaints from St. Albertus's trustees, the bishop ordered Kolasiński to turn over immediately all the parish's financial records to the diocesan chancery.[73]

Having received no response from Father Kolasiński, the bishop on Sunday, 29 November, sent his secretary, Fr. M. J. M. Dempsey, to obtain the account books from the recalcitrant priest. Dempsey arrived at St. Albertus's just as a fiery meeting of parishioners was breaking up at the old church, which now served as the parish schoolhouse and meeting hall. Earlier that day, during his sermon at the late morning mass, Kolasiński had delivered a passionate denunciation of his accusers, whom at one point he had challenged to "step forward and kneel before the altar and swear, if they dared, to the charges they had made." Thereupon the pastor "seized hold of his robe and tore it violently open," an action emblematic of mourning among the Hebrews. The pastor had called the afternoon meeting at the old church following vespers, at which time he again inveighed against his accusers.[74] The bishop's secretary found Kolasiński in a very excited mood, which was further aggravated by Dempsey's intrusion. He refused to hand over the books, saying they were not up-to-date. He supposedly promised to balance them that evening and send them to the episcopal residence the next morning.[75]

Kolasiński's version of his difficulties with the parish books and his reluctance to give them up was given years later by his friend and attorney Feliks A. Lemkie, the first Polish-American to be admitted to the Michigan bar. In 1885 the pastor asked Lemkie to act as accountant and take charge of the parish books, a chore that had never been to Kolasiński's liking. According to Lemkie:

> The first thing I did was to ask Fr. Kolasinski how he had conducted operations in the collection of the [church] building fund. He said that he had divided the parish into ten districts and appointed a committee of two collectors for each district. These collectors went around to houses in their districts and as fast as they collected money they were told to put it down in books that had been provided them, and then they had turned the money over to . . . the treasurer. "Very well," I said, "the first thing I want is those books of the collectors." "What do you want of those books?" asked a collector, who was [also] a trustee, and several other trustees who were also collectors under this system began to look at each other. I told them I wanted the books to find out how much money had been collected. I was then going to compare the amount collected with the amount received by the treasurer, and then I was going to make a copy of all the books, and during church I was going to read off to the congregation the names of the contributors to the building fund and the amounts they were credited with having contributed. . . . From the very minute I told how I was going to work, the trustees said that they would not give up the [collectors'] books and they did not. . . . Shortly after that [meeting] they preferred a charge against Fr. Kolasinski. They told Bishop Borgess that the father had received hundreds and thousands of dollars from parishioners who had come to his home and donated towards the building fund. They said that he had pocketed all this money and never said a word about it. That was an utter falsehood.[76]

The bishop, on the basis of these charges, then demanded a full accounting based on the parish books, and, when the trustees escalated their accusations against the pastor, Borgess dispatched Dempsey to take possession of the records. Such was Kolasiński's version: when the culpable collectors and trustees were threatened with exposure, they banded together and turned against the pastor.

The truth will never be known for certain, and in any case would probably not have altered the course of events. In the absence of hard evidence one way or the other, it is not unreasonable to assume that several building-fund collectors had kept back a portion of their collections, perhaps persuading themselves that the embezzled sums were remuneration for their time and effort. Kolasiński was no less guilty of remissness in monitoring the financial affairs of the parish. He may have occasionally construed a contribution as a personal gift (as it likely was intended to be). In his overriding desire to build a magnificent church for himself and his people, the pastor certainly lost sight of the parish's financial resources, especially after the economic recession set in. On the other hand, he could be generous to a fault and may well have condoned a friend's taking a couple of dollars from the parish funds when he was down and out.

But speculation aside, the actions themselves, culpable as they surely seemed in the eyes of the stern head of the diocese, pale into insignificance when compared to the ignominious scenes that followed. The Kolasiński Affair was a very human tragedy, involving at one and the same time proud and stubborn individuals and the mass of confused and vulnerable but simple and loyal immigrants.

The denouement of the events that were set in motion can now be readily divined. On the following morning, 30 November, when Father Dempsey returned to the St. Albertus's rectory, the pastor "absolutely refused to deliver the books."

"I will not give the books till I am ready," he said.
"Will you give me a verbal statement of the affairs of the parish?" persisted Fr. Dempsey.
"Yes, I will."
"How much is the debt of the parish?"
"Thirty thousand dollars. There may be a few floating debts besides, but they will not exceed a few hundred dollars."
"Are you sure they will not amount to $1,000?"
"I am pretty sure," said Kolasinski.
"Would you take an oath that they do not amount to $2,000?"
"I would."
"To whom is the $30,000 owing?"
"To the building contractors—Spitzley Bros. & Dee."
"All the $30,000?"
"Yes."
"Now, you owe that sum to the contractors, and I know that

you owe $7,500 to the People's savings bank. I know that you owe $3,000 to Mr. Mehling, the other builder."

Kolasinski replied to all this that he would not be questioned as a boy.

The bishop had foreseen that Kolasinski might not obey his orders to give up the books, and had furnished the private secretary with a document to be used in such an emergency.

"Since you will not obey the bishop on the laws of the diocese, I have a painful duty to perform," said Fr. Dempsey drawing forth an order suspending Kolasinski as a priest. Handing it to him he bade him good day.[77]

The Kolasiński Affair had begun.

CHAPTER 2

A SUSPENDED PRIEST FIGHTS BACK

The overwhelming majority of the parishioners at St. Albertus's Church were unaware of the gravity of the crisis developing between their priest and the parish elders on the one hand and the priest and his bishop on the other. The times were not good economically, and many of the most recent, unskilled immigrants had great difficulty in obtaining even irregular employment as day laborers. But they were members of "the finest Polish Church in America," and their pastor's elegant office and manner and his adherence to the ways of the old country provided them with a sense of familiarity and security in this strange new land. Understandably, then, the news that the "German" bishop, Caspar H. Borgess, had suspended "their" priest and directed him to leave the diocese brought consternation and anger to the Polish parishioners.[1] The ostensible reason for the pastor's removal (no formal charges were released by the bishop and no ecclesiastical investigation had been held), that Father Kolasiński had declined to submit the parish's financial records until they could be brought up to date, seemed of little consequence to the essentially peasant congregation and was hardly grounds to remove their adored pastor. Kolasiński's refusal to turn over the books provided an excuse to suspend a man whom the bishop had already decided to remove because of mounting charges of misappropriation and mismanagement of parish funds and allegations of moral turpitude. Details regarding this last charge, certainly the most inflammatory

41

and damaging, came to light only later and fueled an already full-blown crisis.

The parishioners' anger was heightened when, late on 30 November, they learned that the Reverend Józef Dąbrowski had been appointed temporary pastor of St. Albertus's.[2] Most of the recently arrived Poles, who predominated among Kolasiński's adherents, knew of Dąbrowski as the rather drab priest who ministered to the Felician Sisters at their motherhouse across the street from St. Albertus's. Many no doubt recalled that Kolasiński had urged them not to contribute to Dąbrowski's plan to build a seminary to train Polish priests in the new country, a project Kolasiński scorned.[3] Thus, to many of the parishioners, Dąbrowski now appeared in the role of a usurper in league with the bishop.

Opposition to the bishop's decision soon erupted into overt action when Father Dąbrowski attempted to say the six o'clock morning mass at St. Albertus's Church on Tuesday, 1 December 1885. The events of that morning would be characterized in Detroit's English-language newspapers as the first of the numerous "Polish riots" that occurred over the next decade. Though the bells were not rung that morning, a number of parishioners were already in the church. When Dąbrowski attempted to ascend to the altar to commence the celebration, he was seized and held by one man and then bodily ejected from the church by a crowd of women who had surged around him. "Out with him! We want only our own priest!" was their cry. Within a few minutes the church was emptied and the doors locked.

The excited parishioners, whose number quickly swelled as news of the incident spread, continued to mill about outside the church. Then, when the police were summoned at about seven o'clock, the crowd grew more ugly. One woman, identified in the press as "Annie Kuchilski" (Anna Kuchylska?), "rushed upon them, and using an umbrella for a weapon, got in some effective work before she was hustled into the patrol wagon and taken to the station." The confrontation continued for some time, with the police holding the streets and the crowd pushed back into the yards and commons near the church. This stalemate was temporarily broken when Dąbrowski accompanied by his assistant, Fr. Antoni Jaworski, reappeared briefly. Several women in the crowd charged after him, and the unfortunate priest was obliged to beat a retreat down a nearby alleyway. Eventually, around nine o'clock, Captain Mack of the Gratiot Avenue police station decided to disperse the crowd. When the police charged, a wild scene ensued. According to the *Evening News* reporter, "the women fought like tigers, using umbrellas and fists to pound the enemy." Finally, after a twenty-minute melee, the police emerged victorious, though many Poles still milled about in smaller groups. A little later, the suspended priest reached the church. Kolasiński's power over his devoted followers was made manifest when, after saying a few words, the remainder of the excited parishioners dispersed and headed toward their homes. " 'Go home,' he said, 'I am here now, and will remain as your adviser while this trouble lasts.' " He then held out his hands, and the women crowded around, eagerly kissed them, and left contented. Later that evening, however, an angry crowd regrouped to jeer outside the home and grocery-saloon of Tomasz Żółtowski, Kolasiński's principal accuser.[4]

Although Dąbrowski, perhaps understandably, was too upset to discuss the day's difficulties with the press, a reporter for the *Detroit Free Press* was "most graciously received" by Kolasiński, whom he found to be "calm and dignified." In response to the reporter's question, "What is the true cause, briefly, of all this trouble?" the deposed priest laid the blame directly at Dąbrowski's feet.

> The Franciscan [Felician] Sisters in the cloister [convent] across the street have bought a square of land near here and they have paid but little on the large investment. Father Dombrowski . . . is located at the convent, and he is ambitious. . . . He imagines that if he can get possession of the parish, he will thus find an easy way to not only lift the entire debt from the shoulders of the . . . sisters, but throw the entire support of the cloister upon this parish. That's all there is to it. Father Dombrowski wants to incorporate the cloister and its debts as a part of this parish, and my parishioners object to the proceeding.

Kolasiński went on to say that out of his parish of two thousand families only a handful, mostly "saloon-keepers," seemed to be supporting Dąbrowski. When pressed further, Kolasiński voiced disdain for Dąbrowski's "slouchy manners as to attire" and his lack of dignity as a priest. Kolasiński conceded that his own attention to attire, as well as his keeping a carriage and coachman, was necessary to maintain his priestly decorum as pastor of such a large parish. As for the allegations that he had mismanaged parish funds, Kolasiński denied them in all particulars, rejecting as well the accusations that he had been charging his parishioners exorbitant fees. He freely showed the parish books to the reporter, who found them "neatly kept, up to date, with not even the slightest evidence of erasure, interlineation or alteration. More than that," the reporter found, "each page bore the audit and signature of the trustees of the church." But Kolasiński was not planning to turn them over to the bishop until a formal ecclesiastical investigation of the charges against him was undertaken. To yield the books now, the suspended priest believed, would deprive him of his only means of defense.[5]

The next morning, 2 December, when Dąbrowski and Jaworski again made their way from the Felician convent to St. Albertus's Church to celebrate early mass, they were escorted by six policemen. The crowd, even larger than on the previous day and again composed mostly of women, "hissed and hooted and liberally pelted [the priests and police] with chunks of mud and bits of gravel." Twice the priests were forced back from the entrance by the enraged women, who "bit and clawed and slapped . . . like very devils" before the police were able to clear a path into the church. Within the church, "the sacred walls . . . resounded with cat-calls and shouts of anger," and to one observer, "the scene presented was that of a perfect bedlam." When a group of women made a rush toward the altar, the two priests and their escort were forced to escape into the vestry, where they awaited the arrival of additional police. Finally, with over thirty policemen in the aisles, Dąbrowski and Jaworski went through the motions of celebrating mass, despite the intense shouting. But when the two priests left the church, "they were obliged to run a very serious gauntlet of infuriated people, being pelted with stones and other missiles." Though he would nominally remain pastor of St. Albertus's Church for over a year and a half, this was the only time Father Dąbrowski actually celebrated mass there. According to the Detroit newspapers, the second "Polish riot" had occurred.[6]

As on the previous day, Kolasiński appeared a couple of hours later before his flock at the entrance to the parsonage, where he had continued to stay since his suspension. Again he advised his people to disperse to their homes. The amazement of the American reporter on the scene at Kolasiński's authority over his people was evident in his account. "The people crowded about him and bestowed all manner of endearing treatment upon him, even to kissing his hand and the clothes that he wore." Once again, during the afternoon, a hostile crowd estimated at a thousand persons milled around Żółtowski's home and store on Hastings Street. The grocer had by now taken the precaution of boarding up the building and remaining out of sight.[7]

The dispute at St. Albertus's was by no means the first conflict between a parish and the head of the diocese. At St. Anne's there had been a disagreement over parish property, and a more recent

*Intersection of St. Aubin Street and Canfield Avenue, looking south on St. Aubin, ca. 1890.
St. Albertus's Church is on the right; the Felician Sisters' motherhouse and convent is on the left.
Courtesy of the Burton Historical Collection of the Detroit Public Library.*

clash involved St. Joachim's Church. Some lay Catholic leaders freely conceded that the diocese was seething with discontent. Lay critics were particularly outspoken over what they believed was the bishop's excessive support of the religious orders, especially the Franciscans and Jesuits, from funds raised by the parishes. In addition, Bishop Borgess's reputation for stubbornness and authoritarian ways, no less than his refusal to see the press, seemed to contribute to the tensions.[8] Having summarily dismissed three of Kolasiński's four predecessors at St. Albertus's (even if one accepts that Gieryk resigned voluntarily in 1875), the bishop doubtless expected that Kolasiński too would quietly acquiesce to an espiscopal order. Furthermore, perhaps because of the bishop's reluctance to make any formal public statement regarding his reasons for suspending Kolasiński, all the more charges and countercharges by the other principals were being aired in the press. In response to Kolasiński's deprecation of Dąbrowski in his interview with the *Free Press* reporter, an associate of Dąbrowski and one of the first Polish priests to minister in America, the Reverend Leopold Moczygemba, visited the *Free Press* office and volunteered an account of Dąbrowski's career which praised his pastoral devotion and refuted the accusation that he had coveted control of St. Albertus's Parish.[9]

On the following day Dąbrowski contacted the *Free Press* to deny publicly the charges and insinuations Kolasiński had raised. Specifically, he noted that the Felician Sisters had no outstanding debt and, as a separately incorporated church institution with its own trustees, the Felicians, their motherhouse, and their assets and incumbrances could not be joined to St. Albertus's congregation.[10] By nature private and retiring, Dąbrowski, unlike St. Albertus's former pastor, was not comfortable in the limelight. An *Evening News* reporter at this time described him as a man who "lays no claim to personal attractions. He is an older man than the late pastor [actually, he was four years younger], dresses ordinarily in black clothes, and on the street wears a black fur cap pulled down on the left side of his head. His Roman collar is the only mark to distinguish that he is a priest. He has a full dark-complexioned face and expressionless black eyes."[11]

As on the previous two days, a large crowd, predominantly women, gathered in front of St. Albertus's Church on 3 December at six in the morning. But this day Father Dąbrowski made no attempt to celebrate mass and the crowd eventually dispersed. One wonders if there was not a ring of disappointment in the *Evening News* headline that day: "No Polish Riot Today." For his part, though he still had the church keys in his possession, Kolasiński made no attempt to defy the bishop and hold services himself. Rather, he urged his ardent supporters, who again crowded around the rectory, to remain peaceful despite the slanderous charges against him and the interference of the police, on whom he laid the blame for the disturbance. He did, however, retain an attorney, John B. Corliss, to whom he turned over the controversial parish financial records for safekeeping.[12]

But if it was relatively quiet on 3 December in the Polish quarter of Detroit, later in the day the Kolasiński case took on an added dimension when the *Evening News* carried a front-page report to the effect that, in addition to the charges of insubordination and mishandling parish funds (for which the priest ostensibly had been suspended), the bishop had in his possession two notarized affidavits containing accusations of sexual misconduct by Kolasiński. The newspaper had obtained the details of the charges, surprisingly, from Kolasiński himself, who reportedly had been apprised of them by the chancery. The first affidavit, made by Tomasz Żółtowski, alleged that the priest had had "illicit intercourse" with a certain Franciszka Danielska, who had confessed the matter to Father Gutowski of St. Casimir's Church. The second affidavit, of which Kolasiński had only partial recollection, he believed had been brought by the Polish notary Emil Niedomański and alleged intimacy between the priest and the daughter of a Polish family on Dubois Street. Kolasiński stated that Mrs. Danielska had occasionally done washing at the pastoral residence, but he categorically denied the charge and stated that the grocer Żółtowski had been after this poor woman for some time to make some charge against him. The grocer, Kolasiński had subsequently learned, had offered her a barrel of flour and fifty dollars, and eventually she agreed to sign a paper without knowing what it contained.[13]

When a reporter for the *Evening News* located Mrs. Danielska, she denied having signed any affidavit and appeared frightened. Żółtowski purportedly had left the city the previous day.[14] Father Gutowski also denied having had any role in the statement, though he intimated that the charges probably bore an element of truth. In talking to the reporter, Gutowski made no effort to veil his distaste for the suspended priest and his excitable followers. "Is it not a strange fact," he remarked, "that only the women of his church display such inordinate affection for him? Where are the men, and how do they feel? . . . I'll tell you what I would do if I had the power. . . . The city officers should send a fire engine to the scene next time the church is opened. If the women attempt a riot again, turn on the hose and wet them down. It might cool them off; they are too hot." The next day's editorial in the *News* suggested that Gutowski's remarks "would indicate that christian charity is about as scarce among the catholic clergy as anywhere known."[15]

In the space of just a few days, passions on all sides had become so inflamed that any hope of compromise seemed dim. When John Corliss called upon Bishop Borgess to convey his client's willingness to turn over all parish financial records and answer all charges against him if a properly constituted ecclesiastical hearing were convened, he found the bishop unmovable. Borgess reiterated, "I cannot and will not under any circumstances grant Father Kolasinski a hearing until after he resigns and surrenders everything in connection with the church to myself, and brings back the people that he has excited against the lawful authority of the church."[16] A man not known to relent, he would give no hint of yielding to the Poles' wishes to see their priest reinstated. Instead, on Friday, 4 December, the bishop promulgated an official decree of interdiction on St. Albertus's Church, banning all religious functions. The order was read in all the Catholic churches of the city and had almost the same effect as excommunication, since it also closed the doors of these other churches to the "dissident" members of the proscribed parish. Though the interdiction was temporary, it was to remain in effect for almost nineteen months.[17]

Despite the interdiction and the inclement weather in early December, which included a severe snowstorm, a large number of Polish women kept up a daily watch at St. Albertus's Church to prevent any attempt by priests other than Father Kolasiński to conduct services there. The fortitude of these women seemed remarkable to an outside observer. "Their wooden shoes and open slippers were carried in the hand whenever a deep drift was encountered, but the heavy woolen stockings they wear seemed to be as comfortable foot wear as they cared for. Many of them knelt down in the snow to say their prayers."[18] It is to Kolasiński's credit that the first Sunday that the church was closed passed without further upheaval. His counselings to quiet his flock were duly noted in the press.[19] To outside inquirers, the suspended priest answered confidently that he would soon be vindicated and that within a few weeks the church would reopen with him as pastor. Żółtowski and Mrs. Danielska, he noted, had retracted their charges.[20] But when Kolasiński met with Borgess at the bishop's request on 17 December, no resolution to the conflict could be found. The priest insisted that

the charges against him were unfounded and that he must be reinstated before a formal investigation was conducted.[21] The bishop,
for his part, refused to alter his stance.

Meantime, a sharp polarization of attitudes was emerging within
the Polish community. While the vast majority of parishioners
seemed fervently behind their suspended priest, a small but growing
number of Dąbrowskiites was discernible, especially among the
Prussian-Polish elders. Among the Poles, members of the two
factions were known as "Kolachy" and Dąbrochy." What had begun
as a conflict between priest and bishop would cause increasingly
sharp divisions in the fledgling Polish community, and therein lay
the most tragic consequences of the Kolasiński Affair for the Poles
themselves. The crisis did, however, over the next years direct
Detroiters' attention toward what previously had been seen essentially as an exotic, ethnic outpost on the city's fringes.

Kolasiński's claim that his opponents within the parish were only
the grocer-saloonkeepers, though not entirely accurate, did have
substance. His denunciation of the saloonkeepers' greed and his
efforts to close the saloons on Sundays and other holy days had
certainly alienated this small but influential group of prominent
Polish residents.[22] Of course there were others, especially among the
older Prussian Polish and Kashubian settlers, who opposed the
flamboyant priest from Austrian Poland. Many of them resented his
leadership and hold over the steadily mounting number of new
immigrants. "One of the oldest Poles in Detroit" offered the *Evening
News* a description of the new arrivals and Kolasiński's relationship
to them.

> The people who caused the exciting scenes . . . were all Gali-
> cians.. There are about 500 families of these people in the
> parish. They have come principally during the past two years
> of Fr. Kolasinski's pastorate. They represent the poorest class
> of the Polish people in Detroit, and in this respect they hold the
> same position as they did in their native province of Cracow.
> . . . Cracow is also the native place of Fr. Kolasinski. Hence the
> affiliations of the priest and this portion of his congregation
> are complete. Their condition in their native country was one
> of abject slavery. Without a master they would not feel content,
> and so they render to [Kolasiński] the same homage which
> formerly they gave to the nobleman who allowed them to till
> his land in Europe and in return provided for their existence.
> That they still retain many of their customs and habits is quite
> evident. The practice of kissing his hands and garments is a

tribute they formerly paid to their masters. It signifies nothing in this free country except the most abject subjection of the people and a repulsive vanity in the priest who accepts it.

The informant went on to emphasize that in 1882, when Kolasiński had arrived to guide the parish, there were almost no Galicians there and that most of the settlers came from Prussian-held Polish lands.[23] Although Kolasiński, as the crisis developed and in ensuing years, occasionally exploited the limited horizons and experiences of many of his followers, as well as the sense of insecurity and displacement that gripped many of them, it would be a mistake to conclude that the ardent Kolasińskiites were drawn solely from the illiterate or semiliterate former Galician peasants. Many a Detroit Pole supported the controversial priest in the conviction that he was the victim of injustice at the hands of the Detroit Catholic hierarchy and of the jealousy of established elements in the city's Polish community.

As the Christmas holidays approached and no resolution of the conflict seemed in sight, certain elements among Kolasiński's followers, perhaps in frustration at being unable to alter the stalemate, began to threaten violence against their priest's opponents. Notwithstanding the fact that Kolasiński repeatedly urged his supporters to be patient, the *Free Press* reported on 22 December that "a gang of roughs," estimated at fifty persons, had threatened to beat up Father Dąbrowski, who was now saying three masses a day in the Felician convent, and had also staged an ugly demonstration outside the home of Jan Lemke, the patriarch of Detroit's Poles. Having at first taken a neutral position in the church dispute, Lemke was now outspokenly pro-Dąbrowski. There seemed to be a general consensus in the press that, if St. Albertus's Church were not reopened on Christmas Day, then serious trouble would surely occur.[24] But little could they anticipate the remarkable and tragic events that would take place on that day.

When an announced Christmas Eve mass was held at the Felician convent by Father Dąbrowski, about fifty persons attended.[25] The worshipers were jeered at by a group of Kolasińskiites (also numbering about fifty), whom the press described as "roughs and malcontents"; but when two police officers were summoned, a more serious confrontation was averted. From then until about four in the morning, quiet reigned in the vicinity. In the early morning hours, members of the ostracized congregation began to gather; by five o'clock a crowd estimated at eight hundred men, women, and children, "bright and clean in their holiday attire," had assembled about the church hoping that the doors would open to let them celebrate an early Christmas mass, notwithstanding the several notices that had appeared in the press stating that the church would not be reopened. When the hours for mass had passed and the door remained sealed, the crowd, now swelled to several thousand by one estimate, decided to march to the episcopal residence downtown on Washington Avenue to appeal personally to the bishop for permission to hold Christmas services in their church. Separating into several groups, the crowd was subdued and orderly. According to the *Evening News,*

> There was little or no jabbering or demonstration. The faces wore an expression of extreme earnestness. They appeared to feel keenly the fact that while other church bells were ringing, other congregations were bowing before their altars and offering thanks to God, they stood crowded and shivering in the streets with their church cold and silent and with the frown of their bishop upon them. . . . The men were well dressed in the holiday garb of laborers and mechanics. The brilliant red shawls of the women gave a picturesque look to the otherwise sombre appearances of the body.

As nine o'clock approached, the sections converged on the bishop's residence from different directions. The marchers, who now filled the entire block in front of the residence, chose a delegation of six parishioners to convey their wishes to the bishop. Their ringing of the doorbell brought no answer. Then, just as they again began to ring the bell, word came from the fringe of the crowd that the bishop had just been seen entering his carriage in the alleyway behind the residence and was now driving away hurriedly. This apparent act of cowardice further disheartened the crowd.

The bishop had in fact been informed of the crowd's presence but had decided to ignore it and proceed with his morning schedule, which called for him to say mass at St. Joseph's German church. But his precipitate departure via the alleyway signified to the Poles a callous rejection of their appeal. However, they were still determined to confront the bishop and set out to follow him. Their number was now about three thousand, with perhaps an additional thousand curious onlookers. But at St. Joseph's, where the mass was in progress, the Poles were again rebuffed. When the delegates sought admission, their entrance was blocked by members of the lay St. Joseph's Society, who in essence curtly told them to go back to their own church. A reporter for the *Free Press* captured well the mood of the Poles at this juncture.

> Thus balked at every turn and with all their efforts useless, the homeless congregation realized fully that they were debarred entirely from observing the day according to their religious training and belief and it was at this point that women began to cry. . . . Their leaders, however, kept them well in hand so that there was no sign of a disturbance of the peace and so they marched back to the corner of St. Aubin avenue and Fremont street, reaching there about noon. Then the crowd slowly dispersed.

By two o'clock in the afternoon, the Poles started to congregate again, numbering about four hundred. There were a few police on the scene. The most vocal segment of the crowd had gathered a block south of St. Albertus's Church, at the corner of St. Aubin and Willis, in front of the saloon and grocery owned by Jan Lemke and his sons, now identified as leaders of the pro-Dąbrowski faction. For several hours much verbal abuse was directed at the Lemke house, and from time to time objects were thrown. (The report in the *Evening News* that all the windows in the building had been broken at this time was not borne out by later investigation.) About five o'clock a youth, aged about fifteen, ran furtively up to the Lemkes' front door, gave it a hard kick, and scampered away. Almost immediately, the door opened and a man appeared, holding a revolver. Although it was already quite dark, most sources suggested that he was Bazyli Lemke. Other men could be seen behind him in the doorway. Four shots were fired into the crowd. One struck Jan Lewicki just over the left eye, entering the brain and causing instant death. Another shot grazed a woman standing nearby. The police then forced an entrance into the house and arrested all the men inside, except for the elder Lemke, since no one would admit to the shooting. The Lemkes later claimed that the first shots came from the crowd and that they had merely fired in self-defense.

The dead Pole, Jan Lewicki, was in his mid-twenties and, though a member of St. Albertus's Parish, was not known to support either the Kolasiński or Dąbrowski factions. He was described by those who knew him as "an industrious, temperate man who had shown himself to be thrifty and an agreeable neighbor." He had been in Detroit for only two years and left an eighteen-year-old pregnant widow. On the day after the shooting, an *Evening News* reporter sought to learn more about the murdered man, whose story typified the life of many of the recent Polish immigrants. When Lewicki was alive, he had lived with his wife in a shanty on Garfield Avenue. He was an unskilled day laborer, presently out of work due to the economic slump. He and his wife had few possessions. Lewicki had built the house himself from scrap materials, and the land on which it stood was still not fully paid for. In a small shed attached to the rear of the shanty, the dead man lay, still wearing the same clothes as when he was shot down. The blood had been washed from his face, which was bandaged to cover the ugly head wound. His widow did not yet know if he would be permitted a Christian funeral and burial because the interdiction was still in force.[26]

The shooting, coming on the heels of the rejection of the Poles' hopes for reopening their church, understandably contributed to heightened anxiety and bitterness in the Polish community. The following morning, the second day of Christmas for Polish Catholics, a crowd estimated at about two thousand, and less restrained than on the day before, had gathered around the church. After a few hours, a segment of the crowd headed toward the nearby home and grocery of Tomasz Żółtowski, the scene of several earlier disturbances. A fusillade of stones, bricks, and frozen mud quickly smashed all the windows. After some time, the irate Żółtowski himself appeared at a second-story window and fired two shots from a Winchester into the air. Fortunately, at this point a detachment of police arrived and the crowd's wrath was momentarily diverted from Żółtowski to the men in blue. Eventually the situation was brought under control, though the police were unable to disperse the large crowd. Even with upwards of a hundred men, the police succeeded only in shunting the crowd from one street to another in the hope of averting further violence.[27]

In the aftermath of the shooting of Lewicki and the bishop's behavior on Christmas Day, there was an outpouring of criticism of Borgess by prominent Detroit lay Catholics. Most maintained that if he had displayed more flexibility and understanding of people's feelings, the bloodshed probably could have been averted. One critic was quoted in the *Evening News* as saying, "It was certainly not upholding the sacerdotal dignity to retreat through the alleyway, when those poor people, through an excess of faith, called upon him to solicit some services in their church. The bishop ought to remember that it is far easier to drive people out of the church than to drive them back again." An editorial in the *Evening Journal* pointedly concluded that "there was no 'mob' " of Poles on Christmas Day "until the bishop had left his residence by the alleyway without meeting either the committee of the petitioners or the petitioners themselves."[28]

True to his ways, the bishop refused to see reporters, but he did dispatch Father Dempsey to counter the criticism. Since the best defense is usually a rapid counterattack, Dempsey set out to place the blame squarely on Kolasiński, who, it should be noted, had made no public appearance on Christmas Day. Dempsey accused Kolasiński of inspiring the recent violence, and raised a charge not previously made public: the suspended priest had been tried on similar charges of immorality while he was a priest in Poland. As for the bishop's actions on Christmas Day, he was right not to face the "Polish mob" because, in Dempsey's view, he would certainly have been "assassinated" had be gone out on the porch at the time. The bishop was now more adamant than ever that Kolasiński must yield the church keys and vacate the parish residence before any hearing could take place.[29] Bishop Borgess had the canonical right to suspend the priest without a hearing (notwithstanding guidelines promulgated by the Propaganda, the Sacred Congregation for the Propagation of the Faith, for the establishment of investigatory commissions) if he believed the spiritual well-being of his subjects was endangered by the priest's continued presence. In this instance, Borgess had deemed the charges against Kolasiński so devastating as to justify his immediate suspension. The *New York Times* quoted the bishop as saying, "He has been charged with immorality of such a character that he should not be allowed to stand at a Catholic altar for a single hour, and no pure home should permit him to cross its threshold."[30]

Despite the evidence of the bishop's indirect complicity in the Christmas tragedy, the *Evening News*, in an editorial on 27 December 1885, took his side, urging its readers to appreciate the bishop's "delicate position." After removing a recalcitrant subordinate, he "at once finds himself confronted by a violent congregation of ignorant foreigners, instigated, as he believes, in their riotous and criminal conduct by the suspended priest."[31] The *Michigan Catholic*, an organ very close to the episcopate, was similarly uncharitable to the Polish Christmas "rioters," whose "foolish mission of demanding the immediate reinstatement of a priest under stringent ecclesiastical censures . . . proves conclusively that the motives by which they are actuated do not at all spring from religious devotion, but are only the outcome of blind prejudices and deplorable susceptibility to unlimited influence from any individual whom they happen to set up as a chief." Though declining to reply to the "bigoted and ignorance-founded flings" appearing in the city's newspapers against the bishop's conduct, the *Michigan Catholic* lamely tried to place much of the blame for the riotous scenes of 25 and 26 December on the unrestrained press reporting before Christmas of the Polish church troubles.[32]

Kolasiński, as had become his custom, freely agreed to receive reporters, whom by nearly all accounts he charmed with his gracious manner. Though he spoke poor English, he was fluent in German, a language widely understood in Detroit at the time. He responded to the bishop's renewed intransigence by asserting that he was prepared to remain at the parish residence until justice was done, which in his view meant his reinstatement before a hearing was convened. Kolasiński also emphasized what had now become apparent to all, that his parishioners would accept no other priest.[33]

The coroner's inquest into the death of Jan Lewicki was convened on 29 December and carried over into the next day. Throughout the proceedings a large crowd of Poles waited outside the building. The purpose of the inquest was to determine the cause and manner of the victim's death and to guide the authorities in deciding whether to prefer criminal charges against the alleged perpetrators. Although the evidence failed to establish who had fired the fatal shot, it was determined that three persons—Bazyli Lemke, his brother Aleksander, and an August Stieber—had in fact fired shots from the Lemke store and residence. All three were bound over for trial, without bail, though the latter step was probably taken to assure the men's safety. In point of fact, the Lemkes and Stieber were soon set at liberty and did not stand trial until six months later, at which time all three were acquitted.[34]

The continuing crisis was perhaps bound to spill over and embroil Detroit's other ethnic communities, especially the smaller neighboring Bohemian Catholic church of St. Wenceslaus at the corner of Antoine and Leland streets, which counted about one hundred and thirty families or five hundred souls. Its pastor, Fr. W. Koerner, often said services in German, and a small number of Prussian Poles, disenchanted perhaps with the changes taking place at St. Albertus's and the influx of Galicians, had begun to attend St. Wenceslaus's Church. Kolasiński had once called upon Koerner and apparently tried to persuade him—unsuccessfully—not to receive Poles into the Bohemian parish. Thus in the eyes of the most ardent Kolasińskiites, once the crisis at St. Albertus's broke out, Koerner too was an opponent.[35]

A rumor in the *Evening News* to the effect that numerous Poles were purchasing firearms suggests the anxiety Detroiters felt following the Christmas troubles. A clerk at one of the larger gun stores was reported to have sold at least thirty revolvers to Poles over a two-day period. The police launched an immediate inquiry, and officers were detailed to visit the city's gun shops, only to discover that "the dealers were unanimous in saying their business had been unusually dull the past few weeks." Lamely, the *News* now told its readers that the unfounded rumor stemmed from the Poles' "peculiar custom of saluting the birth of the new year with a promiscuous discharge of fire-arms."[36] Be this as it may, the New Year arrived relatively peaceably in the Polish quarter, and the American newspapers could find no cause to report additional disturbances. In fact, for as long as Kolasiński remained at the St. Albertus's parsonage, there would be no further "Polish riot" headlines in Detroit's newspapers, though a storm of controversy continued to surround Kolasiński and Detroit's Poles.

The newspapers, and by no means only the big English-language dailies, contributed greatly to keeping the affair alive. Not only did each faction use the press to air its version of events, but the press had learned that the troubles had whetted their readers' appetites, and thus there was no shortage of aggressive investigatory reporters with a knowledge of German and a smattering of Polish who ventured through the Polish quarter, knocking on doors in search of "news." Already at the end of December an enterprising *Free Press* reporter had followed up a tip from the anti-Kolasiński forces that there was a priest in the Detroit diocese who had firsthand knowledge of Kolasiński's wrongdoings in Kraków. The Reverend Konstanty Domagalski had ministered to the reconstituted Polish congregation in Parisville for about a year. Before coming to America he had served as a notary in the archdiocese of Kraków and purportedly had heard testimony given there against Kolasiński. The reporter set out for Parisville, but encountered the priest at the depot in Port Huron, where he learned that Domagalski was in fact en route to Detroit to confer with Bishop Borgess. Domagalski, however, would only tantalize the reporter with promises of damaging evidence, claiming that he was not at liberty to speak without the bishop's authorization.[37]

A couple of weeks later the bishop apparently agreed to let Domagalski speak. The Polish Catholic weekly, *Pielgrzym Polski* [Polish pilgrim], whose board chairman was Kolasiński's opponent, Fr. Pawel Gutowski, on 12 January 1886 published an interview with Domagalski, and a few days later the English-language papers reprinted his sensational charges. In brief, he alleged that, while an assistant priest in the Kraków diocese, Kolasiński had become "intimately acquainted" with a certain "Sophia Czimara" (Zofia Czymara?), the daughter of a Polish nobleman. Charges of immorality were preferred against the priest, but before the case came to episcopal trial Kolasiński disappeared, possibly to make a retreat. After a year he contacted the bishop, pleaded repentance, and asked forgiveness. This was granted, and after an additional year's penance Kolasiński was reinstated in the priesthood. But, because his usefulness in the Kraków area was impaired, he was encouraged to seek a post in America. He received an exeat and left Poland for New York, where he served as an assistant in a Polish parish before coming to Detroit. Despite his penance, he brought Sophia with him to New York, and later she followed him to Detroit, where she was installed as mistress in his house and introduced as his sister. But after several months, the question of Sophia's relationship to the priest was raised by some recently arrived emigrants from Kraków. The girl then suddenly disappeared; Kolasiński maintained that he had sent her back to Poland.[38]

Domagalski further intimated that Bishop Borgess had received documents from the Kraków archdiocese that substantiated the charges raised there against Father Kolasiński. The implication was clear: if charges of moral turpitude had been confirmed in Poland, then allegations of similar failings in the Detroit diocese were credible. In fairness to Kolasiński, it should be noted that well before any allegations of misdoings had surfaced in Detroit, he had written to a Kraków religious journal that he had come to America in the company of two Belgian priests and had stopped in New York only thirty-six hours.[39] However, it was not uncommon at the time for European bishops to encourage "flawed priests" in their dioceses to assume missions in the United States.

Through his attorney, Kolasiński issued an emphatic denial of Domagalski's allegations, maintaining that he had never known a Sophia Czimara and had never been charged with a moral failing in Poland or elsewhere until the recent troubles. Then several days later, on 21 January, Kolasiński called personally on Superintendent Pittman at police headquarters to state that the publication of Domagalski's spurious charges had raised a furor among St. Albertus's parishioners, who held Gutowski personally responsible for the slanderous attack. If the attack continued, Kolasiński warned, he would no longer be able to control his congregation.[40] It seemed to Kolasiński's opponents, of course, that his action constituted a threat of renewed violence in the Polish quarter if the accusations did not cease.

But despite these polemics, the status of St. Albertus's Church and its suspended pastor remained unchanged. The bishop still hesitated to take the legal steps necessary to eject Kolasiński from the parish residence, and Kolasiński himself went into virtual seclusion and was not seen for over two weeks in February and early March. During this period only one clash between the Kolasińskiites and their opponents was reported in the press. This occurred on 5 March, when a group of Dąbrowskiites, annoyed at the continuing impasse, attempted to organize a broader following. They gathered at Fredro Hall (named for the prolific nineteenth-century Polish dramatist, Count Aleksander Fredro). This hall, intended to serve the Polish community, had recently been constructed at the corner of Russell and Leland streets. The assembly, estimated at four to five hundred persons, including a number of Kolasiński's adherents who occupied the rear of the hall, selected Franciszek Eichler, another grocer-saloonkeeper, (whom the *Tribune* described as "more German than Polish") as its chairman. Though the speakers carefully avoided mentioning Kolasiński's name, the group at the back jeered and shouted down all the prominent anti-Kolasińskiites who attempted to speak.[41]

Finally, after more than three months of stalemate, on 10 March at the beginning of Lent, the bishop initiated steps to remove Kolasiński from the parish residence. He elected to bring a civil action of ejectment, and as his agent chose Jan Wagner, a sewer contractor, an ardent anti-Kolasińskiite, and a trustee of St. Albertus's Church. The bill of complaint sought to establish Borgess as the legal owner of St. Albertus's Church and all its appurtenances and grounds, and maintained that "Dominick Kolasinski is now in possession of said churches, pastoral residence, school house and lands, and that he unlawfully holds the same by force against the rights of said Caspar H. Borgess."[42] The next day a summons was served upon Kolasiński through his guards at the parish residence.[43]

The civil case of Father Kolasiński was tried a week later on 19 March in the circuit court of Judge Joseph Weiss.[44] Kolasiński, who chose not to attend, was represented by John Corliss, who pursued the argument that Kolasiński had not actually been in possession of the church since 3 December of the previous year, when he had turned over the keys to the three church trustees who supported him. (Their spokesman, Antoni Spiegel, was part of the delegation that Borgess refused to see on Christmas Day.) Corliss further maintained that Kolasiński was "a tenant of will or a tenant at suffrance" in the parish residence and therefore entitled to three months' notice before formal eviction could be effected. The attorneys for the complainant, on the other hand, argued that the trustees only had been holding the keys on Kolasiński's behalf. On the critical issue of the pastoral residence, they maintained that no landlord-tenant relationship existed, and that the priest was in fact the bishop's "agent." An agent holding real property against its owner's will was in effect a trespasser. The jury found for the complainant after deliberating for only a half hour. Moreover, it placed an annual rental value on the church properties of $10,000 which thereby set the appeal bond at twice that sum, $20,000, or an amount that the bishop's attorneys believed all but precluded Kolasiński's financial ability to file an appeal. By the court's order he was now given five days to vacate the church premises.

The court order, although it resolved the legal issue, seemed to most observers to render a violent confrontation inevitable. Even if Kolasiński would agree to vacate, his impassioned followers would not allow him to leave; if the police tried to evict him forcibly, violence was sure to ensue. The bishop had to make some concession if further bloodshed was to be averted. Yet when Kolasiński did manage to raise the amount of the appeal bond, in the form of numerous property deeds from his supporters, the bishop's attorneys challenged its sufficiency. At this juncture, Kolasiński appeared to give in. His lawyer offered to withdraw his client's appeal if the bishop would permit him to remain in the parish residence until 4 April. The bishop, through Jan Wagner, accepted the offer.[45]

Although Kolasiński's defeat now seemed complete, the wily priest still had one more stratagem to play. At the end of March he journeyed to Cincinnati in an attempt to enlist the intervention of Archbishop William Henry Elder, whose jurisdiction included the Detroit diocese.[46] Upon his return, Kolasiński let it be known through his followers that the archbishop had given him a letter instructing Bishop Borgess to lift Kolasiński's suspension and allow him to remain in the pastoral residence until the entire matter was resolved in Rome. Father Dempsey, speaking for the bishop, called the idea preposterous, but for a short time the Kolasińskiites were ecstatic; they believed they had won at last. It now appeared that Borgess's refusal of the archbishop's request would galvanize Kolasiński's supporters into frenzy.[47]

But by 29 March, this latest ploy was unmasked when the real contents of the archbishop's letter became known. The letter, to which Kolasiński had been obliged to add his own signature, stated only that he had called upon the archbishop and related his version of the troubles at St. Albertus's Church and his relations with the bishop. The letter further stated that Kolasiński had offered to leave the diocese forthwith if Borgess would provide him with an exeat. The archbishop, however, specifically refrained from rendering any recommendation of these matters. On 1 April the *Michigan Catholic* set out to expose what it regarded as Kolasiński's latest attempt at trickery. The newspaper, having sent a telegram to Cincinnati, published the archbishop's reply, which denounced Kolasiński's version of their exchange as a distortion and lie.[48]

Kolasiński's wish to procure an exeat is understandable for several reasons. Having come to the realization that he would have to leave the parish house and Detroit, he would need the exeat to secure a pastoral mission in another diocese. But more important, perhaps, an exeat would mean that the priest was no longer under sanction and was free of censure. Kolasiński could interpret the document to his adherents as a removal of the suspension and, by implication, of the charges against him. Even in leaving, Kolasiński could show the document as evidence of a victory of sorts, which indeed it would be.

Did the letter episode and the revelations in the *Michigan Catholic* lessen the ardor of Kolasiński's followers? The less worldly recent arrivals were not inclined to trust any pronouncements made by the "foreign" ecclesiastical hierarchy in Detroit. They put faith only in the words of their Galician priest. Their attitude toward their departing priest was perhaps best expressed by a young Pole, identified as Frank Yogalski (Franciszek Jagalski), who, when encountered by a *Free Press* reporter, was "rather the worse for liquor," but still remarkably articulate.

> Our Father Kolasinski is going and he leaves behind him 4,000 Poles who have been from the first faithful to him, have suffered abuse and ill-treatment, been deprived of the solacements of the church for him, and who today would willingly die for him. Fr. Kolasinski has been loyal, true-hearted and faithful to his people. And they love him. He is not quite four years in the country and yet the great St. Albertus Church . . . shows what he has done for us. Bishop Borgess has never been fair to the Polish people and Fr. Kolasinski is the fifth of our priests that he has driven from us. . . . Bishop Borgess' secretary says that only sixteen families hold out for Kolasinski. [But] fully three-fourths of St. Albertus' congregation still warmly support our self-sacrificing pastor. In the block where I live alone . . . there are 120 families who are for Kolasinski to

the end. We have watched his house to keep him from harm. That has been our only rebellion. Now he goes in obedience to the laws of the country. But we are not slaves. Bishop Borgess cannot put Father Dombrowski in the church from which he has driven out our Kolasinski. We can not understand Dombrowski.[49]

But during Kolasiński's last days in St. Albertus's parish house, there were also a few conspicuous defectors among his more prominent supporters, who were inclined to make their peace with the bishop. They included Antoni Spiegel and Kanut Gapczyński, president and secretary respectively of the parish's St. Joseph Society. Among the Kolasiński loyalists the rumor spread that each had received a hundred dollars from the Lemkes for denouncing Kolasiński.[50]

Even for those who may have still doubted that the Kolasiński crisis was really drawing to a close—that the controversial priest was indeed going to leave the parish house—the evidence of impending departure was overwhelming. On 3 April five large boxes were taken from the residence to the warehouses of the Riverside Cartage Company. And Kolasiński had begun to take leave of his closest associates, each of whom received a photograph of St. Albertus's Church with Kolasiński's carriage and team in front. Finally, on 5 April, the crisis which had embroiled Detroit's Poles for over four months seemingly came to a close. At 11:30 in the morning, Father Kolasiński personally delivered the keys to the pastoral residence into the hands of the bishop's attorney, Col. John Atkinson. To the press Kolasiński indicated that he was leaving that day for Berea, Ohio, where his brother served as priest.[51]

The tensions among the Poles did not lessen in the aftermath of Kolasiński's departure. When a group of Kolasiński partisans called a meeting on 9 April at Fredro Hall, it was disrupted and a clash ensued between the two factions, and the *Free Press* reported on 6 May, a month after Kolasiński's departure, that Polish women would still gather every day outside the closed church and accost passersby: "Are you friends of Kolasiński? No? Then we'll smash you when we get a chance." Apparently unwilling to let the issue fade, the *Evening News* on 20 April ran a headline, "Where is Kolasiński?" Was he still in Detroit, staying with friends, as his opponents unanimously asserted, or had he indeed left the city?[52]

Kolasiński had in fact left Detroit, ultimately for the Dakota Territory, where he had obtained a pastoral post. And he had in his possession an exeat, dated 9 April 1886, granted by Bishop

Borgess.[53] Presumably the understanding stemmed from Kolasiński's assurance that he would never come back to Detroit if he were given the document clearing him of censure. But such would not be the case. Two-and-one-half years later, Father Kolasiński would return, establish his own maverick parish, build a church even more magnificent than the "finest Polish Church in America," and embroil Detroit and its Polish community in another decade of controversy. The turmoil of Kolasiński's suspension and departure was but a foretaste of events to come.

CHAPTER 3
A TENSE INTERLUDE

In possession of the exeat that he had finally obtained from Bishop Borgess, Father Kolasiński presented himself to Bishop Martin Marty, vicar-apostolic of the Dakota Territory, who assigned him to the small Prussian-Polish and Kashubian settlement in Warsaw (also known as Pulaski) near Minto. For a person of Kolasiński's urbane and cosmopolitan ways, this remote outpost, with its long, cold winters, must have seemed doubly like banishment. Yet he endured there for over two years with no apparent ill effects. During the controversial priest's absence, however, the splits and tensions within Detroit's Polish community abated little. In retrospect, the thirty-two months of Kolasiński's exile appear to be a tense interlude in the longer saga of Detroit's late-nineteenth-century Polish church troubles. To be sure, Kolasiński's most outspoken opponents, such as Jan Wagner, remained convinced, even three months after the priest's eviction from the rectory of St. Albertus's, that he was still "hovering around Detroit." Wagner even telegraphed Bishop Marty to determine if Kolasiński was in fact serving in the Dakota diocese.[1]

One legacy of the first phase of the Kolasiński crisis was the Lewicki murder trial. The protracted tensions in the Polish community had prompted city officials to delay for almost six months before bringing Bazyli and Aleksander Lemke and August Stieber

63

to trial. Finally opening on 8 July 1886 and lasting almost a week, the proceedings became one of the most celebrated murder trials in late-nineteenth-century Detroit.[2] Judge Swift's courtroom was packed with spectators, many of whom, in the words of a *Free Press* reporter, "bore the unmistakable physiognomy of the Polanders." Among them was Franciszka Lewicka, the slain man's widow, who was now quite visibly with child. For the first two days of the trial the prosecuting attorney paraded witnesses, Poles and policemen, who testified that the crowd outside the Lemkes' store, at least until the shooting, had posed no serious threat to the building's occupants. But these same witnesses were not able to agree on how many shots were fired and by whom. The effect of their collective testimony was to ensure that the person guilty of the fatal shot, whether Bazyli or Aleksander Lemke, could not be positively distinguished. After a weekend's rest, it was the turn of the defense, which called Jan Wagner, Tomasz Żółtowski, and the elder Jan Lemke, all of whom testified to the violent mood of the mob on 25 December and to the repeated threats to the Lemkes from persons whom, they claimed, Kolasiński had inspired directly. On the final day of the trial the three defendants took the stand. The key figure was Bazyli Lemke, who, without showing remorse or contrition, recited a long litany of abuse and threats to which he and his family had been subjected since the onset of the Kolasiński Affair.

Throughout the proceedings the prosecuting attorney had seemed reluctant to press the case for murder, and in fact appeared relieved when the judge in his charge to the jury ruled out a possible verdict of murder, stating that malice aforethought had not been shown, and that the most severe penalty that could be rendered was manslaughter. The jury, which did not include a single Polish-surnamed member, apparently appreciated the claims of self-defense among the allegedly law-abiding Polish element. After only five minutes of deliberation, they returned with a verdict of not guilty for all three defendants. The acquittal of the Lemkes hardly set well with the Kolasińskiites, whose distrust of the "foreign" bishop and the police was now extended to the courts as well. In this respect, Bishop Borgess's intimation shortly after the trial ended that he would reopen St. Albertus's Church, "if the congregation would confess its guilt and promise amendment and obedience to ecclesiastical authority," was certainly ill-timed.[3]

On 16 August 1886, the day following an announcement in the city's Catholic churches of the forthcoming reopening, a large crowd of Kolasiński adherents gathered in front of St. Albertus's. When they learned that no action was to be taken at the church, rather than dispersing they turned their anger on the Felician convent across the street. Several sisters were threatened and stones were thrown through the windows of the orphanage.[4] Outraged by the violence toward the Polish sisters as well as the hostile rejection of his offer of clemency, Bishop Borgess drafted an edict of excommunication of the rebellious faction of St. Albertus's Parish. But then, for some reason, the bishop decided not to promulgate the order and the censure was not put into effect.[5] Eight months later, however, the bishop would no longer hesitate to take this extreme step.

This latest "Polish riot" had taken place during the absence of Father Dąbrowski, who, though still nominally pastor of St. Albertus's Church, had journeyed to Europe in late May. The ostensible purpose of his visit, to partitioned Poland and to Rome, was to secure the services of several Polish priests to teach at the Polish seminary which he planned to open by the end of 1886. Dąbrowski also carried a letter from Bishop Borgess authorizing him "to deliberate with the . . . Bishop of Poland [sic] about . . . adopting two Polish priests for our diocese," most likely to take charge of St. Albertus's.[6] During Dąbrowski's absence, his place as chaplain to the Felician Sisters was taken by Father Domagalski from the Parisville mission. Domagalski, of course, was principally responsible for the charges regarding Kolasiński's moral failings while still in Poland, and his tenure at the Felician convent may have caused the Kolasińskiites in August to turn their anger in his direction.

Construction on the seminary, which during the initial phase of the Kolasiński troubles had been brought "practically . . . to a standstill," was again temporarily halted in early July when an adherent of Kolasiński, a W. Sztybert "who had climbed upon the seminary framework, fell from the structure to the ground and killed himself."[7] Dąbrowski's plans suffered a further setback at about this time when Father Jaworski, who had been serving as Dąbrowski's assistant in the parish as well as on the seminary project, broke with his superior and precipitously left Detroit. While in Kraków, Dąbrowski was able to secure from Archbishop Dunajewski the release of two diocesan priests, the Reverend Wincenty Bronikowski and the Reverend Hipolit Barański, to the Detroit diocese for a period of four years to serve in his stead.[8] But since neither priest had much experience in seminary teaching, the immediate speculation upon Dąbrowski's return to Detroit in early September was that he had in fact brought the two priests to take over St. Albertus's Parish. The response of the Kolasińskiites was by now predictable.

As one of their spokesmen reported to the *Free Press*, "Dombrowski might bring back with him a dozen priests if he felt so inclined, but they would not be recognized."[9]

By fall 1886 it had become apparent that the loyalist faction—that is, the so-called Dąbrowskiites—in the Polish church controversy had grown to such numbers that they could no longer be accommodated for services in the Felicians' chapel and that many had begun attending services in the Bohemian, German, and even French parishes. Since the reopening of St. Albertus's had evidently been postponed indefinitely because of the riotous scenes in August, an addition was made to the Felicians' chapel which greatly expanded its seating capacity.[10]

Upon his return from Europe, Dąbrowski, despite sporadic harassment from the Kolasiński faction, devoted all his attention to readying at least a substantial portion of the seminary for occupancy by the year's end. On 16 December 1886, a year and a half after the laying of the cornerstone, the Polish seminary, the first in the United States to provide Polish-speaking priests for the growing number of Polish immigrants, was ready to be officially opened. For the first time since the outbreak of the Kolasiński troubles, Borgess ventured into the east-side Polish quarter. He was met near the seminary building by members of the lay St. Albertus and St. Stanisław Kostka parish societies, who, "with their banners flying, formed an escort before and behind the Bishop's carriage." A large crowd was in attendance at the seminary, many attracted by the hope of hearing that their church would soon be reopened. But this was not to be. The bishop blessed the new structure and delivered a sermon in German following the mass celebrated by Father Dąbrowski, but he had nothing to say on the church troubles in the Polish quarter. The bishop also met with the group of seminarians who would now commence their studies. Though trouble from the Kolasińskiites had been anticipated at the ceremonies—the expectation of disturbances had become almost axiomatic in the press—nothing of that kind occurred. Kolasiński's name, by all accounts, was never even mentioned, and the only police officer on duty had in fact nothing to do on that day.[11]

The first years of the seminary's existence were especially trying for Father Dąbrowski.[12] In addition to the not insignificant problems of financing, organization, and staffing, the seminary was inescapably buffeted by the ongoing religious division within Detroit's east-side Polish community. Dąbrowski's immediate and paramount concern, however, was to secure a sufficient and competent faculty.

Artist's rendering of the planned SS. Cyril and Methodius Seminary ("the Polish seminary") to be built on the corner of Forest and St. Aubin. Courtesy of the Archives of the Orchard Lake Schools.

The Polish seminary as it was actually built on its Detroit location. Reproduced by permission from the Sunday News-Tribune, *29 May 1898.*

Antoni Długi. Reproduced by permission from the Evening News, *30 November 1888.*

When the seminary officially opened its doors, the faculty consisted solely of Dąbrowski as rector and the two priests from Kraków. Dąbrowski also was director of the Felician Sisters and nominal pastor of St. Albertus's. In the summer of 1887 the pressures on Dąbrowski were eased when Fr. Witold Buhaczkowski arrived from Rome. He would remain at the seminary as a teacher for over thirty years and, following Dąbrowski's death in 1903, would assume the rectorship. But until a sufficient full-time teaching staff could be built up, Dąbrowski had to rely on the help of several local Polish priests, including Fr. Leopold Moczygemba, on a short-term basis. Then, in the fall of 1890, Fr. M. Barabasz from Louvin joined the faculty and also served as vice-rector.

The Polish seminary—officially entitled SS. Cyril and Methodius Seminary—grew rapidly. By the end of its first year, in June 1887, there were twenty-two students, and three years later there were sixty-five. Most of the early students came from Detroit and had been born in partitioned Poland. From the outset, the seminary imitated the classical and religious curriculum of the Roman colleges. Philosophical and theological studies were conducted in Latin, and the classics were taught in English and Polish. In 1888 a preparatory, preseminarian division was added, which took the name St. Mary's. In 1890 the seminary graduated its first three students, who were then ordained in the priesthood. As was perhaps inevitable in the divided Polish-American community of the 1880s, there was some criticism of the seminary's program and especially of what were described as Dąbrowski's strict disciplinarian ways. These criticisms were found especially in publications associated with the lay-oriented Polish National Alliance, which was engaged at the time in a fratricidal struggle with the more clerically minded Polish Roman Catholic Union for the allegiance of the Poles in America. The seminary was obliged to survive on outside contributions, since tuition payments were insufficient to meet the institution's needs and there was no regular support from the diocesan chancery. Additional funds were also obtained through the seminary's press, which published Dąbrowski's many tracts and texts for the education of Polish children in America, as well as studies aimed at the practical enlightenment of the Polish community.

For a while the seminary also housed the St. Albertus's parochial school because of the closing of the school building by Kolasiński's followers at the onset of the church troubles. The children of the loyalist faction were taught by the Felicians at the convent until the new seminary building was opened,[13] while the children of Kola-

siński's followers attended a private school on Riopelle run by
Antoni Długi, of whom more will be said.

In March 1887 rumors again spread through the Polish quarter
that Bishop Borgess was planning to reopen St. Albertus's, at which
time Fathers Bronikowski and Barański would be installed as
pastors. These rumors coincided with a spurious report that had
appeared in the Polish newspaper *Wiarus*, published in Winona,
Minnesota, that "Archbishop Elder [of Cincinnati] had received
instructions from Rome to reinstate Rev. Fr. Kolasinski as pastor of
St. Albertus' and that the latter would at once return to Detroit."
Even though Dąbrowski termed the report a complete fabrication,
possibly planted by Kolasiński himself through a friend at the
Minnesota paper, the Kolasińskiites began to keep a daily guard of
about fifty persons at the church.[14] On 20 March, the day rumored
for the reopening, a crowd of upwards of three thousand people,
separated into Kolasińskiites and Dąbrowskiites, gathered near the
church. The Kolasińskiites grouped themselves at the north side of
the intersection of St. Aubin and Canfield, while the Dąbrowskiites
held the southern side of the intersection and their ranks extended
along St. Aubin in the direction of the Lemke store.[15] Although only
some among the crowd were aware of the fact, Bishop Borgess had
on the previous day relieved Dąbrowski of the pastorship of St.
Albertus's and appointed Bronikowski in his stead, with Barański as
his assistant. The bishop, therefore, initially may well have planned
to reopen St. Albertus's Church on 20 March with the new pastor.
But the mounting evidence over the previous days of the Kolasińskiites' intention to disrupt any such step had decided the bishop
against revoking the closing.[16]

Throughout the day the two sides held their respective ground
as their numbers ebbed and flowed. Then, toward late afternoon,
the police force positioned between the two factions was augmented.
As the time neared for members of the loyalist faction to leave the
services at the Felician chapel, the police attempted to push the
Kolasińskiites further away from the intersection. (The Dąbrowskiites, whom the police referred to as "our people," had welcomed the
reinforcements.) The Kolasiński crowd seemed reluctant to retreat,
and at one point, according to a reporter for the *Free Press*, "a Pole
leaned forward from the crowd and struck Officer Schaffron a
terrible blow in the face with a brick which he held in his hand." The
wounded officer, blood streaming from his face, lunged forward,
seized his assailant, and dragged him to the police lines. At this point
the Kolasińskiites, numbering perhaps a thousand, seemed to erupt

into a frenzy, throwing all sorts of missiles and charging the police in a vain attempt to liberate their compatriot. Fearing for their lives, the officers fired a number of shots into the air in a desperate attempt to slow the onrushing mob. At the same time, keeping their prisoner in tow, they retreated to the nearest call box and sent out an emergency appeal for reinforcements. The line of retreat took the police toward the Dąbrowski faction, whose proximity—and the speedy arrival of more bluecoats—eventually halted the Kolasiński-ites' advance. The fight, though it had lasted perhaps only five minutes, led to the injury of several officers in addition to Schaffron, whose face was terribly disfigured. It was also learned later that one of the Polish bystanders, a girl identified as Annie Wobrack, suffered a painful flesh wound caused by a police bullet.[17] Officer Schaffron was described in the press as being a Pole, and it is likely that his ordering the Poles, in their own tongue, to disperse heightened their anger and helped precipitate the initial clash. By 8:00 P.M. the police, now numbering over fifty officers, had succeeded in clearing the streets immediately adjacent to the church and in separating the two factions.

By the next morning, 21 March, relative quiet had returned to the Polish quarter, though a group of Kolasińskiite women remained on guard in front of the church. It was clear, however, in the aftermath of this latest "Polish riot"—which had made front-page news as far away as in the *Atlanta Constitution*—that the bishop was not about to undertake any immediate move to reopen the church.[18] The first public announcement of Dąbrowski's replacement as temporary pastor of St. Albertus's Church was not made in the local press until 22 March, which gave rise to the false impression that he had resigned or been removed because of the violent disturbances on the previous Sunday.[19]

Within a couple of days after these latest Polish disturbances, the leaders of the Dąbrowski faction and the police authorities had come to the opinion that the best means to handle the "riotous Kolasinskiites" and ensure against further outbreaks was to see that many of their leaders landed in jail. Accordingly, on 24 March the injured Schaffron, accompanied by Bazyli Lemke and Jan Wagner, submitted a lengthy list of Kolasińskiites to Police Court Justice John Miner, who issued, on the basis of their testimony, some thirty arrest warrants. The technical charge in each instance was rioting and assault. To carry out the arrests without provoking a new riot, the police decided to make a silent nighttime sweep through the Polish quarter. A reporter for the *Morning Tribune* who was permitted to accompany the officers gave a melodramatic account of one of the midnight arrests.

> The [arresting] party stopped before a small frame house at 101 Benton street and Roundsman Slater with a patrolman entered. "We wish to see Martin Lavinski," he said to the Polish woman who opened the door. "Where is he?" Lavinski was in bed, but the two officers entered his room and woke him up. When the Pole saw the handcuffs he jumped up suddenly and seizing a . . . saber that stood in a convenient corner of the room made a dash at the officers. Raising the saber in both hands, but forgetting in his excitement to remove it from the scabbard, he brought the weapon with terrific force upon Slater's shoulders. The Pole was quickly disarmed and led outside.[20]

Apparently, word of the police sweep spread quickly through the Polish community, and the police were forced to halt their operation after only nine arrests. That night an extra guard was mounted around the Gratiot Avenue station in case the Poles might attempt to rescue their compatriots. The next morning two more arrests were made, and within a couple of days nearly twenty Poles were in custody on charges of rioting and assault. Stunned perhaps by the sudden loss of their most outspoken members, the Kolasiński faction attempted no disruptions on the following Sunday, 27 March, when Father Bronikowski conducted services at the Felician chapel.[21]

Those arrested in the police roundup were brought up for preliminary examination and indictment on 30 March in Justice Miner's courtroom. As was to be the case in all the legal proceedings involving the Poles during the years of the church troubles, the chamber was overflowing with Polish spectators, and a large crowd of those who had failed to gain admission milled about outside the building. Initially the authorities were hard pressed to separate from the crowd the many defendants, all but two of whom had been out on bail. Eventually eighteen defendants were counted, but the identity of the absent ones was only established with great difficulty. Detroit's English-language papers suggested that local officials were often befuddled in trying to distinguish the Polish surnames, which were usually spelled phonetically because so many immigrants were illiterate. Different spellings in the documents for the name of a single individual occasionally led the authorities to connect a name to the wrong person.

The principal prosecution witness was Captain Mack, chief of the Gratiot Avenue station, who, in two hours of testimony, endeavored to establish that a riot had in fact occurred on 20 March. He also alleged that the first shots had come from the mob. Patrolman Schaffron then identified nine of the defendants who, he said, had thrown bricks at the officers and the Felician convent. Several other officers took the stand to point out other defendants who, they claimed, had incited the crowd and also thrown objects at the police.[22] On the second day of the hearing, more officers were called to identify the alleged ringleaders. They were followed by several Polish witnesses, all Dąbrowskiites, who readily identified the defendants as the leaders of the disruptive forces. The unsuppressible Jan Wagner also testified, using the opportunity to denounce Father Kolasiński's machinations from afar in the current troubles. The Polish witnesses were frequently interrupted by the defendants, and it could be said that court decorum was not always maintained.[23]

As the preliminary examination dragged over the weekend into a third day, it became increasingly apparent that the prosecution was putting on a sort of publicity show to discredit the Kolasińskiites in the public mind. The attention paid to the proceedings in the press in no way had abated. Finally, when the prosecution finished its parade of witnesses, the defense moved for dismissal, which was denied. And when the defendants could produce no witnesses, Justice Miner indicted all of them on the charges of rioting and assault and ordered them bound over for trial. The prosecution asked for stiff bail and the obliging Miner concurred, setting the amount at $1,000 for each defendant. Three of the defendants managed to post this amount. The indicted Poles were brought before Recorder's Court Judge George S. Swift on 3 May for arraignment, at which time all pleaded not guilty; bail was kept at the same amount.[24] As late as 24 June, the day of the reopening of St. Albertus's Church, the defendants were still awaiting trial.

In addition to these legal measures initiated to cool the spirited Kolasińskiites, other actions with worse consequences for them were taken by Bishop Borgess in the aftermath of the 20 March riot. After waiting a month, he issued, on 23 April, a decree of excommunication against the unreconciled Poles. He directed Father Bronikowski to read the order at mass in the Felician chapel on 24 April. *Die Stimme der Wahrheit*, a German Catholic paper very close to the bishop, published the decree in German. The English text was not published until 3 May, the same day on which the bishop's resignation as head of the Detroit diocese was made public. The simultaneous appearances of the two items left the clear impression that the excommunication order was, so to speak, the bishop's parting shot (one report called it a "Parthian shaft") at the Poles who had caused him so much grief.

The bishop's lengthy decree stated that having "already for seventeen months exercised Christian patience in the hope that [the rebellious members of St. Albertus's congregation] would see the error of their ways and would submit in contrition to the Christian authority, but to date have shown no submission but a greater stubbornness, therefore, we are forced, after ·ineffectual public warnings, to punish those insubordinates against the authority of the church with public excommunication, in order that the true believers of . . . [the] congregation and Catholics in general may not take offense." The bishop cited seven categories of offenders, each and all of whom were subject to the order: first, "all those men and women who on December 1 and 2, 1885, took part in the brutal disturbance of the mass in word and deed, and also all those men and women who on the same day forcibly ejected Revs. Joseph Dombrowski and Anton Jaworski from St. Albertus' Church"; second, "all those men and women who caused the public and bloody riot of December 25, 1885, and who took part in the same by advice, word and deed"; third, "the committee, and every single member thereof, which was chosen by the malcontents, or pretended that they were chosen by them, and that represented the faction in meetings and newspapers"; fourth, "all officers and also the several members of the Kosciusko Guard, who took forcible possession of the parsonage of St. Albertus' congregation, and held the same against the authority of the bishop"; fifth, "the committee, and each single member thereof, which disseminated the untruthful reports [directing Kolasiński's reinstatement] which they claimed to have received from Rome and Cincinnati"; sixth, "all those men and women who by advice, word and deed took part in the bloody riot of March 20, 1887"; and seventh, "all those persons who pretended that they were in correspondence with Rev. Dominic Kolasinski, and who from time to time disseminated the report 'that the reverend gentleman exhorted them to persist in their opposition to the authority of the church till he came and opened the church.'" The order concluded: "All above mentioned persons we hereby declare to be formally and publicly excommunicated, and we hereby declare and make known that all above mentioned persons are expelled from the Church of God, and will remain so till each and every one of them, singly, is absolved by us."[25]

A week after issuing this blanket and retroactive decree, Bishop

Borgess informed Father Bronikowski of the specific steps that each excommunicated individual would have to take "to obtain absolution and be reunited with the Church." First, he must enter his name in the register of St. Albertus's Parish; second, he must do public penance for his past wrongdoings on three successive Sundays before high mass; and third, he must observe for eight days strict fast and abstinence, being allowed only one meal a day.[26] But if the bishop's extreme action was intended to cow the remaining Kolasińskiites into submission, it failed. As Joseph Swastek has noted, "The available records do not speak of any public penances or submissions to episcopal authority."[27]

Bishop Borgess's decision to lay down the mitre had been made some weeks earlier, probably in the aftermath of the riotous scenes of 20 March. But the decision was a well-kept secret and was only announced after a letter, dated 16 April, accepting his resignation was received on 2 May from the Propaganda in Rome. Born in Germany, Caspar Borgess had come to America at a young age and settled near Cincinnati. There he had been trained for the priesthood and ordained. When in 1870 he had come to Detroit, the diocese, according to the assessment of the bishop's career that appeared in the *Evening News*, was in disarray: "Priests would walk the streets with cigars in their mouths, wearing slouch hats and rusty coats. They had a free and easy way of doing things . . . [and] did not preserve the dignity of their high calling." To such habits the new bishop had brought an abrupt halt. But his arbitrary ways ruffled many a sensitive spirit and his centralized administration of the diocese was achieved at the expense of harmony, especially between himself and the individual parishes. In the opinion of one lay Catholic critic,

> intellectually [Bishop Borgess] was not a strong man. . . . He was stern and even abusive to those who met with his displeasure and would submit tamely to his authority, while to those who met him boldly he was cringing and timid. His character was that of the traditional bully. . . . He was not a sociable man, except with a few of his intimates, and was frequently rude and blunt. . . . He lately surrounded himself by narrow-minded, incompetent and truckling advisers, through whom he sought to feel the public pulse, and the errors into which they have led him are notorious. It is well that he resigned!

Even the bishop's supporters were obliged to concede that he was "not personally loved."[28] The bishop remained in office until 10

May, when he nominated Rev. Edward Joos as interim administrator of the diocese. Nineteen months would pass before a successor to the bishop would be named, and it would ultimately be that decision which determined Father Kolasiński's return to Detroit.

Despite the turmoil and internecine struggle in the Polish community, the confrontations in court, and the excommunication order, numerous Polish Detroiters assembled peaceably at Fredro Hall on 3 May 1887 to commemorate the ninety-sixth anniversary of the enactment of the Polish constitution of 1791 that had aimed to transform the old Polish-Lithuanian commonwealth into a viable, modern constitutional monarchy that would breathe new life into the crumbling, battered state. (The constitution, however, had in fact led to further dissension among the Polish gentry and become the pretext for further foreign intrigue in Poland and to its extinction through two additional rounds of partition.) The evening's program was organized by the Detroit chapters of the Polish National Alliance.[29]

Notwithstanding the order of excommunication, which the unreconciled faction chose to interpret as the vindictive act of the "German" bishop rather than the true censure of Holy Church, rumors persisted among the Kolasiński faithful that their beloved pastor was returning. On the evening of Ascension Thursday, 19 May, a large crowd, estimated at over a thousand and comprising mostly women, gathered outside the parish rectory, presumably intending to expel publicly Father Bronikowski and his assistants, who had quietly taken up residence there since Bronikowski's appointment as St. Albertus's pastor. As word of the Kolasińskiites' latest action spread, the loyalist faction, who continued to refer to themselves as "Dąbrochy," also began to collect. With the ever-present Jan Wagner in the lead, a group of about one hundred men began to disperse the women by force. Fortunately, the police arrived in time to separate the two factions before more blood was shed.[30] Yet, remarkably, the disturbance on 19 May was the last serious clash involving such large numbers in the Polish quarter for several years. To be sure, the differences between the loyalist parish faction and the unreconciled Kolasińskiites persisted, and in fact intensified, but the latter were for the time being sufficiently intimidated to refrain from more than sporadic individual clashes.[31]

With a new occupant in the diocesan residence, Bronikowski and the parish elders renewed their efforts to find a formula for reopening St. Albertus's Church, one that would satisfy the diocesan hierarchy but not precipitate further disturbances. A serious concern, of course, for Bronikowski and the parish trustees, no less than for

Administrator Joos, was the reality that as long as the church remained closed and under interdict, no real progress could be made in reducing the sizable debt that Kolasiński had incurred in building the new church. Eventually it was decided to initiate a "parish mission," a series of sermons with discussions open to the whole congregation and conducted by an outside priest uninvolved in the factional strife. These religious meetings might pave the way toward a reasonably tranquil reopening. As his choice for a priest suited to lead the mission, Joos turned to a Jesuit, Rev. Władysław Sebastyański, who was widely hailed as "the greatest pulpit orator [of his day] speaking the Polish language." He had come to America a few years earlier at the request of Bishop James O'Connor of Omaha, Nebraska, who at the time was having difficulties with several Polish congregations in his diocese. Word of Sebastyański's successes in reconciling these parishes to episcopal authority prompted Joos to invite him to Detroit.[32]

For more than a week in mid-June, as many as six missions a day were held, with increasing attendance. According to the *Free Press*, Sebastyański's eloquence "literally carried the people by storm.

> In the short time of his ministry [he] has literally out Kola-sinskied Kolasinski. Already he has won the hearts of the people and they hang about his skirts and listen to his every word. At first these meetings were attended only by members of the Dombrowski faction, but the priest labored to break down the spirit of faction and sent his hearers forth to bear the olive branch of peace to the admirers of Kolasinski. [And gradually] members of that faction were induced to attend.

By the evening of 23 June the mission seemed to have reached a climax. According to a contemporary account:

> The crowd numbered fully 8,000; almost every member of the Kolasinski faction was present; the eloquent Jesuit urged brotherly love, peace on earth and good will to men. He vividly portrayed the condition of the Polish people—strangers in a strange land, who should let no enmity supervene to militate against their common weal. The immense throng was melted to tears and when the priest had reached the height of his impassioned appeal he shouted out: "This church does not belong to a faction, but to the Polish people and to God. Shall we occupy it or not?" [At this point] a perfect hurricane of ayes rent the air.[33]

With remarkable rhetorical skill and an innate ability to tap the innermost wishes of his listeners, Sebastyański had paved the way for the opening that finally took place the next day.

But for a while during the morning of Friday, 24 June, it seemed that all the preparatory work by the Jesuit father might have been wasted. Indiscretion and hesitation by Bronikowski and possible second thoughts on the part of Joos—who was informed that a few diehard Kolasińskiites were preaching violence—almost provoked a disturbance where none actually was planned. Although there had been no formal announcement that the church would reopen, it was widely understood that Joos had left the decision to Bronikowski, who was expected to follow the advice of the Jesuit missionary. After celebrating morning mass in the Felician chapel, Bronikowski and his assistants crossed the street to the open space before the church, where he announced to the assembled throng that the church would be opened that very morning. Then, inexplicably, as joy spread through the crowd, he ordered the Kolasińskiites to reconcile themselves or leave. A din and commotion grew, and the police on the scene called for reinforcements. Soon over seventy-five patrolmen were in the vicinity and Sebastyański's good work seemed likely to be undone. At this moment Bronikowski and several parish trustees, including Wagner, left to consult the diocesan administrator. From the reports made by his own informants, Joos was beginning to take the Kolasińskiites' earlier threats seriously and had misgivings about opening the church. When two hours passed and Bronikowski had not returned, the crowd became restless. Then, at about 11:30 A.M. a messenger from Joos arrived with a request for the remaining trustees to come to the bishop's residence. Perhaps still unsure in his new role and understandably fearful of the consequences of his decision to reopen the church, the administrator now wanted formal requests from Bronikowski and the trustees to proceed in the matter.

During this time, about three thousand people remained in the vicinity of the church. A group of Kolasińskiite women, estimated at about two hundred, attempted to foment unrest but were easily isolated by the police. Bronikowski at last returned around 1:00 P.M. to confirm that the church would open. Then, except for one incident when a Kolasińskiite tried to strike Bronikowski in the face (which by church tradition would render him unsuitable to perform mass), the doors that had remained closed since 3 December 1885—over nineteen months—at last opened. A formal procession from the Felician convent to the church was guided by members of the

St. Stanisław Kostka Society in full regalia, while members of the societies of St. Albertus and St. Joseph stood shoulder to shoulder along the way, and Bronikowski led the worshipers through the gates and into the church. Within minutes the church was filled to overflowing. One newspaper estimated the crowd at six thousand. Technically, the church was still under interdict, and therefore no mass was celebrated. As he had during the previous days, Father Sebastyański delivered the sermon.[34] The apparent ease in reopening the church led some observers to wonder how the crisis could have lasted so long; in their surprise they perhaps underestimated the remarkable achievement of the Jesuit father from the Mississippi Valley.[35]

Father Bronikowski, now in fact the pastor of the vast east-side St. Albertus's Parish, had been born in Prussian Poland in 1853. He had begun theological and seminarian studies in Poznań and Gniezno, but as a consequence of Bismarck's anti-Catholic, germanizing policies had left his native province to complete his studies in Vienna and Kraków, where he was ordained. He became pastor of St. Albertus's at age thirty-four.[36]

In the eyes of Administrator Joos, 24 June had been a test which the city's Polish quarter had passed. Accordingly, on the next day he wrote to Father Bronikowski, formally lifting the interdict; mass was celebrated in the formerly proscribed church the same day.[37] An editorial in the *Evening News* proclaimed "Poland Redeemed," and cited "the eloquence of a Jesuit missionary, the firmness and determination of the pastor, the reluctant consent of the [diocesan] administrator, *and* the strong hand of the police department" as having joined together to bring to a happy conclusion the crisis that had long embroiled the city's east-side Polish quarter.[38] This euphoria of the *News* would prove premature, but there was nonetheless every reason for the city and its Polish residents to rejoice over what had been achieved in a little over a week in June 1887. Bronikowski and the police still worried that a disturbance might occur on Sunday, 26 June, around the reopened church, but except for the removal of three unreconciled Kolasińskiites and an occasional skirmish with a handful of intoxicated malcontents outside the church, the two hundred officers stationed in the vicinity on that day had little to do. One sign that boded ill for the future, however, was a report in the *Free Press*, which identified the ringleader of the unreconciled Kolasiński remnant as the schoolteacher "Anton Gluki."[39] Soon this man—actually his name was Długi—would become almost as controversial as his mentor Kolasiński.

As might be expected, over a year of strife within the Polish Catholic community was seized upon as an irresistible opportunity for Protestant proselytizing. A Polish-speaking missionary from the Woodward Avenue Baptist Church tried to hold a revival meeting in Fredro Hall but was hounded from the building. The *Evening News* reported the incident on 3 July 1887: "The preliminary singing in English was tolerated all right, but the moment the missionary began to read from the bible in their native tongue all the curiosity of the listening Poles seemed to change into a fiery hatred and they made a dash for him."[40] Divided as they were over their own religious disputes, the Catholic Poles were united in their abhorrence of "heresy."

Such incidents aside, however, a period of relative quiet and reconsolidation settled over the Detroit east-side Polish quarter, and Poles all but disappeared from the headlines for almost a year. Father Bronikowski saw a steady upswing in the membership of St. Albertus's, especially among the continuing flow of new Polish immigrants.[41] To be sure, a hard core of Kolasiński adherents still remained outside the pale of the Roman Catholic church. And it is fair to say that an even greater number, though ostensibly having made peace with the ecclesiastical authorities, still hoped for the return of the "real" pastor, Kolasiński. The irreconcilables fell into the habit of periodically "taking over a church" on Saturdays. For example, on 14 April 1888, a large group—perhaps a thousand—occupied most of the pews in St. Aloysius's Church, where Fr. Ernest Van Dyke was preparing for a funeral mass. The leader of the Kolasińskiites on this occasion was Antoni Długi. Answering a reporter's question as to why the Poles visited other churches on Saturdays, he said: "Just to show our strength. Our people go to church on Sundays, but not in a body nor all to one church. We have this demonstration on Saturdays because then the children are home from school." He further asserted that only a portion of his people were present, namely those who were out of work.[42]

Finally, in June 1888, almost a year after the reopening of St. Albertus's, Długi was able to deliver on his often stated promise that Father Kolasiński would return to Detroit. Four thousand people gathered outside Długi's school at the corner of Riopelle and Canfield on 7 June to greet their idol. A reporter asked, "Have you come to stay?" The priest replied, "No, I have merely come for a stay of four or five days to see my friends. . . . When my visit is ended I shall return to my parish in Dakota." To the *Evening News* reporter who dogged his trail during this first day, Kolasiński "looked the man content with his lot and at peace with all the world. . . . The greeting [of his loyal followers] was a characteristic one. Men, women and children seemed wild with excitement, and were restrained only by reverence for the man whom they hastened to salute. Strong men held their hats in one hand while with the other they seized that of the priest and showered kisses upon it. The women mingled tears with their kisses and crowded their little ones forward." The priest spent most of the day going from home to home among his followers, but he told his flock, "I am not coming back for good at present. I hope, however, to be with you soon, and to remain with you as long as I live. I have every reason to believe that my appeal to Rome against the course taken in my case will receive the favorable consideration which you and I desire."[43]

Although Kolasiński lodged during his short stay in Detroit with his old friend Józef Przybyłowski, who lived on Michigan Avenue on the city's west side, each day the priest journeyed across town to Długi's schoolhouse to receive the homage of his faithful adherents. The major event of the visit was the so-called Kolasiński picnic held at Burns's grove, about a mile and a half beyond the tollgate on Gratiot Avenue. An estimated five thousand people made the journey, including the members of the Kościuszko Guard in their brilliant uniforms. One hundred kegs of beer were consumed and the priest and Długi collected a reported four thousand dollars from the concessions and in donations. A reporter on the scene wrote that Kolasiński "carries himself as a prince. He is a captivating conversationalist, witty and jolly, and has a pleasant word for all."[44] The brief visit halted the ebb of Kolasiński's support and his self-appointed lieutenants began to prepare his followers for the priest's permanent return. The *Michigan Catholic*, however, had only contempt for Kolasiński's staging his "boisterous picnic" on the Sabbath, thereby violating the sanctity of the day and "pocketing the profits of [his followers'] beer drinking."[45]

The Kolasińskiites' principal leader and spokesman, Antoni Długi, understood well the need to stage periodic rallies to keep up the emotional fervor of the maverick flock and remind the loyalist faction of the undiminished strength of support for the absent priest. And of course Długi constantly made assurances that Kolasiński would soon be returning permanently. Despite a heavy rain, for example, Długi proceeded with a parade on 7 October 1888, in which over one thousand Kolasiński adherents marched.[46] Taking another page from the Kolasiński book, Długi, upon learning that a new bishop had at last been appointed, made a trip to

Baltimore to meet Bishop John S. Foley before he came to Detroit. Although the bishop subsequently maintained that he had merely heard Długi out, the latter triumphantly announced to his people that Foley had "promised him that everything would be managed to the entire satisfaction of the Kolasinski faction."[47] The gullible Kolasińskiites interpreted the message to mean that their priest would be reinstated.

Who was this man whom the press described as the "ringleader of the Kolasinskiites"? In a sketch that appeared in the *Evening News*, he was described as "a most successful agitator." The article went on:

> Like most such characters, he borders on positive ignorance himself, but has a native shrewdness and a knack of inspiring his followers with an idea of his greatness and goodness. The poor, ignorant Poles . . . look upon him in the light of a protector to guard them from spiritual and bodily evils. . . . Dlugi has succeeded in not only alienating his followers from the church, but in making them positively antagonize it. His people kneel down before him in the street and receive his grandiloquent blessing. They kiss his gown, and he is king among them. As a king he draws a good income through their credulity and ignorance, and has put a neat lining into his purse.

He had been born in Poland only slightly above the peasant class. His father was a blacksmith, and young Długi had learned that trade. As a boy he had served as an acolyte in the church and apparently learned a few Latin phrases which he now turned to good use. He arrived in Detroit just shortly before Kolasiński was compelled to leave the city.

> He became a confidant of Kolasinski, and the people who were so devoted to their priest looked with almost reverence upon that priest's friend. He gained a great influence over them after Kolasinski left, and using that name as a war cry, a watch word and countersign, has kept them his devoted servants and subjects and the source of his income. . . . Although so unlearned that he can hardly write his own name, he had the astonishing cheek to set himself up as a school master. . . . Of late he has donned the priestly garb, and has persuaded his followers that he had taken the lower orders of the priesthood. As he passes among the people he bows majestically to them as they bend the knee to him, and mutters the few phrases of Latin he learned as an acolyte. The illusion is com-

plete. The man receives the respect of a pope. No king has more earnest followers. When spiritual comfort is needed by any member of his flock they go to him. He gives them his blessing. They give him money.[48]

Evidence suggests that Długi had in fact been a lay Jesuit brother in Poland for about two years before coming to Detroit. He apparently ended his association with the Society of Jesus when his request to be admitted for study to the priesthood was denied.[49]

Notwithstanding his training, Długi's ignorance was illustrated in a pamphlet he issued, a scathing attack on Dąbrowski. Though supposedly written in his native Polish, it was so badly spelled and composed as to be in a mongrel tongue. Dąbrowski was so upset by the attack, incoherent though it was, that he filed suit against Długi. The schoolmaster responded with a countersuit.[50] To put the lie to Długi's claims and his distortion of their conversation in Baltimore, Bishop Foley, shortly after taking up his post in Detroit in November 1888, categorically stated that Father Kolasiński would "never be reinstated." Through his spokesman, Father Dempsey, the bishop let it be known that Kolasiński had again gotten into trouble in the Dakota Territory. To all questions concerning Kolasiński the bishop replied, "I don't want you to mention that name again in my presence."[51]

Unlike his predecessor, the new bishop decided to take the initiative in bringing an end to the Polish church troubles. Accompanied by Joos, Foley went to the Polish seminary and summoned Dąbrowski, to whom he said, "We are going to all of Kolasinski's followers, and we want you to come along and show us where they live and act as an interpreter." Dąbrowski's first reaction was shock and concern for his and the bishop's safety. But for more than an hour and a half the three men toured the heart of the Kolasiński quarter on Riopelle Street, entering over a dozen of the "squalid homes." The Poles, overawed by the bishop's presence, fell to their knees, and most of them promised faithful obedience. The bishop's bold step was a setback to Długi. If the bishop could lure the last of the Kolasińskiites back to the fold and restore harmony, Długi's ministerings and lucrative school—attended by an estimated four hundred children—would evaporate.[52] Vainly attempting to counter the bishop's inroads into his flock, Długi did the only thing he could; that is, he spread still more rumors that Kolasiński's return was imminent and declared that it was not the bishop who had visited the Polish homes, but only his assistant, Dempsey.[53] Długi's latest "cunning and wicked" ways prompted the *Michigan Catholic* to suggest that Kolasiński's agent "should be in an insane asylum, and we think that if he were not a Pole he would be taken before the Probate Court for examination as to his sanity." This was not the first time, nor would it be the last, that this newspaper, purportedly the voice of Michigan's Catholics, would slander the Poles.[54]

On Saturday, 1 December 1888, Bishop Foley, this time alone, made a second visit to the Polish quarter, staying for about four hours and visiting over thirty Kolasińskiite families. The newspaper headlines read: "The Tide Against Dlugi." In reply to one Pole who had the temerity to call for Kolasiński's reinstatement, the bishop declared, "So long as the sun rises in the heavens, Kolasinski shall not return. Let me assure you of that. It is better for you that you have no priest at all than a bad priest."[55] The new bishop, it must be said, was getting a good press. By Sunday, 2 December, the fortunes of the diminishing band of Kolasiński adherents seemed at their lowest. The *Free Press* reported that among the thousands of worshipers at St. Albertus's on that day, "many of them were reconciled Kolasinskians who had not been in the church for nearly two years." Undaunted, Długi continued his customary Sunday "exercises" at the schoolhouse.[56]

If the new Irish bishop could venture into the notorious Polish quarter, then so could May Bell, one of Detroit's best-known newspaper columnists. Everyone in Detroit had by now heard of "Polacktown," but who, asked May Bell, "can claim to have seen it, to have visited its hovels and its homes, to have mixed with its jabbering children, mangy curs, buxom women and ill-kempt men? Few indeed." But before entering this other Detroit, May Bell was careful to obtain a trusty police officer and an interpreter as companions. Her report treated the readers of the *Sunday News* to a whole page of deprecating pictures of filthy, odorous alleys, "swarming with children," of the sufferings of "blind Albert Petrovsky," of Poles being married behind jail bars, and of the consequences of drunkenness and overcrowding. Perhaps at no time during the long duration of the Kolasiński Affair was a more negative, condescending, and implicitly hostile caricature of the Polish quarter offered to Detroit readers. The account was particularly unfortunate since, on the whole, the press had been providing a remarkably thorough, objective, and even eloquent account of the Polish church troubles, given its limited resources and the delicacy of the subject itself.[57]

May Bell's advice, should her readers find themselves by chance in "Polacktown," was a warning. Though "among themselves the Poles are simple, hospitable folk, to the stranger they are suspiciously ungracious. . . . Visitors are rudely treated to say the least.

Every family keeps a mongrel dog, and the savage curs are allowed to fly at the stranger. The 'lady of the house' answers the door, and if accosted in a foreign tongue it is unceremoniously banged, at which signal the children, who are lurking conveniently near, pelt the intruder with mud and stones, or call out a string of bad names in very bad English." Needless to say, the Kolasiński troubles had led in this instance to reinforcing the worst sorts of stereotypes about the Poles, rather than fostering sympathy and understanding. In fairness it should be said that the considerable attention that the church troubles had brought upon the Poles had understandably led many of the newly arrived immigrants to mistrust and fear the "outside" American world. Believing, and not without some justification, that their way of life and values were under attack, many Poles reacted by turning inward and barricading themselves against alien intrusion. The language barrier and ignorance of urban ways only exacerbated the problem.

On 7 December the lead story in the *Evening News* read, "No more Kolasinski; that's Bishop Foley's final answer to the Poles." But Foley, certainly a more flexible and human leader of the diocese than his predecessor, soon discovered that the Reverend Dominik Kolasiński was a far more difficult challenge than he might at first have thought. A report had reached Detroit from Saint Paul, Minnesota, that Kolasiński had passed through that city on 5 December, en route to Detroit. A large trunk belonging to the deposed priest arrived at the Długi schoolhouse on 7 December.[58]

The trunk's owner was not far behind. At seven-thirty in the evening of 8 December, a smiling Father Kolasiński stepped out through the gates of the Michigan Central depot to the resounding greetings of his adherents. Later in the evening he received a reporter from the *Free Press*, having just finished a late supper at the schoolhouse on Riopelle Street. The reporter wrote that Kolasiński "looks as young as ever, is even ruddier, smiles as winningly, and acts as courteously. . . . Sitting back in an arm chair, puffing vigorously on a cigarette, he was a picture of contentment." His answer to the obvious question, "What are your plans?" was "Oh, I can't say. . . . You'll see it all!" Was all of Bishop Foley's careful work of reconciliation to be undone at a gesture from this priest? Perhaps. As one "tall, respectable-looking Pole" relayed to a *Sunday News* reporter that evening, "No, I don't go to any church, now; I waited for Kolasinski. We won't have any other priest, so it is no use. [The bishop] has got to fetch him back. There are 5,000 of us, besides women and children. We will never have any other priest, so it is no use."[59]

CHAPTER 4

PASTOR OF A MAVERICK PARISH

The ninth of December 1888 was chill and drizzly, but on this, Father Kolasiński's first full day back in Detroit, an estimated three thousand of his followers stood in the cold and mud for hours outside the shabby Długi schoolhouse to catch an occasional glimpse of and hear a brief word from their returned pastor. Though it was Sunday, Kolasiński made no attempt to lead religious services. In his stead, Długi conducted his customary Sunday exercises of singing, prayer, and the muffled intonation of some Latin phrases.[1] For most of the day Kolasiński was closeted with his chief lieutenants, Długi and Jan Karaszewski, receiving a briefing on the current situation in the Polish quarter and an account of Bishop Foley's latest efforts to induce the priest's following to submit to diocesan authority. What Kolasiński's immediate plans would be occupied everyone's mind. The version leaked to the press indicated that the priest intended shortly to call upon the bishop in "humble submission." "He will bow in obedience to any order, submit to a censure and receive a penance. All this, however, is hinged upon this condition. After the penance has been performed he is to be reinstated as pastor of St. Albertus Church."[2] This expectation, of course, ran directly counter to the bishop's adamant statement that Kolasiński would never again minister in the Detroit diocese.

Actually, Kolasiński did call on the bishop at the episcopal residence on Saturday, 15 December, exactly one week after his return to Detroit. He came alone and, as an observer noted, his elegant manner had not changed. "His attire was faultless. A fine beaver overcoat hung down below his knees, his silk hat was new, stylish and glossy, and his hands were encased in a pair of outre yellow kids."[3] His interview with the bishop was brief and, for a purportedly penitent priest, unsatisfactory. According to Father Dempsey, who was head of the diocesan chancery as well as the bishop's assistant, "The bishop met him in the parlor. What little conversation they had was carried on in Latin. Kolasinski asked to be given a hearing and to have his case reopened. 'Your case is settled finally,' said the bishop. 'You can never again officiate as a priest in this diocese. Instead of reinstatement you should go and endeavor to make some reparation for your own sins and for the wrongs you have done the Polish people of this city.' And with that . . . the bishop politely bowed him to the door."[4] The bishop's refusal could not have come as a surprise to Kolasiński and his followers; they had already begun to look for a suitable site on which to build an independent church, free of episcopal authority. In fact, they had in mind a spot on Canfield Avenue between Russell and Riopelle streets, just three blocks west of St. Albertus's.[5]

To those who had been watching closely the personalities and developments in the Kolasiński camp, it was no surprise when Kolasiński and his chief lieutenant, Antoni Długi, soon clashed. Difficulties became evident immediately. During the many months their priest had been absent, the Kolasińskiites had been collecting funds to build a new church in the eventuality that Kolasiński would be forbidden to return to St. Albertus's. Długi, acting as custodian, had opened an account in his own name with the Wayne County Savings Bank, where he had deposited the approximately $3,000 thus far collected. Another Kolasiński "trustee," the captain of the Kościuszko Guard, Stanisław Paszczykowski, acting on his own—or, more likely, at Kolasiński's behest—had initiated on 11 December a suit in the Wayne Circuit Court to block Długi from taking possession of this money. Paszczykowski argued that Długi intended to abscond with the funds and leave the city. The court granted a temporary injunction restraining the bank from releasing the money to the schoolmaster.[6] To the startled Kolasińskiite faithful, Długi sought to explain that the money in question was not from a fund allocated to build a new church, but in fact belonged to him personally. The money, he insisted, came from his teaching (he charged fifty cents a month for each of his more than four hundred pupils) and the contributions made during his Sunday exercises.[7] Be this as it may, the funds were now enjoined and beyond Długi's reach.

Although both Długi and Kolasiński publicly denied to the press that there were any serious difficulties between them, the talk in the Polish quarter by the end of December indicated that very much the contrary was true.[8] The financial issue was symptomatic of a far deeper rift. Essentially, Długi, having acquired material gain and vast personal prestige in his two years of leading the Kolasińskiites, was unable to readjust to the role of subordinate. Kolasiński had come to regard some of Długi's schemes and proposals as particularly reckless; moreover, he saw Długi as only a schoolteacher—not even well qualified for that task—and thought his presumption of continued leadership preposterous. In a contest between these two strong-willed, vain individuals, Długi did not stand a chance. By the first days of the new year, their differences erupted into an open rift. The priest dismissed Długi as schoolmaster and banished him from the Kolasiński fold. Soon a campaign to discredit the ex-schoolmaster was in full swing. For his part, Długi reportedly had in revenge called on Bishop Foley and offered, if the bishop would "commission" him, to bring "all the Kolasinski people back to your flock." But apparently the bishop too wanted nothing more to do with Długi and unceremoniously dismissed him.[9]

The fortunes of the discarded schoolmaster took a decided turn for the worse on 19 January 1889, when he was arrested and jailed on the basis of a capias sworn out in the Wayne Circuit Court. Długi's accuser was Albert Punkey, a Kolasińskiite, who charged him with the paternity of his seventeen-year-old daughter Aggie's child, born in July 1888, and asked for $10,000 damages. Punkey's affidavit alleged that the girl, in the fall of 1887 while a pupil at Długi's school, had been enticed upstairs and seduced. Długi had ordered the girl to say nothing, and her parents, because of his stature among the Kolasińskiites, had remained silent. Judge G. S. Hosmer set bail at $1,000, which a few of Długi's friends were able to raise.[10]

Through an interpreter Długi informed the press that he did know the Punkey family. He said that in early July 1888, shortly after the child's birth, the girl and her mother came to him and accused him of being the father. Długi maintained that they attempted blackmail, and, though he was innocent, he agreed to pay the family $300 to avoid notoriety that might harm the Kolasiński cause. In return he made the girl sign a paper "renouncing all further claims on me." Długi showed the reporters a document in Polish, dated 8 July 1888, that bore the girl's signature. The child in

Kolasiński's chapel and schoolhouse.
Reproduced by permission from the Sunday News, *3 February 1889.*

Joseph René Vilatte.
Reproduced by permission from the
Evening News, *25 December 1893.*

Fr. Dominik H. Kolasiński.
Courtesy of the Eduard Adam Skendzel
Polonian Historical Collection.

Sweetest Heart of Mary's Church.
Courtesy of the Burton Historical Collection
of the Detroit Public Library.

St. Casimir's Church.
Courtesy of the Burton Historical Collection of the Detroit Public Library.

question died shortly thereafter. It should be noted that this incident had occurred just after Kolasiński's four-day visit to Detroit; if the charge of paternity had been made public then, Długi would probably have lost favor in his mentor's eyes.

Kolasiński's other lieutenants now quickly lined up against Długi. Frederick Raeder, identified as the priest's cook and organist, said he had learned of "five or six [other] charges against him of a similar nature, some worse, some not so bad." And Jan Karaszewski, Długi's assistant at the school during Kolasiński's absence, said he had been aware of Długi's misconduct, but likewise had remained silent for fear of harming the absent priest's cause.[11] On Sunday, 20 January, the talk among the Kolasińskiites who milled about the priest's headquarters was solely of Długi and the sensational charge brought against him. A *Tribune* reporter who mingled among the Poles gleaned stories of other moral wrongdoings by Długi. Though most of the Poles seemed to accept his guilt implicitly, a small number still rallied to his defense.[12]

After the notoriety caused by the charges of immorality, Długi found it impossible to remain in the east-side neighborhood. He bought a house—apparently he did not lack for funds—in Springwells, near the smaller west-side Polish community, where, undaunted, he announced plans for a new Polish school similar to the one he had run for the Kolasińskiites.[13] But Długi was apparently unwilling to accept defeat and become simply a humble teacher of young Poles in Springwells. On 11 March 1889 he brought suit in Wayne Circuit Court against his former mentor for $10,000, charging slander. Specifically, Długi contended that the slander occurred in a speech in Polish delivered on 10 February, in which Kolasiński accused him of having "by fraud and deception" misappropriated large sums of money from the Polish people. Długi also brought three other suits against Kolasiński to recover, first, $2,273 in expenses incurred in keeping the priest's flock together; second, $35 that Długi said he lent to Kolasiński's cook with the understanding that the priest would repay him; and third, $200 that Długi had lent the priest during the latter's visit to Detroit in June 1888.[14]

Further, Długi swore out a capias on Kolasiński, which was served on the priest at his new home at 624 Beaubien Street the next morning, 12 March. The "arrested" priest, followed by about two hundred of his close adherents, thereupon marched to the sheriff's office, where Kolasiński's supporters literally vied with one another for the honor of posting the $1,000 bail. To an observer they bragged that they could have put up $50,000 if necessary. Shortly after the crowd left the sheriff's office, Długi arrived with a handful of followers to attend to further legal matters concerning his suits against Kolasiński. To the press he vowed to "expose" Kolasiński, though he admitted that "all the correspondence [to him from Dakota] relating to keeping the [Kolasiński] faction from the catholic church have been stolen from him and destroyed."[15]

As might be expected, a response from the Kolasińskiite faithful to Długi's public attacks on their priest was not long in coming. But rather than chasing Długi out of the city by force, they decided—probably at Kolasiński's suggestion—to harass him by the same means he had invoked, the courts. On 3 April a half-dozen suits were instituted against him for small debts and to recover personal property: Barbara Wituska wanted her $90 music box returned; Stefan Kamiński (an alias for Frederick Raeder) was owed $25 for work done for Długi; Jan Karaszewski, the new schoolmaster, demanded the $37.50 that Długi had appropriated from him. Karaszewski also made Długi's bank a garnishee defendant in the case. These steps, the Poles promised, were only a sample of what was in store for Długi.[16]

Długi's suits against Kolasiński for the $200 and the $35, but not the slander and back salary suits, were heard in the small claims court of Justice of the Peace H. A. Robinson on 12 April, at which time testimony was also taken in ten suits filed against Długi. All the attention was focused on Father Kolasiński, who sat next to his new attorney, Feliks A. Lemkie. Even when Długi took the stand, the crowd watched Kolasiński's every expression and gesture. A frown or shake of the head elicited immediate concurrence from his many followers who had packed the courtroom. Kolasiński also frequently interrupted the proceedings with comments. During his own testimony, he "proved a too willing witness, jumping about the witness box and answering questions with a flood of information that overcame the interpreter." The latter, to the justice's mounting annoyance, could not refrain from laughing at many of the remarks.[17] The frequent digressions and interruptions finally caused the justice to order a continuance of the case into the next week. At last, having heard enough, a harassed Justice Robinson on 17 April ruled that the funds raised at the picnic the previous summer rightfully belonged to Kolasiński, and Długi was ordered to pay the priest an additional $153.[18] Action on the other suits by and against Długi was continued.

Eventually the public quarrels, so demeaning to Detroit's Poles, between Kolasiński and his former associate ended when Długi left the city. A lead story in the *Sunday News* of 12 May 1889 read: "Dlugi has fled; the once proud Polish leader is on the Atlantic; Polacktown had got too hot for him; Kolasinski is now left supreme over the rebellious faction." One of Dlugi's acquaintances told the press that Dlugi had come to realize that if he didn't leave he would soon be killed by some fanatical Kolasińskiite.[19] By his precipitous departure, Dlugi of course forfeited the $1,000 bond that his friend, Jan Hansz, had posted in the Punkey paternity suit. Dlugi's career in Detroit had been marked by a phenomenal rise and an equally phenomenal fall. Three years earlier he had arrived poorly attired and half-starved. But he had befriended Kolasiński, and the many months of the priest's enforced absence had enabled Dlugi to attain total mastery over the rebellious faction. He had profited materially and had certainly used to his own advantage those who had trusted him. Now he had fled the city in disgrace.

The internecine strife between Kolasiński and Dlugi had not been the only issue that again focused the public eye on the recently returned priest. After Bishop Foley's categorical refusal to reinstate him into the Detroit diocese, Kolasiński quietly began to organize his maverick congregation, ostensibly loyal to Rome but denying the authority of the diocesan head. He converted the rear of his house on Beaubien Street into a makeshift chapel and proclaimed to his followers that the exeat he had received from Bishop Marty of Dakota gave him the authority to consecrate the sacraments at any location. In a dramatic ceremony on 23 January 1889, he administered first communion to over 250 children. Frederick Raeder, who apparently had replaced Dlugi as Kolasiński's chief spokesman, explained that many parents in the parish, refusing to go to Father Bronikowski, had waited for Kolasiński to receive their children into the mysteries of Holy Church. It was estimated that Kolasiński also performed over six hundred baptisms shortly after his return. The diocesan authorities, however, were unequivocally opposed to his pastoral ministrations. By administering the sacraments without the bishop's sanction—actually in defiance of Foley's orders—Kolasiński had in effect excommunicated himself, as well as all those communicants who knowingly participated in the service.[20] To emphasize the gravity of Kolasiński's action, the bishop issued a warning in Polish and German which was posted on the door of St. Albertus's Church. Two thousand copies were distributed to warn the faithful of "all dangers which menace your welfare."

> We are . . . in duty bound to declare that a certain Kolasinski is
> not a priest of this diocese, nor that he will ever be looked upon

as such. He has no jurisdiction. He cannot serve holy mass; nor can he administer any of the sacraments. We further declare that if you participate in any services performed by the said Kolasinski you will be cut off from the communion of the Roman catholic church.[21]

But would this new threat of excommunication bring the Poles to their senses, since most of the rebellious faction was under order of excommunication several times over from Foley's predecessor?

The day following the bishop's warning and renewed threat of excommunication, the Kolasińskiites drafted their own pronouncement, a copy of which Raeder brought to the *News* office. It read in part: "Bishop Foley! At present we announce to you in the name of 12,000 Polanders—Kolasinski side—that neither with you nor with your stubbornness we wish to have anything to do. We are not afraid of any excommunication." Raeder went on to say that the Kolasińskiites were making a new appeal to Rome, and in the meantime they were laying plans to build a magnificent church which might cost as much as $100,000. Though he was "accompanied by a large glass bottle and a decidedly alcoholic odor," Raeder's parting comment captured well the sentiments of the simple peasant parishioners on whose behalf he spoke: "Bishop Foley ain't got hell in one pocket and heaven in the other any more, and put Polacks in which pocket he likes."[22] Raeder's gesture was typical of the Kolasińskiites' defiance. Already in late January, barely a month and a half since Kolasiński's return, the treasurer of the ostracized flock, Kazimierz Nowak, announced that $17,000 had been raised in cash pledges toward a new church.[23]

Baptism and first communion were by no means the only sacraments that Kolasiński had celebrated in the first months of his return. City officials in February 1889 reported that about two-thirds of the marriage licenses being issued were to Poles. Just as with the other religious celebrations, many Polish couples had postponed their weddings until Kolasiński's return. It was reported that he was performing upwards of twenty weddings a week, and the pace was mounting as Lent approached. The *Evening News* for 20 February recorded that on the previous day "from early morning until the afternoon the wedding parties thronged the little house of the priest on Beaubien street. He would say the words which made two one, dismiss them and begin again." The Kolasińskiites estimated that about eighty families had been added to the flock in February alone.[24]

Inevitably perhaps, Kolasiński's notoriety led some of his opponents to consider more extreme means to rid themselves and Detroit of the troublesome priest. In early March 1889 Kolasiński personally appeared at the police court to state that he had learned that a group of his enemies, especially in the Toledo area, were organizing a band of "Polish white caps"—vigilantes—to harass him. He also claimed that an attempt had been made to poison him.[25] In fact, Kolasiński was now experiencing the kind of annoyances, especially from street urchins, that Father Dąbrowski, for one, had undergone from the Kolasiński faction.

Notwithstanding his falling out with Długi and the opposition of Bishop Foley, Kolasiński had already announced at the beginning of February, less than two months after his return, his plans for an interim church and school building for his maverick flock. The brick and stone structure, modern in design, was to cost $15,000. The ground level, with a seating capacity of one thousand, would be used as a chapel, while the first floor would have four classrooms and Kolasiński's living quarters. From the outset, however, the Kolasińskiites emphasized that this structure was only temporary until a new church of "cathedral proportions" could be constructed, perhaps within a year.[26] Four months after announcing these plans, Kolasiński was ready to dedicate and formally open the new shelter for his dissident parish, which now took the name "Sweetest Heart of Mary" (Najsłodsze Serce Marii Panny).[27] The last items to be installed were three large bells, weighing a total of five tons, which had come from Saint Louis, Missouri. On the morning of 10 June, a procession led by the Kościuszko Guard and comprising members of the new parish's St. Joseph's, St. Lawrence's, and Rosary societies, accompanied by two bands, escorted Father Kolasiński from his home on Beaubien Street to the new church. The priest rode in a magnificent carriage, drawn by a pair of fine horses, which the press described as a "gift"—costing over $1,000—to Kolasiński from his adoring adherents.[28]

The *Evening News* estimated the "entire contingent of Kolasinskians" at fifteen to twenty thousand, although this figure undoubtedly included many curious onlookers. (Five months earlier Kolasiński had claimed twelve thousand adherents, a figure at which Bishop Foley had scoffed.) During the dedication ceremony, Kolasiński spoke of "2,783 families" in his flock. It was not uncommon for some Polish families to have eight or ten children. Kolasiński consecrated the chapel-schoolhouse building, following carefully the Roman Catholic rite. In his sermon, delivered with his customary emotional appeal, he asserted that, despite oppression, his parishioners now had a church from which no earthly power could eject them. He called upon the congregation to pray for their enemies and continue to live in peace and harmony. Then from noon until two o'clock, Kolasiński celebrated high mass in the new chapel. Though about thirty militant anti-Kolasińskiites showed up, they contented themselves with sneering at the proceedings and no untoward incident occurred. The only levity during the solemn occasion was provided by a *News* reporter who had gained access to the building via a ladder to the second story. During the lengthy services, the Poles, described as great users of snuff, passed a snuff-box to the reporter. He politely took a sizable pinch and had to be removed lest his violent sneezing disrupt the ceremony.[29]

About a month later, an enterprising *News* reporter (perhaps the same unfortunate taker of snuff) was conducted through Kolasiński's "princely" personal quarters, consisting of a "handsomely furnished" reception room, bedroom and bath on the second floor of the schoolhouse-chapel. "A gaily colored Brussels covers the floors of the reception and sleeping rooms." In addition to a marble fireplace and fine oil paintings, "richly cushioned divans, the furniture of finest walnut, . . . are aranged about the room. A walnut secretary . . . inlaid with rosewood, occupies a place between two windows, from which float curtains of filmy lace. A pretty bronze clock, of French design ticks merrily on the mantelpiece." The reporter was then shown the bedroom, which he found "still more cheerful. Fr. Kolasinski is a great lover of birds, and a dozen of these musical little creatures occupy cages in this room. There is a talking parrot and a mischievous mocking-bird. The others are canaries, . . . The couch . . . has a coverlid of lace and is overhung with a princely canopy of rich material. Even a king," the reporter mused, "might rest easy in such gorgeous quarters. A soft hair rug is spread in the doorway between these two rooms, which are separated by heavy tapestry curtains." The reporter could only conclude, "Nothing is too good for Kolasinski."[30]

In the wake of Kolasiński's return and the renewed ferment in the east-side Polish section, Bishop Foley had decided that he would have to replace Bronikowski, who, though not involved in the initial troubles, was nevertheless considered a usurper by the Kolasiński-ites. Still believing that the rebellious faction could be led back to the fold of the legitimate church, the bishop intended to bring in a new priest who had no previous association with the disturbances. He was also annoyed over Bronikowski's several lengthy absences from the parish; in addition, he was concerned over the dropping off in the number of families listed in the St. Albertus's parish register since Kolasiński's return.[31] So despite his achievements in holding together the loyalist faction of St. Albertus's Church under trying circumstances, and the request of a group of parishioners that he not be removed, Foley formally ended Bronikowski's pastorate on 5 March 1889.[32]

Foley presented the new pastor, the eighth since the founding of St. Albertus's to his congregation on 11 March. The Reverend Kazimierz Rohowski had been raised in the ethnically mixed (Polish, German, Czech) region of Austrian Silesia. He had come to Detroit at the invitation of Bishop Borgess, and for thirteen years prior to his appointment to St. Albertus's he had guided the largely German St. Joseph's Parish in Adrian.[33] In retrospect it is plain that the bishop made an unfortunate choice in bringing the stern, essentially Germanized Rohowski to lead St. Albertus's Parish at this troubled time. In just over two years the majority of the congregation would be in open rebellion against this "foreign" pastor whom the bishop had imposed on it.

An event which coincided with Rohowski's appointment, however, was a source of particular pride for Detroit's Polish community and especially Father Dąbrowski. On 10 March 1889, John A. Lemke, the youngest son and namesake of Detroit's Polish pioneer, Jan Lemke, following seminarian and theological studies in Baltimore and Monroe, Michigan, was ordained by Bishop Foley in St. Albertus's Church. It is widely believed that he was "the first native-born American of Polish descent to be ordained to the Catholic priesthood in the United States." Soon after his ordination, Father Lemke was appointed assistant pastor at the city's west-side St. Casimir's Parish.[34]

Shortly after Fr. Kolasiński had begun construction of an interim home for his maverick parish—just three blocks west of St. Albertus's—diocesan permission was granted to found a second, "legitimate" parish in the neighborhood. The offshoot parish would ostensibly accommodate the growing Polish population between the railway line on Dequindre and Woodward Avenue. To be sure, even without the Kolasińskiites, St. Albertus's had become overcrowded. But Kolasiński's plans for a new church had certainly been a factor in the timing of the decision to move ahead with a second diocesan church, and especially in determining its location.

According to Swastek, a group of parishioners from the western fringes of the Polish neighborhood appealed to Rohowski for a church and school nearer their homes. Rohowski obtained Foley's permission and convened a meeting of the area's more prominent parishioners to choose a building committee. To chair the committee the assembly selected Tomasz Żółtowski, who will be remembered from his role in the early stages of the Kolasiński crisis. With the committee established, Foley authorized Rohowski in June 1889 "to buy a site for the new Polish church on or near Hastings and Fremont streets and as soon as possible to begin erection of a school and chapel thereon." As chance would have it, Żółtowski owned sixteen lots near this site and donated twelve of them to the parish. At Rohowski's suggestion, the name of Saint Josaphat (Św. Jozafat), the archbishop of Płock martyred in 1623 and canonized in 1867, was taken for the new parish.[35] St. Josaphat's Church was located five blocks west of St. Albertus's and just two blocks west of Kolasiński's Sweetest Heart of Mary's. Its proximity to Kolasiński's church was occasioned not so much by the expectation of winning over the Kolasińskiites as to avert their gaining additional communicants among the new Polish immigrants who were moving into the area west of St. Albertus's. These three churches stand today in a vastly changed physical and ethnic setting, enduring monuments to the vibrant and turbulent first decades of Polish settlement in Detroit.

The cornerstone for St. Josaphat's was blessed by the bishop himself on 6 October 1889, and the church opened its doors in February of the following year. The first pastor of the new parish was Fr. Antoni Leks, who had been Rohowski's assistant at St. Albertus's. He was apparently ill suited for his assignment and failed to attract sufficient Polish residents from the immediate neighborhood. Within a short time he left for Buffalo and was replaced by Fr. Marynian Możejewski (Modrzejewski), who immediately began to build up the new parish and reportedly even made some inroads among the Kolasińskiites. Soon after, however, Możejewski also left Detroit for mission work among the Polish immigrants in Brazil. The third pastor of St. Josaphat's in as many years, Fr. Jan Rzadkowolski, would oversee the building of a new, permanent church in 1900–1901 and would guide the parish for twenty-four years.[36]

The year 1889 proved especially active for the Polish churches in Detroit. In addition to the establishment of St. Josaphat's and Sweetest Heart of Mary's, the cornerstone was laid on 28 July for the new St. Casimir's Church at Myrtle and Twenty-third streets on the city's west side. To counter the attention that had been accorded Kolasiński's opening of his chapel just over a month earlier, the diocesan authorities staged a stunning and impressive demonstration, hailed as the largest Roman Catholic ceremony ever held in Detroit.[37] The dedication, in which representatives of all the city's loyal Catholic parishes and organizations took part, was staged primarily as an endorsement of and tribute to Bishop Foley and his policies since assuming control of the diocese eight months before. In his sermon Foley commended the harmonious spirit of Detroit's Catholics: "the faithful sons of Erin, the sturdy sons of Germany, the children of sunny France, the sons of Poland, and the liberty-loving children of our own dear republic. . . . All nationality is buried to-day, and we stand around this first stone as Catholics. . . . Here no bitter Czar rules; here is no raging lion to crush the sons of Erin. Here we are all freemen. All that is asked is that we be good citizens." The harmony of which the bishop spoke was achieved, however, largely by denying Kolasiński and his followers their place in the ceremonial procession.

A year and a half later, on 21 December 1890, Foley and Detroit's Catholic faithful again turned out in force for the formal dedication and opening of the newly completed St. Casimir's Church. Designed by the versatile architect Henry Engelbert, who had also prepared the plans for the neo-Gothic St. Albertus's, the new St. Casimir's Church was modeled after the Romanesque cathedral at Pisa and the eighteenth-century basilica at Trzemeszno near Gniezno. Its dominant feature was the central dome, which rose 170 feet and was flanked by two lesser domes. On this occasion the bishop, by now perhaps more hardened to the dogged persistence and survival of the Kolasińskiites, had less to say concerning harmony among Detroit's Catholics. He congratulated Father Gutowski and St. Casimir's congregation for following the true church "and not a hireling [Kolasiński] whose sole ambition was to lead the faithful Poles from the path of religion and snatch their souls for eternal damnation; one who is actuated through malice against the church and plays the role of a hypocrite."[38]

But by late 1890, Kolasiński was already well advanced in his preparation to build a permanent church of "cathedral proportions" for his flock. Needless to say, the new structure was to be larger and more ornate than St. Albertus's. On 25 July 1890 Kolasiński had signed a contract with the builders and released details on the proposed construction. It was to be the largest church building in the city. The nave would be 90 feet wide, at the transept 118 feet, and its total length 222 feet. The two bell towers would rise 220 feet. The style would be similar to the brick and stone neo-Gothic of St. Albertus's. The church would face on Russell Street, with a side entrance on Canfield Avenue. The seating capacity was estimated at 2,400. The architect and contractors, according to the *Evening News*, did not seem worried that the Kolasińskiites would be able to raise the $120,000 (excluding the cost of the land) for this project, despite their recent expenditure of over forty thousand dollars on the school-chapel structure.[39] (The new St. Casimir's Church had cost about sixty thousand.)

But if Kolasiński's plans for his cathedral were progressing, he was continually meeting hurdles on other fronts, including renewed dissension within his own ranks. At the end of October 1889 Kolasiński was back in the headlines, this time for a preliminary hearing in Justice Miner's police court on the charge of assault and battery. The complainant was Józef Skupiński, editor of the anti-Kolasiński Polish weekly *Gwiazda Detroicka* [The Detroit star], who charged that Kolasiński, while riding in his carriage, had verbally abused him and then stopped the carriage and struck him. Kolasiński pleaded not guilty and was released on his own recognizance. Trial was set for 9 November.[40]

As during the Długi suits, Kolasiński cut a dashing and unclerical figure in court, playing to the crowd which was composed mainly of his faithful supporters. Accompanying the priest, who arrived late for the hearing, were his new schoolmaster, Jan Karaszewski, and Frederick Raeder. Kolasiński excused his tardiness by cockily stating that it was still ten o'clock until the clock struck eleven. An array of witnesses confirmed that Skupiński had in fact been struck in an altercation with Kolasiński and his companions. Raeder then took the stand for the defense and dramatically proclaimed that it was he, not Kolasiński, who hit the editor after he had denounced the priest as a robber. Karaszewski's testimony neatly confirmed Raeder's version. When Kolasiński's turn came to testify, he emphatically denied that he had struck Skupiński, to which the aggrieved editor cried out "liar." At this point, according to the *Evening News*, "[Kolasiński] shook his head, rolled his eyes, compressed his lips, clenched his hands and appeared deadly in earnest." Three persons had sworn that Raeder had committed the assault. Was it credible that all three would have lied? The court presumably did not think so and directed that the accused be discharged. The priest then made a graceful exit, accompanied by the good wishes of his followers. A dismayed and bitter Skupiński could only say that he would get a warrant for Raeder's arrest.[41]

By the following June, however, the man who in November had courted jail for Kolasiński's sake publicly and dramatically broke with his former mentor. The falling out between Kolasiński and his

latest trusted lieutenant was probably precipitated by money matters. On the other hand, the reason could simply have been
Kolasiński's reluctance—as in the case of Długi—to allow any associate to gain too much power and influence. Whatever the cause, the
rupture was dramatically revealed when Kolasiński, fleeing from a
shotgun-wielding Raeder, locked himself on the second-story bal-
cony of the school-chapel, whence he cried out for aid. After
passersby raised the alarm and Kolasiński was liberated, he pressed
charges against Raeder, who was hauled into court. Raeder pro-
tested that he had simply called on the priest to retrieve several
books that he had left at the school. Raeder explained that a friend
had given him a broken shotgun to fix and he just happened to be
carrying it when he encountered Kolasiński. Released from jail, an
enraged Raeder swore vengeance on the priest who had thrown him
out in disgrace.

Having acquired a smattering of technical skills, Raeder fixed
upon the idea of using a small printing outfit, originally purchased
for parish use but for which, according to Raeder, Kolasiński had
refused to pay. Raeder laboriously composed and printed two
hundred copies of a manifesto denouncing Kolasiński. The main
text consisted of twenty-six questions directed at the priest, each of
which was phrased to imply wrongdoing on his part. The more
tantalizing allusions to Kolasiński's behavior on Raeder's list included false representation of appeals to Rome; drinking and smok-
ing in the chapel; marrying couples without their first going to
confession; falsification of his exeat from Bishop Marty; the burning
of the letters sent to Długi from Dakota; collapsing from drink
before the altar while administering the holy sacrament; and incit-
ing a Polish parish in Buffalo to resist their bishop. Raeder closed his
circular with a ringing denunciation of the priest, whom he challenged to respond.

> You loafer and fool and, at the same time, traitor of the Poles in
> Detroit! Your measure is already full. Damned devil, prove
> your position. Show to the innocent people what kind of a
> Roman catholic spirit there is in your body. Your own brother
> is ashamed of you for being such a cheat. If I am lying, then
> you may sue me. God and my conscience demand that I should
> say the truth, for terrible is the judgment of God.[42]

Kolasiński's opponents found merriment and satisfaction in the
circular, while his adherents probably destroyed any copies they

found. A copy was delivered to the *News*, which not only printed an English translation but Raeder's Polish as well. This step now made the *News* not just an avid chronicler but an active instrument in the Polish church troubles. When the newspaper's wagons attempted to distribute the issue containing Raeder's *défi* in Polish, they were stopped and stoned by angry Kolasińskiites. Still, it claimed to have distributed thousands of copies in the Polish quarter.[43]

The day after Raeder's opus appeared in the *Evening News*, Kolasiński and his attorney, Feliks Lemkie, visited the newspaper office. The priest had, he said, only one item he wanted to offer to dispel Raeder's malicious charges: the true copy of the exeat given him by Bishop Marty, which Raeder alleged had been falsely translated and misrepresented to the priest's adherents. Kolasiński indicated that he would not lower himself to reply to the other charges. While waiting for the newspaper's artist to copy the exeat, Kolasiński belittled the charge often raised by his opponents that he ministered to his people only for money and to satisfy his expensive tastes. He maintained that his 500-acre farm in Dakota had in the past year netted him $6,000. "All I care for here," he told the reporters, "is the spiritual welfare of my children. I believe that I will be ultimately recognized by the constituted authorities of the catholic church."[44]

Although Raeder's charges did Kolasiński's public image no good, their effect on his followers is difficult to determine. Certainly they were talked about in private, and Kolasiński likely had to offer his flock some soothing explanations to quiet doubts and maintain his image. One defection that may have been triggered by Raeder's attack was that of Fr. Wiktor Prowdzicki, an assistant priest in Sweetest Heart of Mary's Parish, whom Kolasiński had lured to Detroit from Buffalo a half-year earlier. For some time before he left Kolasiński, loyal Polish prelates in Detroit had been laboring to convince Prowdzicki of his heresy. Two weeks after Raeder's disclosures, Prowdzicki announced, "Kolasinski deceived me." Though Kolasiński had repeatedly told Prowdzicki that he possessed special dispensation from the Propaganda in Rome to conduct his parish, he kept finding excuses for not showing this authorization to his new assistant. To escape recrimination and make amends for his error in judgment, Prowdzicki was secluded in the Polish seminary, where he did penance under the watchful eye of Father Dąbrowski.[45]

Prowdzicki's arrival in Detroit in February 1890, which coincided with Kolasiński's announcement of plans to build a huge permanent church for his congregation, led at that time to widespread speculation that the flamboyant priest planned to make his cathedral the locus of the nascent "independent" movement among Polish Catholics in America and set himself up as their bishop.[46] Clashes between individual Polish parishes and episcopal authority, similar to the outbreak at St. Albertus's in December 1885, had occurred over the previous two decades with growing frequency in a number of American cities, notably Cleveland, Buffalo, Chicago, Milwaukee, and Scranton. The Polish immigrants found the Catholic hierarchy in America to be German- or Irish-dominated, and hence insensitive to Polish religious traditions and expressions. And they often felt slighted and bewildered when obliged to join a multi-ethnic parish because their numbers were too few to achieve a separate Polish congregation. Bishops frequently were suspicious of the Poles' desire for ethnic exclusivity, especially in matters of language.[47] Nonetheless, most instances of Polish parish rebellions had been speedily quelled and diocesan authority reimposed.

Whether Kolasiński did in fact envisage a role for himself in leading America's independent Polish Catholics is not known. Raeder charged, and Prowdzicki confirmed, that Kolasiński did encourage the Poles in St. Stanisław's Parish in Buffalo in their open dispute with their bishop, but there is no evidence that he actually attempted to organize them. In the next decades, however, when an organized "national" Polish Catholic movement did crystallize, many of its members looked back on Kolasiński as a sort of alter ego, even though he had in the meantime made peace with the Roman church. It seems reasonable to conclude, however, that Kolasiński's overriding goal was to be vindicated and reinstated with his adherents in the Detroit diocese. He well knew that to proclaim himself an independent Catholic bishop would certainly block all paths of return to the established church.

Following the defections of Raeder and Prowdzicki, the newspapers began to monitor Kolasiński's every move for signs of further error or failure. On 4 July 1890 the *Evening News*, playing the part of expert on canonical practice, triumphantly proclaimed on its front page that Kolasiński had violated two firmly rooted Catholic practices. Not only had he celebrated high mass after a full breakfast, but he had also celebrated it after one o'clock—two apparently cardinal transgressions.[48] Of far more serious consequence for Kolasiński's reputation, however, were the disclosures of his attempts to deceive his followers about his authority to minister in Detroit. In the history of the Kolasiński Affair, the second half of 1890 is perhaps best remembered for the "forgeries controversy." On two separate occasions, Detroiters were given the opportunity to examine and weigh documents relating to Kolasiński's affairs that one faction or the other labeled forgeries. On the first occasion it was his opponents who cried foul; on the second, it was his opponents who had most likely concocted pronouncements attributed to the priest.

The first incident began in July, when a group of apostate Kolasińskiites decided to expose their former leader's lies regarding a special dispensation from Rome to set up his parish. On 13 July 1890 a letter signed by eight ex-Kolasińskiites was sent to Archbishop Albin Dunajewski of Kraków. It read in part:

> There is no doubt that you are well acquainted with the lamentable affairs in our city and among the Poles, created by one D. Kolasinski. . . . In order to make peace and show the people misled by said Kolasinski and to bring them back to the right way, we ask you very devoutly that you may answer us in the Polish language and under seal, if said Kolasinski has authority without the order and consent of Bishop Foley and of this diocese (but claiming to have said authority received directly from Rome) to perform the duties of a priest.

A similar letter was sent to Mieczysław Cardinal Ledóchowski in Rome.[49] The authors believed that a reply from these two highest Polish prelates would have a greater impact on the Kolasińskiites than one from an American cardinal or, for that matter, from the head of the Propaganda.

Two other former members of the Kolasiński flock, Józef Modlaff and Jan Tetka, addressed similar inquiries to Giovanni Cardinal Simeoni, the prefect of the Propaganda, taking the precaution of requesting separate replies by registered mail. Modlaff was not at home when the reply from Rome arrived in late September, and the postman, contrary to postal regulations, delivered the registered letter to his wife. As fate would have it, Mrs. Modlaff, still a confirmed believer in Kolasiński, took the unopened letter to the priest, ostensibly to have him read it to her. Kolasiński, however, asked her to leave it with him, stating that he would return it later to her husband. While the letter was in Kolasiński's possession, Dąbrowski learned that Foley had received from Cardinal Simeoni what was described as a copy of the identical letters, dated 6 September, that had been sent to Modlaff and Tetka. Dąbrowski, upon further inquiry, was surprised to learn that Tetka had not yet received his letter and that Modlaff had only just gotten his back— three days after the bishop received his copy—and from the hand of a Kolasiński schoolteacher. When Dąbrowski examined what was purported to be Simeoni's reply to Modlaff, he saw that the envelope had been opened and clumsily resealed. The letter was not in ecclesiastical Latin but in modern Polish and written on ordinary American notepaper instead of Vatican stationery. It pronounced Kolasiński to be a bona fide priest and strongly warned the two authors and their kind to desist from meddling in affairs beyond their concern and to trust Kolasiński. Dąbrowski at once showed Modlaff's letter to Foley, who compared it with his copy. Not only were the signatures different, but the bishop's copy was in Latin and conveyed a completely different message from Modlaff's Polish letter. In the bishop's copy, Cardinal Simeoni noted that already in 1886 and 1887 he had answered inquiries from concerned Detroit Catholics regarding Kolasiński's status. At that time Simeoni had stated that Bishop Borgess had acted "most correctly and for just reasons" in suspending him. "Now," the cardinal continued,

> it is not without much surprise and grief that I learn the said Kolasinski has become so perverse as to dare to exercise the sacred ministry in the mission of St. Albert's, although he has been suspended from all exercise of the ministry; and, abusing the credulity of the people he has deliberately led them into error, saying that he has been exempted from the jurisdiction of the bishop of Detroit and is immediately subject to the holy see.

To put an end to all further doubt regarding Kolasiński's claims, Simeoni concluded:

> The priest, Dominic Kolasinski, has been justly punished by the bishop of Detroit with censures; he has no jurisdiction whatsoever from the holy see. . . . As to the church which Kolasinski wishes to build, let it be understood that neither mass can be celebrated there, nor the sacraments administered, nor any sacred functions be performed, without the express permission of the bishop of Detroit.

Further investigations revealed that Przybyłowski, the postman who had delivered Modlaff's letter, was also a member of the Kolasiński faction. The letter to Tetka was located at the post office, undelivered. It proved to be identical to Bishop Foley's copy.[50]

The federal postal authorities found it impossible to take action against the perpetrators of the presumed forgery. After all, Mrs. Modlaff had freely given the unopened letter to Kolasiński. To

prove conclusively that forgery had actually occurred would probably have necessitated calling Cardinal Simeoni as a witness, which
was hardly feasible. So the only person to be punished was the
hapless Przybyłowski, who was suspended by the postmaster.[51]

Was there a falling off in fervor or a wave of defections among
Kolasiński's congregation, as his opponents expected? Certainly
there was no evidence of any reduction in Kolasiński's followers in
the aftermath of the affair. On the contrary, as the *Evening News*
reported a few days after the exposure, "if ever a man [is] looked
upon as a little earthly deity[,] Kolasinski is by his followers."[52] By
1890, it can be said, those persons who might be swayed to leave
Kolasiński on the basis of rational evidence had probably already
departed. The remaining devotees were too emotionally committed
to believe any evidence emanating from the hostile ecclesiastical
authorities. Their vision of their struggle and survival against per-
secution was expressed in an open letter of 27 September 1890, in
which the trustees of the Sweetest Heart of Mary's Church announced that the congregation of 2,870 families would "proceed
with the building of our church and not in the least care for those
that promise us heaven and threaten us with hell."[53]

In his sermon the next day, Kolasiński inveighed against the
bishop, whom he accused of sending false reports to Rome and
persecuting him and his following. He further charged that the
letter purportedly from the head of the Propoganda had not been
written in Rome but was in fact composed at the Polish seminary at
Bishop Foley's instigation. Kolasiński spared his adherents further
details, not wishing to expose them to such calumnies. Rather, he
spoke of how the constant struggles on behalf of his people were
exhausting and aging him and, he feared, leading him to an early
grave. By invoking the subject of his death, Kolasiński played
directly upon his people's greatest fear—of being cast adrift again,
alone and unguided in an alien world. The women in the church
sobbed and rocked their heads back and forth; the men lowered
their faces between their hands.[54] Any doubts that may have been
harbored within this assembly were dissipated by the emotional
bond that was again cemented between the pastor and his flock.
Kolasiński's complete hold over his congregation and the adoration
he basked in are explicable when one considers that throughout his
ministry Kolasiński endeavored to recreate the religious ambiance
of rural southern Poland. When the pews and aisles were packed
and the congregation's anticipation stretched taut, he would make a
dramatic entrance, regally attired in a white lace gown over his black

robe. His preaching displayed full mastery of the modulations of the human voice, from a whisper to a great crescendo. The impact was equal to that of America's most popular evangelical preachers. Moreover, Kolasiński was able to merge his struggle for vindication with the struggle of his parishioners in their new land.[55] The splendid appearance of their pastor and the mystery of the religious service diminished the feelings of helplessness and the drabness of the peasant immigrants' daily toil and provided a cloak of security. With considerable insight, the *Sunday News* observed that "religion is as necessary to the hard lives of these people as the oxygen of the atmosphere."[56]

The second incident of alleged forgery involved a circular, purportedly issued by Kolasiński to his supporters but signed only "your priest," which first appeared in the Polish quarter on 11 December 1890. The document, translated and published by the *Evening News* in its Friday, 12 December editions, described the author's pastoral martyrdom to his Polish flock in terms uncharacteristic of Kolasiński. The writer declared his wish to convert the entire world, to have his sermons heard by all mankind, and claimed that "by special blessings and grace" he had been sent by the Lord to His people. His sacrifices were like those of "Christ, who associated with lowly people, and despised the rich pharisees; Moses who forced the people of Israel from the tyranny of the kings of Egypt; [and] Martin Luther, the great apostle of Germany, who, by parting with the papists, clericals and damned nuns and monks, brought his native land to the highest point of intelligence." Having proclaimed his special mission, he maintained that he could better dedicate his new church—a task which only a bishop or higher prelate could perform—"than even the pope himself, who did give me the power for all this." Rising to the climax, the writer proclaimed himself the apostle of all Poles in Detroit and America.

> Give only money enough to finish the church and so I and you will be happy and will not need to bow before anyone like those who live on Woodward avenue. Other Poles, when they will see our happiness, will demand that I become their bishop! Oh! if I had the voice of an archangel and could be heard in all Polish colonies, I would call and say, "Polish people! . . . Why do you listen to those united enemies of our language? Why do you bow, before those foreign born gods, when I—blood from blood, Pole from Pole—can become thy shepherd![57]

The use of a circular, no less than its language and tone, was certainly unlike Kolasiński's previous way of communicating with his parishioners; he had always used the pulpit. Though the circular had a populist and patriotic ring, the comparison to Luther, the prophet of German Protestantism who was anathema to Polish Catholics in the Prussian-held portions of their partitioned homeland, was sure to alienate Polish readers. On the day following the publication of the circular, Kolasiński issued a public denial of authorship and attributed it to an unidentified priest in "the other faction." His repudiation provoked a counterresponse from Father Możejewski, Leks's successor at St. Josaphat's. In a pronouncement addressed to "the heretic of Detroit," Możejewski challenged Kolasiński to identify this so-called priest who had written what was now dubbed the "Martin Luther circular." Możejewski believed this priest was Kolasiński himself, motivated by the desire to deceive his flock into believing that no bishop was in fact necessary to dedicate the church he was building for his apostate congregation. He informed the Kolasińskiites that their heretic priest had "now, publicly, . . . become a Lutheran, and is forcing you to do also."[58] But this latest and most ingenuous attempt to discredit Kolasiński in his adherents' eyes likewise failed.

Their parishes being just a few blocks apart, each faction had fallen into the habit of trying to impress and outrival the other on the way to church on Sundays. One such scene was described by an American observer who ventured into the east-side quarter one Sunday morning in the early fall of 1890.

> The sidewalks in Polacktown were occupied by continuous processions of Poles, both factions being intent on showing their relative strength and apparently their ability to outdress each other. They presented a picturesque scene—the men wearing their best clothes of rough make and the women with their royal purple and blue skirts and handsomely figured head shawls . . . —as they wended their way to the two edifices of worship. . . . Occasionally two crowds of opposite convictions would meet, and as they wound through each other the expressions of determination in their faces were an interesting study.[59]

The competition between the two sides was still very much in evidence the following spring, when Detroit's Poles celebrated the hundredth anniversary of the constitution of 3 May 1791. Though the celebration was in a sense for a lost cause, the *Evening News* noted that in the Poles' minds the constitution had marked a high point in their nation's contribution to the cause of liberty, and as such was very dear to Polish hearts.[60]

Since the anniversary fell on a Sunday, it was decided to limit the commemoration on that day to a religious memorial and hold the major public celebration on Monday. The loyalist church faction, which included almost all of the more prosperous and influential in the Polish community, had firm control of organizing both the lay and the religious demonstrations. They decided to use the recently established St. Josaphat's Church and parish grounds for both celebrations. On Sunday Bishop Foley celebrated a pontifical high mass in that church. As had become his custom, he laid much emphasis on the boundless opportunities that "a great and prosperous land" could offer the Polish immigrants: "[Though] the Polish people were tyrannically deprived of a constitution at home, they still had one in America." But to profit fully from its benefits, he stressed, they must remain law-abiding and not allow Kolasiński and his kind to lead them astray.[61] The bishop's message was clear; not only was Kolasiński leading his people into religious deviation, but his ways were contrary to the ideals of the Poles' newly adopted country.

On Monday morning, 4 May, the Polish quarter was active early. Some men were putting on uniforms; others were fastening badges to their jackets. Almost all the homes were cheerfully decorated and flying the white and red of Poland and, in most cases, the American flag. At ten o'clock, in the commons adjacent to St. Josaphat's, final touches were being put on the many floats that would be part of the parade. Bands were holding last-minute rehearsals, while members of the parish and lay societies sorted out their order of march. In addition to Detroit's Poles, there was a sizable contingent from Toledo, attired and drilled as a company of hussars, and delegations from as far away as Chicago and Toronto. Uniforms representing all types of Polish soldiers were in evidence, though the greatest sensation was made by "a company of mounted men, with blue flowing cloaks, helmets, and each man with a large pair of bronzed wings, representing the mythological soldier, the flying hussar." One eye-catching float, donated by the Polish brewer Jan Zynda, depicted the mythical King Gambrinus in regal robes seated astride an immense frothy bowl of beer, whose invention is attributed to him. Another float, "The Twenty Provinces of Poland," contained a score of boys and girls, each dressed in the bright colors and carrying the emblem of one of the provinces. Still other floats invoked famous personages and events of Poland's past, including Copernicus; the union of

Horodło with Lithuania in 1386; King Stanisław August swearing an oath to the constitution of 3 May; Tadeusz Kościuszko, who fought for both American and Polish freedom; and King Jan Sobieski, who defended Vienna and Christian Europe from the seventeenth-century onslaught of the Turks.[62]

It might have been expected that the magnitude of the celebration would bring a temporary truce between the rival Polish factions; in fact, the organizers extended a last-minute invitation to the Kolasińskiites to participate, but "the line was drawn at Kolasinski himself or the societies of [his] church carrying the distinctive emblems." Late Sunday evening, incensed at this further attempt to divide him from his congregation, Kolasiński's "mandate went forth forbidding them to participate and counseling them to hold aloof." Thus when the parade got underway shortly before two o'clock on Monday, there were no representatives of the ostracized parish among the floats, bands, dignitaries, or marchers. As the procession left the marshaling grounds at St. Josaphat's, the path of march across Canfield passed Kolasiński's church, where "in the enclosure in front of Kolasinski's premises a large crowd of his adherents gathered and sullenly watched the parade. When some carriages containing the clergy passed, there were a few jeers, but that was all. Directly in front of the [Sweetest Heart of Mary's] church, guarding the entrance, was a squad of the Kosciusko Guard, in full uniform and with fixed bayonets, as though to repel any invasion."[63]

Upon reaching St. Aubin the procession, accompanied by an estimated twenty thousand marchers, headed south out of the Polish quarter toward the city proper, where for over two hours it wound its way through the downtown streets. Late in the afternoon the procession returned to St. Josaphat's common, now transformed into a vast picnic area. The speech-making began at six-thirty in the evening and the merry- making continued well into the night. At dusk candles were lit in all the windows and doors of the neighboring Polish homes. Though vast quantities of food and drink were consumed, the next day's *Evening News* expressed amazement that "only seven Poles" had been brought into police court the previous evening on charges of disturbing the peace.[64]

In a little over a month after the impressive celebrations commemorating Poland's liberal constitution, the harmony within the loyalist, proepiscopal faction of Detroit's Poles was shattered by an outbreak of dissension within St. Albertus's Parish. Not unlike the beginning of the Kolasiński Affair six years earlier, the new trouble stemmed from some of the congregation's dissatisfaction with their pastor. Opposition to Rohowski, Bishop Foley's choice to succeed Bronikowski in 1889, flared up after an altercation on 7 June between the pastor and his assistant, Fr. Kazimierz Wałajtys, a young graduate of the Polish seminary who was popular with many of the parishioners. Opposition also extended to the pastor's cook and housekeeper, Susanna, a former nun from the Felician convent. Her devotion to Rohowski led her to give her version of the dispute to the inquisitive reporters who were always on the lookout for news in the Polish quarter. Naturally she put the blame on the young assistant priest. The housekeeper, whom the trustees had already come to view as a sort of gray eminence in the rectory, was described as "a very well preserved woman of about 40, with flashing black eyes, black hair and a swarthy complexion."[65]

The row between Rohowski and Wałajtys served as a catalyst to bring into the open the smoldering grievances and long-standing resentments that a sizable number of St. Albertus's parishioners harbored against their latest pastor. In part they derived from Rohowski's high-handed financial administration of the parish, but more especially from what was perceived to be his lack of "Polishness." Rohowski, it will be recalled, both was a native of the ethnically mixed borderland of Austrian Silesia and had headed a German parish in Adrian, Michigan, for many years before coming to St. Albertus's. What Polish, or Czech for that matter, he may have learned in his native region would have been a dialect incomprehensible to most Poles.[66] His sermons at St. Albertus's were usually in German, which many of his parishioners, and especially the new immigrants from Russian Poland, did not understand. Trustee Antoni Spiegel, whom the pastor had forced to resign, first gave public voice to the underlying grievance. "We don't want a priest that cannot talk the Polish language. There is no respect for him in the parish; everybody knows him by the nickname 'Old Fritz' because of his being German." Because of Rohowski's "alien ways," his opponents claimed, Kolasiński was reaping a rich harvest of disgruntled St. Albertus's parishioners.[67]

After news of the new trouble at St. Albertus's broke in the press, Bishop Foley and Father Dempsey made a special visit to the Polish quarter to confer with the two priests. In front of the rectory they were buttonholed by some thirty parishioners who urged the bishop to replace the pastor "with a priest of our own nationality, not a German." To complaints that Rohowski could not communicate with many of his flock, the bishop replied that it was his understanding that the pastor spoke excellent Polish. After listening to the two priests, Foley decided to remove Wałajtys and place him tem-

porarily in the monastery of the Capuchin Fathers on Mt. Elliott
Avenue to await a new assignment.[68] When word of his action
spread, what had begun as the grievance of a vociferous group
became cause for a full-fledged rebellion against Rohowski's continued pastorship. A spokesman for the disaffected congregation,
Dr. Józef Iłowiecki, in an interview with reporters, likened the
bishop's actions to "proceedings in Russia. . . . First condemn a man
and then try him." Echoing the sentiments of many others, Iłowiecki
added: "We are only asking what is our right, that we be given a
priest who can talk our language and who has feelings that coincide
with our own." The Kolasińskiites, he pointed out, were now
ridiculing the members of St. Albertus's in the streets. "Here is an
example of what you get for sticking to the church. You are given a
German priest, and your bishop gives you no satisfaction when you
ask for a change." Others among the discontented were heard to
remark that they "would sooner have a priest who would talk
English to them than a servant of Bismarck."[69] When asked for
comment on Wałajtys's removal, Foley was adamant. "Fr. Rohowski
will remain. I cannot," he added, "listen to the complaints of a few
malcontents. . . . Fr. Rohowski has been in this country for 16 years,
and I cannot find anything in his record to justify the complaints
being made."[70]

Angered by the bishop's disregard of their grievances, Rohowski's opponents, led by Iłowiecki and most of the trustees, drafted a
petition in English asking Foley for a proper hearing for Wałajtys
and that Rohowski be replaced "by a Polish priest, who can read and
write the Polish language, and who will be Polish in his feelings and
sympathies."[71] The bishop received the petitioners on Monday, 15
June. He gave no indication of changing his mind, but did assure
them that he would carefully consider their petition.[72] That evening
the disgruntled faction held another meeting. Some of those present
pledged to leave St. Albertus's and join St. Josaphat's Parish if the
bishop denied their demands. Others called for a boycott on re-
newing the rents on their church pews until they received satisfaction.[73] To avoid exacerbating the tension, Rohowski had absented
himself from Sunday services on the previous day. He was replaced
by Fr. Romuald Byzewski, pastor of the new west-side Polish church
of St. Francis. When no reply was forthcoming from the bishop, the
opposition printed their grievances in the form of a circular and
distributed a thousand copies.[74] By the second week of the new crisis
at St. Albertus's, the only person who seemed to be profiting from
the affair was Kolasiński, who announced that "at least 100 families
have come to me."[75]

A new twist was added to the unpleasant situation; on 24 June it was reported that the Kashubs, estimated at perhaps one-third of St. Albertus's parishioners, had aligned themselves behind the pastor. This action was attributed to the overriding influence among the Kashubs of Jan Wagner, who had played so decisive a role at the beginning of the Kolasiński troubles. The Kashubs, who had settled mainly in the Polish quarter east of St. Aubin, seemed less upset over Rohowski's use of German in the church, since they had been accustomed to hearing and using German in their native district of Pomerelia. To Wagner's claim that Rohowski spoke Polish well, Iłowiecki countered, "Wagner cannot know whether Rochowski speaks good Polish or not, as the contractor can not talk Polish himself." To substantiate his claim, Iłowiecki deposited twenty dollars with the *News*, saying he would gladly forfeit it "if Wagner will correctly translate a sentence of 20 words from English into Polish."[76]

Bishop Foley had taken the position that, notwithstanding the strong feelings of St. Albertus's parishioners, he could not bring himself to remove a pastor under pressure from his congregation. Nonetheless, by early July Rohowski's situation within the parish was so untenable that he was granted an extended leave of absence in the hope that a respite might cool the passions of his congregation. Fr. Florian Chodniewicz took over his parish duties. But Rohowski's departure—he was reported to have gone to Milwaukee—failed to pacify the parishioners; they now demanded that Wałajtys be made permanent pastor. Chodniewicz, they felt, was too young and lacked Wałajtys's close ties to the congregation.[77]

By midsummer the dispute seemed to be working itself out; the disgruntled parishioners were beginning to accept Chodniewicz. Unfortunately, on 18 July Bishop Foley announced that Rohowski was returning to resume his pastoral duties, and the congregation must reconcile itself to this fact. However, Rohowski, his health undermined by strain, had had enough; on 11 August he resigned, but the bishop made him stay on until 9 October, when Chodniewicz was to take over as permanent pastor.[78] Rohowski probably did not deserve the untempered abuse directed at him. As Swastek has remarked, "after spending most of his priesthood in non-Polish ministries, he retained little of the Polish dialect he might have learned in his native village. . . . After the fashion of most pastors of his generation, he might have been stern and authoritarian but he most decidedly was not 'a servant of Bismarck.' "[79] However, the latest crisis at St. Albertus's revealed that the bishop who had begun his labors in Detroit in a spirit of conciliation had now, like his predecessors, succumbed to insensitivity and high-handedness in dealing with the Poles' grievances.

Despite the benefits that accrued to Father Kolasiński from the troubles at St. Albertus's, the maverick priest faced considerable problems of his own during the summer of 1891. The immediate effect of the row had been to enhance Kolasiński's fortunes: a month after the storm broke at St. Albertus's, the *Evening News* reported that "money again flows into Kolasinski's coffers, the number of workmen on the church has tripled, and the structure begins to climb into the air."[80] But, according to his opponents, he was also compelling many of his adherents to mortgage their homes. Furthermore, as construction proceeded on his "cathedral," the matter of laying and blessing the cornerstone was causing growing anxiety for those parishioners who believed that only a bishop could officiate at the ceremony. Kolasiński took the position that a bishop's presence was not mandatory and continued to delay action on the matter. To outsiders it appeared that Kolasiński intended "to finish the building before the cornerstone is laid, if it is ever laid at all."[81]

To resolve for the time being the thorny dilemma posed by the cornerstone, Kolasiński, it was reliably reported, resorted to a simple ruse. The *Evening News* of 16 July 1891 revealed the priest's "sly scheme."

The bricklayers employed on the church building received secret instructions to lay brick about the cornerstone, without waiting for the ceremony of blessing to be performed. This was done. A few days later Kolasinski was inspecting the work, commending here, and criticizing there. The sight of the comfortable and well-beloved figure of Kolasinski walking about the church soon drew a number of his parishioners about, as Kolasinski had reckoned would be the case. Gradually he approached the spot where the cornerstone was imbedded in brick. When the ex-priest got within sight of the spot where the stone had last been seen, he suddenly stopped in the midst of a witticism he was delivering to the admiring ears of the people about him. He stopped short in his walk; his eyes bulged out, and the expression of his face showed as finely the marks of surprise, mortification, etc., as was ever pictured in the physiognomy of an actor. He drew off his spectacles, wiped them, looked again, and then threw up both hands, crying to the bricklayers: "Good gracious! What have you done? You have bricked in the corner-stone and the bishop has not yet given it his holy blessing!" Of course, the people were horror-struck. But they saw, of course, that it was not their beloved pastor's fault. Kolasinski stormed about with the boss of the work, but finally said: "Well, it is done now. Let it go thus."[82]

Thus did Kolasiński manage to stave off his problem a while longer.

Nonetheless, the newspaper's disclosure of Kolasiński's "artful dodge" so infuriated the priest that, in the midst of his sermon three days later, he stopped suddenly to denounce two persons in the congregation as spies. The unfortunate parishioners were hustled out of the church by several trustees. To the handful of his flock who had the temerity to suggest that the cornerstone be dug out so it could be blessed, Kolasiński responded that they must either allow him to do it himself or wait until a Polish bishop was sent to Detroit.[83]

Once things had quieted down in St. Albertus's Parish, however, Kolasiński's financial problems returned. Work on his church again became spasmodic; sometimes weeks passed without any workmen showing up, while the contractors awaited further payments. So, with an eye to inspiring his flock to further sacrifice and contributions (or perhaps from sincere feelings of contrition), Kolasiński in August 1891 initiated steps that suggested his willingness to make peace with the Roman church. Learning that James Cardinal Gibbons planned a visit to Detroit, Kolasiński traveled to Baltimore in early August to call on the highest Catholic prelate in America. When asked later about Kolasiński's visit, Gibbons acknowledged that the priest had called but was refused admission; only a written statement from the priest would be acceptable to the cardinal. He stated that he assumed that "Kolasinski wants to make peace with the church," but he made it clear that any action regarding Kolasiński "is a matter for Bishop Foley to decide."[84]

Annoyed at what he felt were misrepresentations in the press of his overture to Cardinal Gibbons, Kolasiński issued a public statement on 4 September 1891 in which he conceded that he had "submitted to Cardinal Gibbons in writing the conditions under which I would submit to Bishop Foley" and restore his congregation of "2,873 families" to the authority of the Church. In an interview, Kolasiński declined to say what these conditions were. Foley, on the other hand, was in a talkative mood. " 'So he wants to submit?' laughed the bishop. 'Well, he can't submit to me. I don't want him. The only way he can submit is to leave the diocese and never come back. . . . The idea of his making any conditions is absurd.' " At best, the bishop speculated, Kolasiński, after years of seclusion and penance, might be allowed to perform some minor chores somewhere in the Church. And even if he abandoned his church and congregation tomorrow, the bishop would have nothing to do with the maverick parish unless it was "absolutely free of debt." With St. Josaphat's just two blocks away, there was no need for Kolasiński's church anyway.[85]

The *Evening News* speculated, as it had earlier, that Kolasiński and his flock, overburdened with debt and discredited over the cornerstone fiasco, were just about washed up. As proof that the priest had given up all hope, the newspaper noted that lately he had been seen frequenting downtown saloons. Three months later, however, the same paper reported, "The scare of the threatened uprising of Kolasinski's 'children' . . . seems to have passed and left the fat ex-priest in his former bland serenity."[86] Once again Kolasiński's resiliency in adversity was manifested. For most of the next year he kept quiet and out of the public eye while work continued on the new Sweetest Heart of Mary's Church and his already large flock continued to grow.

Then, in the first days of June 1892, it was learned that Kolasiński had "imported" a bishop and was ready, two years after construction began, to relay and bless the cornerstone. The ceremony was planned for Pentecost Sunday, 5 June. All that was immediately known was that Kolasiński's bishop was one Mieczysław Hordniecki, identified as the bishop of Podolia in Russian Poland. Upon learning of the priest's intentions, the anti-Kolasiński faction printed and distributed three thousand copies in Polish of a circular addressed to their "Polish Brothers," warning them to beware of Kolasiński's latest trickery. Hordniecki, if indeed he was a bishop, must be a Greek, not a Roman Catholic prelate. For his part, Bishop Foley announced that he had never heard of the Podolian, adding that "no bishop in communion with the Church of Rome would dare to lay that corner-stone."[87]

Although in advance of the ceremony Father Kolasiński had remained very tight-lipped regarding his bishop, he laid out with special care the day's program, which began at ten o'clock with high mass in the school-chapel building adjacent to the new Sweetest Heart of Mary's Church.[88] The laying and blessing of the cornerstone was scheduled for noon and attracted an enormous crowd of twelve to fifteen thousand people. The crowd doubtless included a sizable number of curious onlookers, who were sure to be attracted by any occasion involving the celebrated priest. About sixty police officers were also on hand, principally to discourage any counter-move by the anti-Kolasiński faction. The first suspicion that something might be amiss began to spread when Kolasiński, his bishop, and a priest identified as the bishop's secretary appeared. Contrary to established ritual, the bishop did not march either around the outside or through the partially completed interior of the church to begin the ceremony. His attire, however, caused the most consternation; he carried no crozier, wore no mitre, and sported a cape of white silk instead of purple. The ceremony itself was hastily performed, and the bishop kept his back to the curious crowd throughout the proceedings. Then, after the lowering of the stone and the sprinkling of holy water, it was the secretary who addressed the crowd. (Kolasiński had taken the precaution of informing the reporters in advance that the bishop spoke only Russian.) Speaking in Polish, the secretary told the assembly to "pay no attention to [Foley] nor to the pope. Look only to the great God for comfort." To Him alone were they responsible for their actions. "Bishop Foley has refused to bless the church for Fr. Kolasinski, but you see he has had a bishop anyway, and now you will have a church of your own instead of having to beg for a seat in Bishop Foley's churches." Throughout the ceremonies, "Fr. Kolasinski kept close to his [bishop's] side."[89]

After the ceremonies the priestly trio quickly retreated into the parish residence, and most of the crowd dispersed to their homes for dinner, to reassemble later in the afternoon for a massive procession by the congregation. It had been announced that the bishop would be leaving Detroit that very day by train at five o'clock, so the procession was planned to escort the holy visitor to the Michigan Central depot. The parade was described as "one of the largest processions in point of numbers that has been seen on Detroit's streets," with the number in line estimated at forty-five hundred, with perhaps twice that number tagging along. Kolasiński had laid out the route of march to pass Foley's episcopal residence on Washington Avenue. Foley was not at home, and the residence showed no sign of life.

After the parade reached the depot, Kolasiński's well-laid plans began to come apart. The bands were directed to play Polish tunes, while the trio of priests entered the depot to make inquiries. There they learned that the next train for Chicago (presumably the bishop's destination) would not leave until nine o'clock. Kolasiński then asked about departures to Cleveland and on the Wabash Line, possibly to confuse the curious reporters dogging their steps. To all questions concerning the bishop's identity and future plans,

Kolasiński remained uninformative. Seeing that nothing more could be accomplished at the depot, he announced, "We will make a few visits and then come back in time for the train."[90] But, according to those reporters who remained in the station, the trio did not return, and none of the trains Kolasiński had inquired about carried any of the three out of Detroit.

The trio next entered a closed carriage and Kolasiński instructed the procession to continue. The carriage soon left the line of march, and when it reappeared several hours later at Sweetest Heart of Mary's, Kolasiński was its only occupant. Only the *News*, of the major dailies which covered the proceedings in detail, claimed to have solved the mystery of the destination and whereabouts of the two visitors after they left the marchers. Following close behind, a *News* reporter had traced the carriage to an alleyway in the west-side Polish neighborhood, on Michigan Avenue between Tillman and Twenty-third Street. There Kolasiński alighted from the carriage and, following a route he seemed to know well, disappeared into a nearby one-story brick building. Ten minutes later the other two passengers followed him. After some time elapsed, Kolasiński reappeared alone and ordered the driver to take him back to his own residence, where he dismissed the driver. The house where the two guests presumably spent the night, protected from prying reporters, "belongs to Joseph Przybylowski, a sidewalk inspector of the board of public works, who is known as a warm friend of Kolasinski."[91] The apparent scoop by the *News* only heightened the mystery and underlined the question, "Who was Kolasinski's 'bishop'?"

To all inquirers Kolasiński steadfastly maintained that it was the "bishop of Podolia" who had blessed the cornerstone. But the press as well as Kolasiński's opponents were unwilling to let him get away with what they were convinced was blatant deception. After much conjecture, on 4 July the *Evening News* triumphantly announced that it had at last uncovered the true "identity of Kolasinski's cornerstone layer." He was, the paper proclaimed, an ordinary priest of Polish background, "with a record that won't stand inspection." His name was Ladislaus Dempski (Władysław Dębski), and he came from Spring Valley, Illinois.[92] His story, as relayed through the *News*, went as follows: Dębski left his native Poland when still a young priest and was given a small congregation in Switzerland, but he was forced to leave that country after it was alleged that he had taken a wife. He next turned up in Canada, where he convinced Bishop Narcisse Z. Lorrain of the diocese of Pembroke to give him a mission in a remote northern area of Ontario. There Dębski labored for eight years until he fell out of the bishop's good graces and left Canada. He came to Chicago, where he tried unsuccessfully to obtain a post at the Polish Holy Trinity Parish, then involved in a dispute with the bishop of Chicago. Without a congregation and lacking funds, Dębski was forced to work as a journeyman tailor. He reportedly had approached Kolasiński in Detroit about the possibility of becoming his assistant; at the time, however, Kolasiński did not need one, so the hapless Dębski had returned to Chicago. Then, not too long before the June 1892 cornerstone-laying at Sweetest Heart of Mary's, Dębski had obtained from Bishop John L. Spalding of Peoria a temporary assignment to a small Polish mission in Spring Valley. Knowing that he would soon be unmasked when the bishop checked his record, Dębski took what little money he had acquired during his brief stay in Spring Valley and returned to Chicago, saying only that he was going there to buy certain articles necessary for his church. In Chicago Dębski met a real estate dealer from Detroit, who recounted Kolasiński's difficulties concerning the cornerstone. Whether Kolasiński subsequently approached Dębski, or whether the itinerant priest offered his services on his own initiative, could not be certainly determined. Dębski, however, on leaving Chicago for Detroit, was apparently too short of money to buy a mitre; he brought only the white silk robe he had worn during the ceremonies on 5 June.

Dębski apparently escaped detection on the morning after the cornerstone blessing and returned to Spring Valley "flush with money." He confided in a certain Rinka, with whom he lodged because his parish was too poor to afford a rectory, "what an excellent trick he had played on the Detroiters." But knowing that inquiries would probably follow from Detroit, Dębski decamped a day later, without so much as a good-bye to his flock. So anxious was he to cover his tracks that he left no forwarding address. This, then, was the "bishop" who had blessed Kolasiński's cornerstone!

Six months later the *News*, which had taken on the Kolasiński Affair almost as its own special project, showed itself to be far less thorough or accurate on the subject than it had been diligent in tracking down the pseudobishop. The 23 January 1893 edition announced that Kolasiński had been "summoned" to Washington to confer with the recently appointed apostolic delegate to North America, Msgr. Francesco Satolli. On the basis of this supposed audience with the plenipotentiary and confidant of Leo XIII, the *Evening News* concluded, "It is accepted to mean that amnesty is to be extended to the Detroit Polish priest."[93] Such a likelihood was especially probable in view of Satolli's recent reinstatement of the celebrated Fr. Edward McGlynn to priestly duties without notifying Archbishop Michael A. Corrigan of New York, who had excommunicated the liberal priest. The possibility of restoring Kolasiński's large congregation into Holy Church was worth the slight loss of face by a local bishop. The *News* was essentially correct in assessing Vatican priorities in halting schismatic tendencies among ethnic Catholic parishes in America, although in Kolasiński's case the announcement was a year premature.

The day after the prophecy about Kolasiński's improved prospects appeared, it was learned that Foley and Dempsey had also gone to Washington to consult Satolli. A spokesman for the bishop, however, pointed out that the cases of McGlynn and Kolasiński were quite different. The former had never been contumacious and schismatic after being censured.[94] In spite of the renewed speculation regarding his reconciliation with the Church, Kolasiński remained silent and out of reach of reporters. Only when confronted at night in his bedroom by an eager *Tribune* reporter did Kolasiński state, heatedly: "I was in Washington and saw Mgr. Satolli. I have done my errand well. That's all I will say."[95] By 26 January, three days after its revelation of Kolasiński's forthcoming reconciliation, the *Evening News* was forced to make an about-face and report that Kolasiński "was not invited to come to Washington" and "did not get an audience with Satolli." This corrected version came from Bishop John J. Keane, rector of the newly founded Catholic University in Washington, where Satolli had his headquarters. According to Keane:

> Kolasinski has not been here. He had not been asked to come, and he will not be asked. . . . The idea of summoning him here has not been even remotely considered. . . . No, we wish to have nothing to do with that man. He has shown himself to be utterly unreliable and unworthy of belief. . . . There is only one thing for Kolasinski to do. . . . Let him go away somewhere and hide himself in a monastery and do penance for his acts. That is the only course open to him.[96]

Upon Foley's return to Detroit, it became possible to piece together the chain of events giving rise to this second round of speculation that Kolasiński might be reinstated. It seems likely that Kolasiński, having learned of Satolli's presence in Washington and his decision upholding Father McGlynn against archdiocesan censure, had submitted a statement of his maltreatment by Detroit diocesan authorities to the papal ablegate and then leaked word that he had been invited to Washington. After reading Kolasiński's brief, Satolli had invited Foley to comment. The bishop felt it was prudent to meet Satolli personally and lay out the accumulated charges of Kolasiński's wrongdoing in the strongest terms. And likely the bishop's case had, for the time being, convinced Satolli to give no further consideration to Kolasiński's appeal.[97] But for a few days the prospect that Kolasiński and his flock might be reconciled to the Roman church had stirred up much excitement in the Polish community. There was ample reason to believe that many persons in the loyalist faction would welcome such a step as much as the Kolasiński-ites themselves. An end to the divisive religious strife, now entering its eighth year, was widely hoped for. Every means to force the priest and his following to submit had failed, and after all Kolasiński's church was nearing completion. The exterior was finished except for the windows, and the structure was becoming the fine mini-cathedral that its pastor had promised.[98]

Monsignor Satolli wielded the power—if he chose to use it—to reinstate Kolasiński despite the opposition of the bishop of Detroit, the archbishop of Cincinnati, and even the Propaganda. Pope Leo XIII's decision to appoint his adviser, the fifty-two-year-old Vatican diplomat Satolli, to head the newly created North American apostolic legation was taken after a mounting number of disputes between individual priests and parishes and their superiors had overburdened the ponderous adjudicating machinery within the Propaganda, which nominally held jurisdiction over Catholics in the United States. Satolli was known to sympathize with the "Americanizing" tendencies among some higher prelates in the United States, including Cardinal Gibbons and the new, controversial archbishop of Saint Paul, Minnesota, John Ireland, with whom Satolli had become acquainted in 1889 during the hundredth anniversary of the Catholic hierarchy in the United States and the founding of Catholic University. The pope was believed to be sympathetic to the liberal tendencies of the American hierarchy, and Satolli reflected his views. Modernism, it should be noted, conflicted with the aim of most Polish Catholics in America, to preserve their language and religious customs within their parishes and parochial schools. (Several years later Satolli's views became far more conservative.)

Satolli held wide-ranging authority to resolve disputes and administer discipline among the faithful in America. His appointment not only tacitly acknowledged the significance for the Vatican of the Roman church in America, but was perceived as a threat to the more traditionalist prelates led by Archbishop Corrigan of New York. On the surface, it seemed that traditionalist, ethnic priests like Kolasiński could expect little sympathy from Satolli. Much bargaining and convincing argument by the maverick pastor of Sweetest Heart of Mary's Parish would take place before Satolli would put pressure on the "modernist" bishop of Detroit to reaccept Kolasiński on the priest's terms.[99]

As 1893 drew to a close, so did construction on Kolasiński's church. Reports began to circulate that Satolli planned to visit Detroit, one reason being to try to end the deadlock for Kolasiński's schismatic parish. He and the diocesan authorities could no longer ignore the fact that Kolasiński was about to open "the most magnificent church in the Detroit diocese" for the city's largest parish, nearing five thousand families. The *Detroit Journal* noted that "hunger may knock at the door of many of [Sweetest Heart of Mary's] parishioners, but when the silver reward of heavy toil comes into their humble homes, the hand that gives to Kolasinski is more liberal than the hand that helps the grocer." The times indeed were bad economically, but seemingly no expense was being spared in outfitting the new church: the seven bells in the steeples cost $12,000 and the two front stained glass windows $2,000. The cost of adorning the main altar was estimated at $5,000.[100] Furthermore, the rumor was alive among the Kolasińskiites, possibly spread by their pastor, that Satolli in person would dedicate the church building and would reinstate both pastor and congregation into communion with Holy Church. To put the lie to these rumors, Stefan Kamiński (better remembered as Frederick Raeder, formerly Kolasiński's cook, organist, chief lieutenant, and, later, denouncer) had written the papal ablegate to ask if the rumor was true. Satolli's reply, dated 21 October 1893, categorically stated that "what has been said there concerning my coming to your church is wholly false."[101]

Despite Satolli's public disavowal of having anything further to do with the dissident priest, it was learned in late 1893 that a preliminary exchange of correspondence had taken place between the two men. Having decided in October to reopen Kolasiński's case, Satolli's office had requested several priests in the Detroit diocese to explain their understanding of conditions among the city's Polish Catholics and Kolasiński's role.[102] Meanwhile, Kolasiński had written again to Satolli; this letter, unlike the one sent to Washington in January, conceded "irregularities" in his handling of the congregation's affairs. Kolasiński went to great lengths to explain and justify why he had returned to Detroit in 1888 and organized his followers into a new congregation outside the pale of diocesan authority. He charged that the late Bishop Borgess and Administrator Joos had tried to force his supporters to receive the sacraments from Father Dąbrowski, whom they refused to accept under any circumstances. Kolasiński argued that, had he not returned, thousands of devout Poles would have remained unministered to. He defended himself against the accusations of financial mismanagement and conducting parish affairs for his personal profit. He was willing to accept whatever judgment and penance Satolli chose to impose, as long as the sentence would "not disgrace him with his people."[103]

On 1 December Satolli replied to Kolasiński in a noncommittal letter that urged him to do all in his power to remove the scandal surrounding him and his parish. But the monsignor did forward copies to Bishop Foley of the information his office had received, along with a request for the bishop to consider what resolution might be acceptable. Although still not ready to demand a solution to the conflict from the bishop of Detroit, Satolli was moving in that direction. In any case, Foley's attitude had not changed. In an interview in mid-December 1893, he reiterated his long-standing opinion that the only way to resolve the issue was for Kolasiński to vacate the diocese voluntarily and throw himself on the mercy of the church authorities. To support the bishop's stance, and perhaps to stave off what was now perceived to be subtle pressure from Satolli, some priests in the diocese circulated a petition in which they strongly expressed their opposition to Kolasiński's reinstatement, which "would place a premium on clerical crime, rebellion and schism, . . . would be a degradation to the honorable priesthood of this diocese, . . . [and] would be a scandal of dire consequences to the faithful laity."[104]

But as Christmas approached, the only talk among the Kolasińskiites was about their new church and its imminent opening. Daily a crowd of Poles could be found inside the church, minutely inspecting the recently installed pews, which were being rented so rapidly that, it was speculated, the annual income from rentals alone would net close to twenty-four thousand dollars. At last Kolasiński announced that on Sunday, 24 December, the church would be dedicated. To his adherents he let it be known that either Monsignor Satolli or his personal representative would lead the ceremony.[105] Kolasiński's announcement prompted Bishop Foley on 22 December to issue a denial. Neither Satolli, his representative nor, for that matter, any prelate in communion with Holy Church would officiate at the dedication of Sweetest Heart of Mary's Church. Moreover, if Kolasiński proceeded with his plan, "it will be a fraud and a deception."[106] The *Evening News* printed a Polish translation of the bishop's pronouncement in its 23 December edition.[107]

On the eve of the dedication at Sweetest Heart of Mary's, the Detroit newspapers, determined to forestall another hoax by Kolasiński, revealed the identity of the bishop who would officiate. Naturally Kolasiński was unable to call upon the discredited "Podolian bishop." For this occasion he chose Joseph René Vilatte, a former priest of controversial reputation who claimed to be the "archbishop of the Old Catholics in America." Vilatte had set up a kind of mini-bishopric in a remote area of northern Wisconsin. His Old Catholics were not part of that body of worshipers in Europe who were nominally guided by the Jansenist archbishop in Utrecht. Vilatte's group was one of a smattering of schismatic parishes no longer in communion with the Roman church. The Anglican bishop of Fond du Lac, Wisconsin, had prevailed on the Swiss Old Catholic Bishop Eduard Herzog to ordain Vilatte in 1885. Not content with this arrangement, Vilatte journeyed to India and Ceylon, where, in 1892, he induced several Jacobite bishops attached to the patriarch of the Syrian rite to consecrate him bishop for America. Still later, the Episcopal church, with which Vilatte had tried to associate his flock, declared his powers to consecrate null and void. Upon learning of Kolasiński's choice, an astute lay Catholic observer in Detroit was heard to remark that Kolasiński was "equal to fishing up a cardinal if he ever wants one."[108]

On Saturday, 23 December, Kolasiński was observed scurrying back and forth between his parish headquarters and the telegraph office, where he was supposedly receiving a stream of cables signed "Satolli." Bishop Foley considered the so-called Satolli telegrams just one more fraud, perpetrated by the priest to convince his flock that the archbishop invited to officiate at the dedication was the ablegate's appointee.[109]

On 24 December 1893 Fr. Dominik Kolasiński at long last fulfilled his promise to his parishioners: the doors of the most magnificent place of worship in Detroit were opened.[110] Bishop Foley's last-ditch attempt to warn the congregation—through a circular printed in Polish—that Kolasiński and his "archbishop" were defying the Holy Roman church had, in one observer's opinion, "no more effect than water on a duck's back." Of course, there were a few disappointments: the church bells, one weighing four tons, had not arrived from Saint Louis, and the gas company had failed to extend the mains to hook up the chandeliers, which meant that thousands of candles had to be used to light the interior. Also delayed in shipment was the nine-foot statue of the Virgin Mother, intended to adorn the main altar. But these shortcomings were overlooked. The unseasonably warm Christmas Eve dawned sunny and springlike, resulting in a sea of mud outside the church where the faithful would stand.

By the appointed hour of ten o'clock, a throng of parishioners, estimated at five thousand, surrounded the church. A large contingent of police restrained the crowd of a thousand anti-Kolasińskiites gathered nearby. Mindful of the tragic Christmas events eight years earlier, the police closed every saloon in the Polish quarter. If Kolasiński's opponents hoped that exposing his archbishop would disturb his followers, they were naïve. By this point, the Kolasińskiites generally were indifferent to who dedicated the church as long as the occasion was marked by ceremony. A reporter captured well the prevailing sentiments of Kolasiński's adherents.

> Most of them are poor day laborers, with large families to support, and yet their nickels, dimes and dollars have erected this splendid church—the largest, and in some respects the finest in Michigan. Many are now out of employment and receiving aid from the poor commission. It is said that scores of families mortgaged their little homes to help pay on the church. No wonder that after having almost starved themselves for years, they were anxious to have it dedicated. As they stood with bared heads, gazing at the pomp and panoply of the archbishop's (?) procession, it was probably the proudest moment in their lives.[111]

At twenty minutes after ten, Kolasiński emerged from the school residence, followed by several priests. Then there appeared "a strange man in all the splendor of a bishop's vestments. On the front of his mitre [described as several sizes too large] of cloth of gold was an embroidered crucifix. . . . He was a man of large stature, with rather florid face, coarse features and bold, brown eyes." With Kolasiński close by his side, the archbishop made the sign of blessing and liberally sprinkled holy water. As he reached the front of the church the anti-Kolasińskiites jeered loudly, and for a moment it appeared that a melee would commence. But the Kolasińskiites' attention was firmly fixed on the archbishop as he made his way around the church, sprinkling holy water on the walls, buttresses, towers, and windows. Then the officiating party entered the church. After a few minutes, the main doors were thrown open and a crush of humanity pressed in. Vilatte read a brief sermon in English (with a heavy French accent), in which he assured the people that they had been right to adhere to their pastor. "I am a duly appointed and consecrated archbishop of the Old Catholic congregation of Geneva, Switzerland," he told the assembly, and "I declare all the sacraments conferred by Fr. Kolasinski valid and good. He has, with the help of God, brought together this great congregation. . . . God is with the Polish people of Fr. Kolasinski's church." Then archbishop and priests changed their vestments and high mass was celebrated. The sermon was delivered by Kolasiński's recently acquired assistant, the aged Fr. Ignacy Barszcz, who exhorted the people "to stand by their pastor." He likened the new church to a "ship in a storm." The people were the passengers, the priest their captain who would bring them safe into harbor. Throughout the ceremony and the mass, the rattle of the collection plate was heard. Periodically, Kolasiński emptied it.

After the ceremonies, Kolasiński kept the press away from Vilatte, saying that he was staying at the church over Christmas and that reporters could talk to him later. The church was a scene of activity all that day. Vespers were held in the afternoon and a Christmas Eve mass was celebrated at midnight. On the morrow Kolasiński's parishioners would celebrate Christmas in their own church for the first time in nine years.

Though there were those who were ready to cavil at the errors and shortcomings of the ceremony, rituals, and vestments, and even speculate that Kolasiński had paid $6,000 for the bogus archbishop's services, the prevailing judgment in the press was expressed by the *Evening News*, which grudgingly admitted "a victory for Kolasinski, [who] indicated very well that he could get along without Bishop Foley's sanction."[112] The immediate crisis had passed for Kolasiński and his faithful. In possession of the finest Catholic church in Detroit and, by one reckoning, with over fifteen thousand devoted parishioners, Father Kolasiński could take his time in squaring himself with Bishop Foley and the Roman Catholic hierarchy. In fact, the hierarchy would now make overtures of reconciliation, and the priest would have much to say concerning the terms governing his eventual reinstatement in the diocese.

CHAPTER 5

RECONCILIATION AND
FURTHER TRIALS

The 1890s were a period of momentous transition for the Roman Catholic church in America. Stormy debates raged over "Americanization," "modernism," and especially the thorny subject of parochial schools. Not only were there sharp divisions of opinion within the church hierarchy in the United States, but frequent disputes occurred between parish priests and their immediate superiors. The appointment of Msgr. Francesco Satolli as permanent apostolic delegate to North America added to the confusion.[1] Despite directions to the contrary from the Third Plenary Council of the American hierarchy in Baltimore in 1884, many priests and prelates continued to air their views in the columns of the secular press.

Thus it was that in the first week of January 1894 newspaper readers in Detroit were treated to a series of vitriolic—at times almost libelous—exchanges between members of the priesthood in the Detroit diocese over the question of Fr. Dominik Kolasiński's reinstatement. The polemics were mostly in the form of irate replies to a lengthy report entitled "The Unfortunate Kolasinski Case," by Fr. Peter A. Baart of Marshall, Michigan, which first appeared on 28 December 1893 as an open letter to the *Catholic Mutual Benefit Association Weekly*. Baart's letter, soon reprinted in the *Evening News* and the *Detroit Tribune*, reviewed the history of the Kolasiński Affair.

While not specifically defending the "schismatic" priest, the letter pointed to several factors, notably Bishop Borgess's high-handedness, that had unnecessarily aggravated the situation. Baart believed that "too much personality and too little charity . . . began to be mixed in the case." In particular, the "libelous" petition against Kolasiński's reinstatement that circulated among the diocesan priests had inflamed the issue. Baart maintained that even priests with no knowledge of the affair were coerced into signing, and some priests had been given a blank form to sign. He readily conceded that "discipline is necessary in the organization of the church," but he implied that some of the church authorities might have lost sight of the fact that "the main reason for the existence of the church is to bring souls back to God." And one should not ignore Kolasiński's many thousands of parishioners.[2]

The first voice to challenge Baart was anonymous. A diocesan priest, signing himself "Sacerdos," penned an angry response in a letter to the editor of the *Evening News*. Stripped of its veil of piousness and good will, Sacerdos stated, Baart's article was "a gross impeachment of the conduct of the highly esteemed bishop of Detroit." As to the petition which Baart deemed so harmful, Sacerdos maintained that it "was the spontaneous outcome of the moral sense of the clergy." A "Catholic layman," writing in the *Michigan Catholic*, saw "his duty . . . to call the spade the spade," to offer "no apologetic whine," and to "denounce Kolasinski," whose incitement of rioting was "glossed over" by Father Baart. The *Angelus*, a Catholic weekly very close to the bishop, joined the chorus of criticism directed at Baart's "strange defense of a law-breaker." Not only was his account "a grave aspersion on the Episcopal administration," it was "an outrageous charge of stupid dishonesty against the whole body of the diocesan clergy." The *Angelus* commended the bishop's "generosity [and] leniency" throughout the difficult affair, and chastised Kolasiński as "the poor Polish disturber, with his tribe of pseudo Bishops and priests, with his mockery of religious rites, his horrible profanation of the most holy things of God, [and] his hoyden[ish] defiance and pompous display."[3]

But by far the most vitriolic and scathing denunciation came from Baart's fellow diocesan priest, Fr. Robert Doman, a legal adviser to Bishop Foley. His open letter to the *Evening News*, published on 5 January, characterized Baart's statement as a "monstrosity" of "deceit, double-dealing" and "mendacity." Doman accused Baart of "playing the sycophant to Mgr. Satolli," apparently in the hope of obtaining a promotion. Satolli, too, he suggested in a hardly subtle attempt at verse, was angling for a cardinal's hat.

> I see through the mist, and the haze,
>   and the gloom
> A round, red hat, I will capture
>   it soon.
> It's mine.
> O, stop monsignor, dear soggart aroon,
> You're riding an ass, and chasing the moon.
> Decline.[4]

Doman's denunciation of Baart for criticizing Foley's handling of diocesan affairs referred to Satolli's request for more information on the Kolasiński case. Baart's letter, which Satolli had forwarded to Foley in December along with other materials on Kolasiński, had not, from the standpoint of canonical law, been entirely unfavorable to Kolasiński.[5] And judging from Doman's ranting against Baart, the bishop had apparently shown to his close associates Baart's letter to Satolli.

The exchange of caustic letters prompted one reader of the *News*, who described himself as a "long suffering layman," to suggest that Baart, Doman, and company would do better to "inclose their fists in five-ounce gloves, retire to a barn and settle their differences according to marquis of Queensberry rules."[6] For his part, Foley apparently now realized that the overly enthusiastic defense of his administration by loyal subordinates had become an embarrassment. Therefore, on 8 January he issued a statement expressing disapproval of the public exchanges by priests of his diocese and dissociated himself from their opinions, which meant principally from Doman's.[7] He also took the precaution of telegraphing Satolli in Washington to "repudiate the abusive Doman article."[8]

Unfortunately, the bishop's belated disavowals failed to quell the tempest unleashed by such partisans as Sacerdos and Doman, especially when Satolli had been personally maligned. Baart, who had already acquired a reputation as an eloquent defender of priests in difficulty with their ordinaries, was received on 9 January by the apostolic delegate in Washington, ostensibly to give a report on the Kolasiński case since the opening of Sweetest Heart of Mary's Church. Baart took the occasion to provide him with copies of the Sacerdos and Doman letters. Satolli responded by giving his guest a letter vindicating Baart's statements in the Kolasiński article that originally fired the newspaper polemics. Satolli noted that he had already expressed to Foley his disapproval of the petition against

Kolasiński's reinstatement, and added that "the writings of 'Sacer-dos' and especially of Rev. R. F. M. Doman . . . are unjust, untruth-ful and disrespectful . . . as well as uncharitable and unpriestly."[9]

Satolli's intervention had the immediate effect of damaging the anti-Kolasińskiites' credibility in Detroit—including Foley's—and encouraged speculation that a resolution to the Kolasiński case might finally be at hand, especially when it was found that Satolli had now directed Foley to return all the documents relative to the schismatic priest to his Washington office. The *News*, which had been covering this aspect of the case more closely than the other Detroit papers, speculated on 10 January:

> While Satolli has [still] made no statement on which a predic-tion can be based, all inferences to be drawn as to his attitude must be favorable to the Polish priest's cause. The argument that the restoration of 10,000 people can be led back to the bosom of the church is one which is said to appeal to him strongly.[10]

Also indicative of the new respectability that Kolasinski and his congregation had gained since the dedication of their church was a public organ recital staged in Sweetest Heart of Mary's on Sunday afternoon, 4 February, to inaugurate the impressive organ that had been recently installed. The organist was Theodore G. Beach, from St. John's Church. The press described the event as a "triumph for Kolasinski," and though the loyalist Poles held aloof, there was a large turnout "from the city at large."[11]

Kolasiński's satisfaction over the successful organ concert was undoubtedly heightened by his knowledge that on the previous evening Satolli's personal representative, Msgr. Donato Sbaretti, who was also a curial prelate, had arrived in Detroit with authority to negotiate a settlement with him. The thirty-eight-year-old Sbaretti, formerly a *minutante* (auditor) at the Propaganda and now holding that position with the apostolic delegation to North America, was conversant with Satolli's reopening of the Kolasiński case in January and with the correspondence between the priest and the papal ablegate. It was also reliably reported that Kolasiński's case had been reviewed by the Propaganda, which had given its blessing to opening direct negotiations with Kolasiński with a view toward reconciling him and his flock with legitimate church authority.[12]

A first meeting between Sbaretti and Kolasiński was arranged for 6 February at the residence of the Reverend John F. Friedland, dean of the German St. Joseph's Parish. (Certainly Kolasiński would not have been welcome at the episcopal residence where Sbaretti was staying.) Neither man wore clerical garb at this three-hour meeting. To Sbaretti's proposal, already stated in a letter from Satolli, that Kolasiński must close his church and do penance for two weeks, the priest declared that he would neither do penance nor close his church for a single day. He allegedly said that he was entitled to a promotion but would forgo that if he were taken back into the church without penalty. Clearly the inconclusive first meeting did not deflate Kolasiński's confidence; according to a *Tribune* reporter, later that same day he appeared to be "beaming with delight." Though he would not comment specifically on the negotiations, Kolasiński did say, in broken English, "It's all right, everything is settled, I'm all right," which led the reporter to conclude that a "full reconciliation would take place tomorrow." Friedland seemed to confirm this conclusion in a later interview.[13] But as it turned out, the optimism was premature.

The principal obstacle to Kolasiński's reinstatement, according to canonical law, was his decision to return to Detroit in 1888 and act as a priest in defiance of Foley's ruling. In his negotiations with Sbaretti, Kolasiński argued that, although Borgess had provided him with an exeat in April 1888, the bishop had failed to supply an ineat confirming his entrance into the Dakota diocese; therefore, under ecclesiastical law, Kolasiński had technically remained a subject of the Detroit diocese during his absence.[14]

A second meeting between Sbaretti and Kolasiński on 7 February apparently brought both sides a little closer to an understanding. Although all parties involved were more reserved in their comments to the press after this second meeting, Father Kessler of Foley's household did allow it to leak out that all issues of dispute had been resolved save the matter of penance and the temporary closing of the church. The idea of doing penance, as long as it was not in Detroit, seemed less repellent than closing the church, which would be a clear indication to his congregation that their pastor was in the wrong.[15] By 9 February, however, it was clear that substantial progress had been made in breaking the deadlock, and the outline of a settlement was emerging. Kolasiński, it was now reported, had agreed to "begin a course of spiritual exercises at a monastery in an adjacent city" for one week. On Sunday, 18 February, he would return to Sweetest Heart of Mary's Church, which in the meantime would have been blessed and rededicated in a private ceremony by a representative of the bishop. At the reconciliation ceremony, Kolasiński would publicly recant his errors and activities as a schismatic. Then Sbaretti would celebrate a high mass, after which Kolasiński and his flock would be formally reunited with the Holy Roman church. The church property would remain in the name of the trustees until it was free of debt. The major issue unresolved was whether the church should be closed during its pastor's week of penance. Foley and his advisers were insisting on this point so that "there may be a formal and open indication made that the previous conduct of the church had been schismatic, and that the Polanders may understand that there has been a complete break with the old order." Kolasiński was still refusing to budge on this point.[16]

The likelihood, however, that final agreement was near, and incidentally that Kolasiński might be willing to make some further concessions, was reflected in a report that he had arranged for a new mortgage loan of $60,000 on the outstanding church indebtedness, conditional on his first being restored to good standing in the Roman Catholic church.[17] Needless to say, the Kolasińskiites were overjoyed at the prospect of reconciliation with the diocesan authorities (they had never believed they had not been acting as good Catholics), but among Kolasiński's opponents the news provoked mixed reactions. Resistance to Kolasiński's reinstatement was especially pronounced among the other Polish priests in the diocese, who in fact attempted to organize a protest meeting. Their opposition, one assumes, derived in part from their knowledge that Kolasiński had considerable oratorical skills in the pulpit and that a "legitimized" Kolasiński with a magnificent church might siphon off some of their parishioners. But among business and professional people in the loyalist camp, the idea of a reconciliation was well received. A *News* reporter talked to a grocer-saloonkeeper on Chene Street who was convinced that an end to the "church war" would be good for business. He was said (in the reporter's phonetic rendition) to have remarked:

> Mit Kolashinski priest once more I vill know how I should talk to customers. Now I know not how I zgold. If I zay Kolashinski he is all right, maybe I get me a glass beer in face. Den comes de customer no more. If I say Kolashinski he is no goot, de mans maybe he say you tam liar; den is a fight an I git my zaloon smash. Ven kin I say Kolashinski is fine man and Dombrofski, he is goot, den iss all right.[18]

At a third meeting between Sbaretti and Kolasiński on Saturday, 10 February, the Italian prelate presented what he termed his final offer. The church would not be closed and the period of penance

Fr. Peter A. Baart.
Reproduced by permission from the
Evening News, *17 June 1893.*

The crowd at the entrance to Sweetest Heart of Mary's Church on the occasion of
Kolasiński's public apology and reconciliation with the Roman Catholic hierarchy.
Reproduced by permission from the Detroit Free Press, *19 February 1894.*

Kolasiński reading his public apology.
Reproduced by permission from the Detroit Free Press, *19 February 1894.*

136

The scene at Kolasiński's bier. Reproduced by permission from the Evening News, *13 April 1898.*

Kolasiński's mausoleum at Sacred Heart Cemetery.
Reproduced by permission from the Evening News, *19 December 1898.*

Ladislaus Weidner.
Reproduced by permission from the
Evening News, *15 April 1898.*

was reduced from two weeks to one, but the schismatic priest would have to read his recantation in three languages—Polish, German, and English—before his congregation. He also would have to make an annual accounting of his parish's financial affairs. It was reliably reported that Kolasiński acceded to these terms and that an agreement was signed on Saturday evening.[19]

In the face of this imminent settlement, the forces—essentially clerical—opposed to Kolasiński's reinstatement called a meeting at St. Albertus's school on Sunday afternoon, 11 February. But when Bishop Foley learned of the meeting, he ordered it canceled.[20] It is fair to say that by this time he was reconciled to Kolasiński's reinstatement on Satolli and Sbaretti's terms, and, whatever his personal feelings, he did not care to antagonize further the powerful apostolic delegate. On the same day, Kolasiński announced during his sermon that he would be away until the following Sunday, but made no reference to his penance. He did indicate that agreement had been reached with the papal representative and that "now there are no longer Kolasinskiites or Dombrowskis. All are one people." The consensus in the press seemed to be that Kolasiński was "getting out easier than it was thought he would."[21] His penance would take place at St. Michael's Benedictine monastery in Chicago, and he would have to present a certificate from the preceptor of the monastery to Sbaretti before the formal reconciliation on 18 February could be effected.[22]

Kolasiński's week in Chicago called forth considerable grumbling about the light penance among the Detroit clergy and within the bishop's household. It was openly admitted that Foley was not voluntarily readmitting Kolasiński; this step was being forced upon him by the papal ablegate through Monsignor Sbaretti, with the full backing of the Propaganda.[23] One priest who asked to remain anonymous freely voiced his displeasure to a *Free Press* reporter and was bitter because "foreigners, an Italian" who "can hardly speak a word of English" and knew nothing of the affair, could impose a settlement. The priest suggested, not unlike Father Doman earlier, that Sbaretti was acting to impress Rome and obtain a promotion. Another anonymous source called the settlement one of "the most scandalous things that has occurred in the history of American Catholicism," adding that, whatever Satolli ordered, "no amount of recantation will ever bring back to [Kolasiński] the respect of Catholics."[24] A Catholic weekly, the *Angelus*, added its voice to the general discontent: "Every catholic feels himself the subject of a personal outrage" at this "shocking surprise."[25]

Final details of the conditions and the ceremony of reconciliation and reinstatement of Kolasiński and his congregation were made public on 17 February. Just before the reconciliation, Sbaretti would rededicate the church publicly, rather than in the quiet, private manner Kolasiński desired. Bishop Foley would not attend the ceremony, but Kolasiński would have to visit the episcopal residence after the events at Sweetest Heart of Mary's Church and make a personal apology to him. It was also a tacit condition that Kolasiński would make no attempt to induce others to join his parish. Foley would have full authority regarding the assignment or removal of assistant priests, but it was understood that Kolasiński, unless he was in gross violation of ecclesiastical law, would not be removed as pastor of the parish.[26] Kolasiński's adherents seemed firmly convinced that their pastor had won a "big victory" over the bishop. (And, as it turned out, Kolasiński would do nothing to discourage their belief.) His people had been informed that he had spent the week in Washington patching up things with Satolli; no mention was made of his doing penance in Chicago. There were also indications that in his absence Kolasiński's associates had been preparing his flock to receive his apology as only a meaningless ritual.[27]

Well before ten o'clock on 18 February, the hour announced for the ceremonies to begin, an enormous throng, estimated at ten thousand, had gathered outside Sweetest Heart of Mary's Church.[28] The program began with the rededication, in order to regularize the rite performed by the spurious archbishop. Despite the hope of Kolasiński's opponents that the repetition of the episcopal blessing would call forth some reaction from the Kolasińskiites, the ceremony was conducted too hastily for the crowd to grasp its implications. That the second celebration was much less elaborate than the first also seemed to reassure the parishioners. Furthermore, Sbaretti was not entirely familiar with the prescribed ritual for such occasions, and more than once had to be guided by Kolasiński, who in recent years had made himself a sort of expert on blessing and dedicating churches. The official party also included the Reverend Witold Buhaczkowski, vice-rector of the Polish seminary, who served as deacon; the Reverend Zygmund Kolkiewicz, assistant pastor at St. Casimir's, who acted as subdeacon; and Fr. Charles Hutter of St. Joseph's Church, who was master of ceremonies.

When the rededication of the interior was completed and the main portals were opened, a crush of humanity poured into the church. Several people fainted from the press of the crowd and the long service was punctuated with cries from those who were knocked against the walls or buttresses in the ebb and flow. The greatest concentration was near the main entrance, where people were periodically pushed through the doors, only later to be swept out again. When the mass finally began after a long delay, Sbaretti could barely be heard above the noise of the crowd. The crucial part of the service was reached when Father Kolasiński slowly and dramatically ascended the pulpit to deliver the sermon and, presumably, his apology. While the crowd was quieting at his appearance, Kolasiński read a prayer in Latin, then lifted his hands to the audience and began to speak in Polish. A few words, and anxiety vanished from the faces of his adherents to be replaced by a look of beatification. Quiet reigned, and it was said that Kolasiński could be heard even outside the church. "It was the voice and manner of a great general at the head of his army. There was not a faltering note, not an inaudible sentence. It was an address of impassioned eloquence, . . . full of tragic attitudes, bristling with stage effect."[29] He spoke as one without regrets, sure of the righteousness of his actions. His ostensible subject was the Transfiguration of Our Lord, but the real theme was the transfiguration of Dominik Kolasiński. Emotionally, he recounted the travails that he and his people had endured and proclaimed that God had heard their prayers, had granted them mercy, and was leading them along the paths of happiness and peace. The pope had not turned a deaf ear but had sent Monsignor Sbaretti to light the way. In their beautiful church, built by their great sacrifices, they could now worship undisturbed. Implicit in the message was that it was he, their pastor, who had been their redeemer. He had not bowed beneath the injustices done to him and his people; rather, the true Church had seen their plight and now reached out to gather them again into its bosom. At times tears rolled down the priest's cheeks and his face became flushed with emotion. He closed his sermon with the words, "Let us forgive everybody, as we have been forgiven. I did not tell you to separate mother from child and divide a family. Some did not like our church and left us, but we forgive them."[30] Kolasiński now stood silent for a moment, "erect, defiant, triumphant."

Then, with a sudden movement of his hand, he extracted several pages of manuscript from his vestments. His followers sensed that some momentous point was at hand; the time had come for the public apology in three languages. Yet the audience still did not understand the meaning of what was about to occur and Kolasiński was determined not to enlighten them. He leaned forward, grasping the papers with both hands; his lips moved, but no sound was audible beyond several feet. Though his words a moment before had carried throughout the church, he now spoke barely above a whisper as he read the document Sbaretti and Foley had prepared.

> I Dominic Kolasinski, anxious to be reconciled with the church, to make my submission to the right reverend bishop of this diocese, do hereby make this my solemn retraction of all errors, and satisfaction for the evils and disorders which may justly be laid to my charge. I humbly ask pardon of God and His church, of the bishop and the people of this diocese, for all the scandal I have given during the last five years by disobedience to my lawful superiors, and by the exercise of priestly functions against the will and rightful authority of the right reverend bishop. I protest before God and before this congregation and all the people, that I am truly and sincerely sorry for all I have done contrary to the laws of God and the canons of the holy church. I retract whatsoever I have said or done in opposition to the authority and jurisdiction of the right reverend bishop of this diocese. Moreover, in my own name and in the name of this parish, from this time forth I promise true obedience to the laws and canons of the church and full submission to the rules and regulations of this diocese. I will labor to promote peace and harmony between the people of this parish and their chief pastor, the right reverend bishop.
>
> I pray God and His representative, the bishop, to accept this my humble reparation and submission; and I beg of God through the intercession of the most sweet heart of Mary, the grace to keep these promises for the honor of God and the good of souls. Amen.[31]

First he read the statement in Polish, then quickly in German, and finally in English. Those who may have expected him to beat his breast and raise his voice in public repentance were understandably annoyed. But the agreement with Sbaretti had said nothing of whether the apology was to be delivered fortissimo or pianissimo!

As Kolasiński's tactic became evident to the official party, Sbaretti's voice was heard: "Pater Kolasinski, elevari vocem tuam," ("Father Kolasiński, elevate your voice"). Disregarding this command, the priest continued to whisper. Again Sbaretti spoke: "Pater Kolasinski, faveas loqui altius" ("Father Kolasiński, speak up louder").[32] This order too was ignored and, the whispering ended, Kolasiński contemptuously thrust the papers back inside his garments. Then, rapidly, in only slightly more audible tones, he pronounced the profession of faith—that of converts—in Polish and descended from the pulpit. As he rejoined the official party, Hutter informed him that he must kneel before the altar and repeat the profession of faith in English. Kolasiński replied that he had already said it in Polish and that Father Buhaczkowski had heard him. And when Sbaretti also directed him to repeat the profession, Kolasiński angrily retorted that it was unnecessary and defiantly moved away. Sbaretti was forced to accept his refusal and to conclude the mass.

After the service a calm and composed Kolasiński invited the guests to the parish residence for refreshments. They emerged about one o'clock to confront the enormous crowd that, at Kolasiński's direction, still surrounded the church. Sbaretti was about to enter a hack, but Kolasiński, gently taking his arm, invited him to ride in his own splended carriage to the episcopal residence for the conclusion of the day's proceedings. Sbaretti smiled and concurred, fully comprehending that the wily priest wished to be seen driving away triumphantly with the distinguished visitor.

The last act of the drama was about to unfold. In the privacy of the episcopal residence, Kolasiński knelt before Bishop Foley to kiss the seal of the episcopal ring. The priest professed sincere repentance and pledged full obedience for the future. The bishop, formally and somewhat perfunctorily, pronounced Kolasiński to be welcome into the diocesan family. Then, without inviting him to remain for refreshments, he led the priest to the door. Before departing, the "reconciled" priest invited the bishop to say mass in Sweetest Heart of Mary's Church so that the congregation could share in the happiness of reconciliation. The bishop agreed but without specifying a definite time. Later, replying to a reporter's question of when he would, Foley was still vague. "Not very soon; I've a great many engagements to be filled. . . . By and by I will get around to Fr. Kolasinski's church, but not soon." Asked if he was satisfied with the manner in which Kolasiński made his retraction, Foley answered "with good humored indulgence": "Oh, yes, I suppose so. I understand he didn't speak very loud, but that doesn't matter. I have his retraction, signed with his own hands, and of course a good many copies will be published, so whether he was heard in church or not makes no particular difference."[33]

Despite his cool reception at the episcopal residence, the verdict in the press was that Kolasiński had prevailed, especially in the eyes of his adherents, which was after all what mattered most for the priest. He had in effect turned a potentially humiliating affair into a kind of victory. The Kolasińskiites were convinced that Holy Church had reached out to them and their adored pastor; consequently, the ceremony gave Kolasiński a stronger hold on his flock than ever before. A magnanimous Monsignor Sbaretti, apparently unperturbed by Kolasiński's maneuverings, also appeared pleased with the day's events, and that very evening boarded a train for Washington.

After Kolasiński's reinstatement, Bishop Foley directed the loyalist elements within the diocese not to criticize further the actions of Monsignor Satolli and his deputy Sbaretti. But the loyalists were apparently not restrained from commenting on Kolasiński's behavior on 18 February. The *Michigan Catholic*, for example, characterized his bearing on that day as "impudent, insolent and audacious." The truth, as the *Michigan Catholic* saw it, was that the proceedings were "farcical" and constituted "another scandal" perpetrated by Kolasiński. But now, the paper noted with pleasure, Kolasiński was under Bishop Foley's authority and he would soon have to "come down from his lofty pedestal."[34]

Reconciliation and reinstatement with the Holy Roman church did not end the attention and notoriety directed at Kolasiński. Unresolved financial problems resulting from the massive indebtedness entailed in building Sweetest Heart of Mary's were his chief difficulty during his last years. Moreover, just two months after his reinstatement, Kolasiński and his ways again attracted public attention and, in this case, ridicule.

The difficulty concerned the burial ground Kolasiński had been obliged to set up soon after establishing his maverick parish. The schismatic Kolasińskiites, according to canon law, were debarred from interment in consecrated ground. (To be sure, a few families of the priest's followers who had relatives near death had made temporary peace with the church authorities, but after their loved ones were buried, many had quietly returned to Kolasiński's fold.) But the majority of his adherents stood by their pastor, who, soon after organizing his flock into Sweetest Heart of Mary's Parish, purchased several acres of land north of the city and personally consecrated it as a Roman Catholic cemetery. The graveyard was in the area known as Norris (later North Detroit), then a part of Hamtramck Township. Within the first year after Kolasiński's return, about sixty persons were buried there, most of whom the press described as the "humble dead," whose graves were designated only by "cheap wooden crosses."[35]

At the time Kolasiński purchased the land, he was anxious to take deed to it as quickly and cheaply as possible—it was said that a deceased parishioner had been awaiting burial for several days.

Acting in haste, he purchased a swampy plot, telling the seller that he planned to build a factory there. In an attempt to drain the area, trenches were laid out and a small reservoir dug on the lowest portion. A windmill was erected to carry the excess water to a drainage canal that ran along an adjacent road. These measures were only partially successful, and frequently, especially after a heavy rain, the area flooded. The coffins often had to be held down with poles while dirt was shoveled on top. By the summer of 1893, the local residents had begun to complain of foul odors emanating from the reservoir and canal and had petitioned the state board of health for relief. In April 1894 reporters on the lookout for news relating to the celebrated Polish priest heard about the complaints and launched their own investigation. A *Tribune* reporter, using a steel rod as a probe, found that in most of the some two hundred plots, the caskets were buried only eight to twenty-eight inches deep, although state law required a minimum of six feet. And worse, passersby were seen drinking the possibly contaminated water. The local residents, of course, described Father Kolasiński and his burial ground in extremely unpleasant words.[36]

Once the story broke in the city's newspapers, a fury of legal activity commenced. It appeared that a public cemetery must be incorporated by at least ten persons, and the board of health of the locality technically held the property in trust to ensure obedience to all state and local laws. Kolasiński apparently had taken the deed in his own name and had not told Hamtramck Township that he intended to start a cemetery. Nor could the burial ground qualify as a private cemetery, since it exceeded one acre. The township, it was reported, was initiating legal steps to exhume the bodies and have the cemetery vacated. In addition, Bishop Foley was taking the position that those bodies interred before Kolasiński's reinstatement could not now be given burial in a regular Catholic cemetery, since "those persons died outside the church and they could not be placed in consecrated ground." To a reporter's question whether there was no ceremony or dispensation that might rectify the tragic situation, a "smiling" bishop replied: "Oh, no. It is too late for that. They're dead now."[37]

Kolasiński responded defiantly to the agitation, charging that it was but another example of the attacks on him inspired by his enemies. The cemetery had been in use for five years and no one had complained. There was no evidence that the "revelations" had caused uneasiness among his congregation, who had apparently accepted the shortcomings of their cemetery. But on 21 April 1894 the Hamtramck Township Board of Health was granted an injunction temporarily enjoining Kolasiński from permitting further interments. The township also asked the court to declare the burial ground a public nuisance and order that the bodies already there be relocated.[38] Eventually, Kolasiński was permitted to improve the cemetery sufficiently to satisfy the requirements of the township and to incorporate the property as a public cemetery, referred to as Greenwood. Today, considerably expanded, it is known as Sacred Heart Cemetery, located on Mound between East McNichols and Davison.[39]

Scarcely had this storm abated when, in August 1894, "the clouds of war [were] again hanging over the Church of the Sweetest Heart of Mary." The cause this time was remarkably reminiscent of Kolasiński's earlier battles with his disaffected former lieutenants, Długi and Raeder. The pastor fell out with Fr. Ignacy Barszcz, his assistant of not quite a year. The split appeared to be over money, specifically over what compensation the elderly assistant pastor had expected to receive. The rift became public when Father Barszcz called at police headquarters on the evening of 21 August to request protection. A *News* reporter happened to be there, and the irate Barszcz was only too willing to air his differences with the pastor of Sweetest Heart of Mary's Church. He claimed that Kolasiński had failed to keep the promises he had made at the time he induced Barszcz to leave New Jersey. In addition to a monthly stipend of fifty dollars, Barszcz said he was supposed to receive five dollars for every funeral mass and one dollar for every common mass he conducted. Now Kolasiński had announced that, because of the parish's large debt, Barszcz's salary would be reduced by half. Worse, Barszcz considered Kolasiński to be a "rascal" who drank to excess. He also echoed the old but never proven charge that, by means of exorbitant fees, Kolasiński extorted money for his personal use. Escorted by a policeman, Barszcz returned to the parish residence to collect his personal effects but found that his room was locked and the key was in the possession of the pastor, who was not at home.[40]

This was not the first time that Barszcz had sought the limelight; he had already become known as somewhat of a troublemaker to Catholic church leaders. In 1887, while pastor of St. Anthony of Padua's Church in Jersey City, Barszcz had addressed an appeal to the Propaganda to establish a separate diocesan administration in America for Catholics of Slavic origin. Then Barszcz took his proposal to Cardinal Gibbons but was rebuffed. As a last resort, the priest appealed directly to President Grover Cleveland, who referred the request back to Gibbons. The cardinal apologized to the president for the annoyance of Barszcz's request and implied that the priest was "something of a crank" and merited no further attention.[41]

On the morrow of his visit to police headquarters, Barszcz returned to the pastoral residence, again accompanied by an officer and this time by the *News* reporter as well. Kolasiński appeared, greeted the Polish-speaking Patrolman Balowski, whom he knew well, and willingly unlocked his ex-assistant's room. Finding that his belongings were intact, Barszcz left to hire a wagon to remove them. Only when Kolasiński noticed the reporter lurking in the background did his mood turn ugly.[42] His once cordial relations with the press had soured, especially since the exposure of the several "dedications" of his church. Later that day Kolasiński, accompanied by his new attorney, Adam Bloom, filed suit in Wayne County Court for $20,000 damages against Barszcz for "defamation of character" and swore out a capias on him. It was soon learned, however, that Barszcz had left for Cleveland by steamer. But by repeating his customary method of summarily dismissing an assistant and filing charges against him, Kolasiński had unwittingly run afoul of the diocesan authority to which he was now subject. The Third Baltimore Council had specifically prohibited a priest from bringing civil action against another priest, and, according to the understanding with Sbaretti, Kolasiński had agreed that only the bishop would have the authority to appoint and dismiss his assistants.[43] As his opponents had prophesied, Kolasiński had not taken long to fall into conflict with his nominal superior, the bishop of Detroit.

At almost the same time that Kolasiński was ridding himself of Barszcz, his former associate Stefan Kamiński was entering the priesthood, though not in a ceremony recognized by the Roman church. After breaking with Kolasiński, Kamiński had set up "a little tinkering shop on Leland Street," where he made a living repairing clocks and cobbling shoes. He often spoke of someday becoming a priest, although his friends recalled most vividly his propensity for drink. During these years Kamiński frequently absented himself from Detroit, but it still came as a complete surprise to his old acquaintances when they learned that he had been ordained in a ceremony performed in Cleveland under the patronage of the schismatic Polish priest, Franciszek Kolaszewski. The ordination was conducted by two persons well known to Polish Detroiters: "Archbishop" Joseph René Vilatte, assisted by Fr. Władysław Dębski. Thus, though there was no evidence that he ever studied theology or attended a seminary, Kamiński had obtained his heart's desire.[44]

Kamiński was soon to play an important role in the organization of the independent Polish Catholic movement (what he had once denounced Kolasiński for doing). In 1896 he left a schismatic parish in Freeland, Pennsylvania, to take control of the independent parish set up in Buffalo by Fr. Antoni Klawiter. Then in 1898 Kamiński claimed the title of "Jacobite bishop." Upon his death in 1911, his followers joined the Polish National Catholic Church in America, founded several years earlier by the Reverend Franciszek Hodur.[45]

The difficulties over Kolasiński's graveyard and the clashes between the pastor and his associates at Sweetest Heart of Mary's Church paled into insignificance, however, when compared to the financial problems of the parish. The total cost of the magnificent new church had come close to $150,000. The congregation, according to its attorney, Adam Bloom, had raised about $92,000. In mid-1896 the outstanding debt was placed at $56,450; $40,000 of it was owed the American Savings Bank, which had provided a mortgage at the time of Kolasiński's reconciliation. The remaining indebtedness was spread among several mechanics and contractors. Bishop Foley, it will be recalled, had made clear that Kolasiński could expect no aid from diocesan coffers in resolving his financial obligations.[46]

More than once the congregation had narrowly averted forfeiture of its property and the auctioneer's gavel by making last-minute partial payments on the smaller liens and thereby obtaining further adjournments. But in 1896 the attorneys for American Savings, which was preparing to go out of existence, secured a judgment of foreclosure (well before the original mortgage was to expire) and an order for the sale of the property.[47] Finally, on 1 February 1897 the church was put up for sale. Just as the bidding began an agent from Toronto, identified as Archibald McLellan, announced that he was arranging a scheme whereby about forty prominent members of the parish would execute bonds as security. But the bidding continued, the highest offer of $38,000 being tendered by the bank's attorneys. Nonetheless, they agreed to grant the Canadian representative a thirty-day adjournment to demonstrate precisely how he planned to refinance the mortgage. To secure this delay, the parish tendered $1,500 on the outstanding indebtedness.[48]

A month later McLellan, although stating that he was in contact with an English syndicate that would underwrite a mortgage for $65,000 at 4½ percent per annum for fifteen years, was not yet able to produce a bona fide to substantiate his scheme. Hence the church property was formally sold at auction on 4 March to the attorneys of the American Savings Bank for the sum of $40,000, subject to various liens that raised the aggregate claim to about $65,000. Since the law provided eight days before a forefeiture sale at auction could be confirmed, the congregation was assured of at least one more Sunday in their church. It seemed likely, however, that if the parish trustees were not able to negotiate a new loan within the eight days, the bank's agents would be willing to work out a rental arrangement to allow the congregation to use the church for the time being.[49] The new owners well understood the intense feelings of the parishioners and that any attempt to evict them would certainly lead to a repetition of the bloody scenes in the Polish quarter of twelve years earlier. News of the sale, needless to say, had stunned the Kolasińskiites. There was also mounting evidence of disaffection and opposition to the pastor, especially among the more well-to-do parishioners, including several of the trustees, over his purported bungling of the parish's financial affairs. But for most of the congregation, the greatest fear seemed to be that they might now fall into the grasp of their "step-father," as they had come to call Bishop Foley. Kolasiński, as in other crises, outwardly exuded confidence and maintained that he would soon secure a new loan through McLellan.[50]

Three weeks later the parish still had not obtained a new loan, but neither were they paying rent to the new owners. After the formal sale, Kolasiński's attorney had gotten a court order granting the congregation until Friday, 26 March to file a bill of exception to the sale, a step they had in fact taken, charging irregularities in the proceedings. This measure had the effect of providing ten additional days to obtain a new loan. The bank's attorneys seemed sincerely to hope that the parish would succeed in refinancing, since they viewed the property, despite its valuation, as a white elephant. At the first hearing on 29 March on the parish's bill of exception to the sale, Kolasiński's lawyer argued that, in offering to sell back the property for $47,000, the bank was endeavoring to realize a windfall profit. As the hearing dragged into April, the bank's attorneys countered that several smaller claims had had to be paid off. The bank might realize about $1,000 at the most, a not exorbitant sum in view of the legal fees incurred. Since it was to the interest of both parties not to have the sale finally recorded, the court on 12 April granted a further thirty-day adjournment to give the parish more time to redeem the property.[51]

On 20 April Adam Bloom announced that the congregation had at last obtained a loan of $65,000 through Archibald McLellan, on the terms previously stated, with the Law Union and Crown Fire and Life Insurance Company of London. To secure the mortgage the church property was reevaluated at $215,000. Bloom let it be known that, after covering the outstanding debts, the loan would also provide some $9,000 for a parsonage, since the pastor was still occupying the quarters on the second floor of the original school-chapel.[52] Father Kolasiński had survived the latest, and in many ways most serious, threat to his hold on his flock.

But six months later, as the first semiannual installment on the new loan came due, the congregation was involved in a new crisis, which would culminate in a full-fledged challenge to the pastor and a repudiation of his management of parish financial affairs. The trouble began when Franciszek Potrzuski, a trustee and the treasurer for the parish, refused to turn over the $3,209.90 installment that had come due on 8 November. Although all or nearly all of that amount was on hand, Potrzuski had taken $2,400 for himself, maintaining his right to recover most of the $2,500 he had personally put up earlier in the year to delay the foreclosure on the church. According to him, other parishioners also had not been repaid sums they had advanced. McLellan, on behalf of the London financiers, proposed a moratorium until the parishioners' claims could be untangled. In his own defense, Potrzuski said he was not merely serving his own interests but wished to dramatize what he believed was Kolasiński's gross maladministration. He claimed the pastor was pocketing enormous sums for his personal expenses from fees and the parish school's earnings at a time when the annual parish revenues were only $11,000 in pew rentals and the Sunday collections, although salaries and interest payments exceeded that amount by $3,000. Kolasiński countered Potrzuski's charges from the pulpit, alleging that the treasurer was in fact channeling church funds into his own pocket.[53]

Potrzuski, one of the wealthiest and most influential men in the Polish community, was worth an estimated thirty to fifty thousand dollars, derived mostly from his meat market at 839 Riopelle Street, which was described as "a veritable gold mine, crowded with customers all day long." It was acknowledged that the majority of the trustees backed his effort to force Kolasiński to account for his personal revenues and expenses. The treasurer insisted, however, that "in a religious sense" he stood loyally by his pastor and church.[54] But Kolasiński, accustomed for years to having total control and a free hand in all his church's affairs, could not conceive of such a distinction between the spiritual and the material. Tempers rose and charges and countercharges flew between the principal disputants. In an attempt to recover the money still owed him, Potrzuski had his lawyer swear out a writ of execution against Kolasiński's personal property, particularly his cherished "span of creams" and ornate carriage. When several of the pastor's loyal supporters put up bonds (secured by their homes) to cover Potrzuski's claims on Kolasiński, the butcher tried, unsuccessfully, to challenge their solvency.[55]

As the new year dawned, Potrzuski and the other trustees turned to Bishop Foley to see if some way could be found to force Kolasiński to disclose his personal receipts and expenditures. Specifically, they hoped to secure the financial books of the parish school, which Kolasiński had always handled himself. According to the agreement made when Kolasiński was reinstated, the bishop only had authority to receive a periodic accounting of the parish's pew rentals and collections, but presumably he did instruct the trustees on ways to introduce formal resolutions at the forthcoming annual parish meeting. Since the parish was a legally organized corporation, passage of such resolutions might circumscribe Kolasiński's power.[56]

The trustees put the bishop's advice to good use at what proved to be a stormy gathering at the parish schoolhouse on 3 January 1898. The *Evening News* and the *Tribune* described the meeting as a complete victory of Kolasiński's opponents, who succeeded in "trimming the priest's sails."[57] Close to three thousand people crowded into the building. The majority sentiment, once the voting began, was clearly on the side of the challenging trustees; they were all unanimously reelected to a new term over a Kolasiński-sponsored slate. Potrzuski, however, declined to accept reelection as treasurer and was replaced by Antoni Granke, a grocer. As a result of the resolutions passed at the meeting, management of the parish's financial affairs was taken completely out of Kolasiński's hands. The proceeds from the parochial school were to be turned over directly to the new treasurer to help liquidate the church's indebtedness, as were all fees collected from baptisms, marriages, burials, and other ceremonies. Kolasiński was to receive only a small fixed percentage of these fees. Authority to hire the organist and other church officials also was taken from him; in essence, he was to confine his duties to the spiritual needs of his flock. From what one dissident trustee estimated to have been an annual income of $15,000, the priest would now have to make do with $720 in salary, free rent and fuel, and perhaps $1,000 as his percentage of fees for special services. The *Evening News* could not resist the conclusion that Potrzuski and the trustees had at long last succeeded in doing what Bishop Foley and the power of the Roman church had failed to do: bring the celebrated priest to an accounting. Kolasiński, surprisingly, seemed to accept his defeat—though he refused to concede it was a defeat—with remarkable magnanimity. To a reporter who saw him shortly after the meeting, "he was even more cheerful than usual."[58]

In the aftermath of the showdown, both sides seemed to be willing to patch up differences and restore harmony. No move was made, despite considerable speculation in the press, to challenge Kolasiński's continued pastorship of Sweetest Heart of Mary's Church. Publicly, Kolasiński insisted that no real change had taken place. "I shall . . . insist on knowing what is done with the money and what is done by the trustees at their meetings," he remarked to reporters.[59]

To be sure, twelve years of almost constant struggle and tension had taken much of the fight out of the fiery priest. As would soon become evident, Father Kolasiński was not well. For several years he had suffered from a heart ailment which often brought on severe choking seizures. Because he was nervous and high-strung to begin with, the recent troubles undoubtedly had aggravated his condition. On Monday, 4 April, his personal physician, Dr. Gustav Nicolai, was summoned to the pastoral residence. Kolasiński was having difficulty breathing. Tuesday his condition was improved, and the doctor prescribed rest and medicine. Then on Good Friday the priest suffered a stroke that paralyzed the left side of his body. He was often unconscious, and the doctor feared he would not recover.[60]

By Easter Sunday the congregation and especially the members of the household were anxious. Not comprehending why Nicolai could not restore their beloved pastor to health, a group from the church, led by the coachman, invaded the sickroom and, shouting "Gift" ("poison"), prevented the German doctor from administering medicine. As evidence that it was not poison, the doctor took some himself, but the crowd was not convinced. In desperation, Nicolai sent for Bishop Foley. The bishop had spent two hours the previous afternoon at the priest's bedside, during which time Kolasiński had briefly regained consciousness and recognized his old nemesis. When the bishop arrived this time, he alternately ordered and pleaded with the priest's followers to stand back and allow the doctor to do his work. The group refused, saying that they would nurse the priest and administer his medicine. With the help of another Polish priest, who ordered the crowd to kneel, the bishop was able to offer a blessing and take his leave of the dying pastor. The reconciliation between bishop and priest seemed sincere, and Kolasiński, in a moment of consciousness, reached for the bishop's hand and kissed the seal on the episcopal ring.

Dr. Nicolai managed to see his patient, now comatose, very early the next morning, but at seven-thirty on Easter Monday, 11 April 1898, Father Kolasiński died. The immediate cause of death was attributed to "apoplexy brought on of valvular insufficiency of the heart."[61]

As word of their beloved pastor's passing spread through the parish, there were moving scenes of grief and mourning, especially around the church and the priest's residence. Foley came shortly before ten o'clock and led the multitude in prayer. The church was draped in black crepe and evergreens for the funeral, which was planned for Wednesday, 13 April. The mourners gathered outside the parish school, waiting for a last glimpse of their pastor, who, dressed in priestly vestments, was laid out in a simple casket. On Tuesday evening Kolasiński lay in state in Sweetest Heart of Mary's Church, while fully fifteen thousand mourners filed past the bier. An elaborate ceremony took place when the casket was brought from the school building to the church. A pathway from the school to the church was lined with children holding lighted candles. The casket was borne by members of the Kościuszko Guard, preceded by six priests led by Kolasiński's old rival, Fr. Józef Dąbrowski.[62] Just two weeks earlier the old antagonists had apparently made their peace, when Kolasiński hosted a banquet for Dąbrowski and the faculty of the Polish seminary at Detroit's Richter Hotel. The occasion was Kolasiński's receiving a recent graduate of the seminary, Fr. Józef Fołta, as his assistant at Sweetest Heart of Mary's Church.[63]

Well over an hour before the time set for the requiem mass, the church was packed. Reporters noticed that many curious non-Poles were present. The *Journal* estimated the crowd in and around the church at thirty-five thousand persons, unquestionably the largest throng ever seen at a Detroit funeral. For nearly three hours the people waited for the priests who were to celebrate the mass. Hysterical sobbing broke out as Fr. Romuald Byzewski, pastor of St. Francis's, ascended the pulpit to deliver the eulogy for the deceased. Speaking in Polish, in a "dramatic and resonant voice," Byzewski extolled Kolasiński's virtues. Pointing to the many children gathered near the altar, he spoke movingly of the late pastor's special devotion to the young and his love for his people. But Kolasiński's greatest and most enduring gift to his people was the church in which they were now assembled to mourn his passing. Before the blessing, Bishop Foley said a few words in English that were significant because they implicitly challenged the feelings of the Polish congregation. "If it is wholesome to pray for the dead, it is doubly so for a dead priest, who must give an account, a strict account, of the administration of his flock. Don't waste your energies in expressing your grief, but give proof of your affection by sincere prayers for the soul of the departed."[64] At the end of the mass, more than two hundred and fifty carriages and about twenty thousand people followed the hearse to Greenwood Cemetery, where at two o'clock Kolasiński's remains were laid to rest. Fr. Nikodem Kolasiński delivered a graveside eulogy in which he exhorted the congregation of Sweetest Heart of Mary's to follow the path his brother had charted. Eight months later the casket was reinterred in a stone mausoleum erected at the gravesite at a cost of $2,000 contributed by Kolasiński's followers in a special collection.[65]

The day after the funeral the talk in the east-side Polish quarter concerned the previous day's events and speculation over who would succeed the late pastor. Some Kolasińskiites were bitter at what they felt had been a lack of compassion in Bishop Foley's remarks. One Pole remarked that even in death "it was plain that the bishop had no use for Fr. Kolasinski. He did not even mention his name." But the most hated person in the Polish quarter appeared to be Franciszek Potrzuski, who, it was said, had hastened Kolasiński's death. Potrzuski's butcher shop was no longer a thriving business. The unanimous choice among the parishioners for Kolasiński's successor appeared to be Father Byzewski, who had delivered the moving funeral oration the day before. In his favor were his oratory and the fact that he had not been identified with either of the warring religious factions. Of course the decision was in Foley's hands, and he seemed in no hurry to make an appointment. The late priest's brother was also mentioned as a candidate. He had been pastor of several Polish parishes in Ohio and in the summer of 1893 had temporarily taken over the pastoral duties at Sweetest Heart of Mary's Church while his brother was absent. Father Nikodem, however, had on occasion had his own difficulties with episcopal authority and had recently been given a mission in Wisconsin. He had taken possession of Father Dominik's birds and animals, but he had shown no interest in his late brother's parish and in fact had returned immediately to Wisconsin.[66]

To those who had maintained that the pastor of Sweetest Heart of Mary's Church had amassed a fortune from his parishioners, the revelation of Kolasiński's modest estate came as an eye-opener. His estate was estimated at $10,000, of which $7,000 was the value placed on his farm near Minto, North Dakota. The other assets were a $1,000 life insurance policy, $1,400 back salary, and about $500 in personal property (including his horses). But his debts were estimated at $7,500, including $2,000 outstanding on the farm's mortgage, $2,000 owed his sister in formal notes, $1,500 owed to Dr. Nicolai (who had not been paid since 1896), and sundry personal obligations totaling $2,000. Thus, when the funeral expenses were deducted, his heirs stood to gain very little, even if the farm could be sold. Nonetheless, the late priest's friend and attorney, Feliks Lemkie, filed a petition in probate court to appoint Kolasiński's widowed sister, Mrs. Sophia Weidner (the same much maligned "Sophia" of Father Domagalski's imagination of thirteen years earlier?), administrator of the estate. The greatest concern among Kolasiński's close friends centered on his twelve-year-old nephew and adopted son, Ladislaus (Władysław) Weidner, who had received much attention and devotion from the priest during his last years. For the time being, the boy was being cared for by Dr. Nicolai.[67] A final and sad footnote came a month later, when Kolasiński's beloved pair of creams, the symbol to Detroiters of his dignity and flamboyance, were sold at auction for a mere $150.[68]

For over twelve years, Fr. Dominik Kolasiński had been the object of attention in Detroit at large, no less than in the rapidly expanding Polish community. The day following his death the *News*, which, more than any other Detroit newspaper regardless of language, had recorded the life and activities of the late priest, printed an editorial titled "Rev. Kolasinski's Remarkable Characteristics," in which it paid high tribute to the man it had so often chastised.

Detroit could scarcely lose a citizen other than Rev. Dominick H. Kolasinski whose life and doings occupied so large a place in the public interest for a decade. Kolasinski's abilities were suggestive of genius, but genius commonly concentrates talent in some one direction, leaving the remainder of the man commonplace. Kolasinski was in no direction commonplace, and though his talents were masterful in many directions, the play of his multifarious gift was so rapid that it was always doubtful where his particular genius lay. By the power of his oratory he was able to call about himself multitudes of simple, truthful parishioners and hold them in loyalty almost phenomenal. . . . But Kolasinski was more than this. His was an invincible nature under all circumstances. Whether it were a strong man, or a person of high official power, or the impersonal forces of nature and circumstance that withstood him, Kolasinski was the same tower of strength that had to be reckoned with. . . . He was as incapable of taking a subordinate place before any sort of power as it is for others to lead. . . .

The load of his spiritual cares and difficulties could have been borne only by a giant in character. The well-known face of the famous priest never betrayed the anxiety of his soul. . . .

Detroit loses a most remarkable man.[69]

The *Detroit Tribune*'s comments on Kolasiński's passing echoed the sentiment that "one of the most remarkable lives that Detroit has known has gone out," and reminded its readers that the priest's death "is first of all a deep personal bereavement to the hundreds of devoted people to whom he sustained the relation of spiritual shepherd." But not all public voices were so charitable. The *Detroit Journal*, on the day of his death, remarked, "He was a large man only in his pugnacity and perseverance." And the *Michigan Catholic* used Kolasiński's passing to laud the "extreme charity, gentility and humility of the present Bishop of Detroit," who had endured with so much patience the doings of the late pastor of Sweetest Heart of Mary's Parish. It expressed the hope that with Kolasiński dead, "the troubles . . . of Little Poland in our midst are gone never to return."[70]

Certainly few could deny Kolasiński's forceful character, persistence, tenacity, indomitable will, and remarkable hold over his devoted followers. As circumstances dictated, he could be shrewd and crafty, and he certainly possessed the uncanny sense of timing of a successful politician. But he was no less vain, haughty, and given to ostentatious display, traits which, though they often earned him the derision of outsiders, seemed not to diminish the loyalty of his adherents. Although his knowledge of Latin, ecclesiastical practice, and canon law was perhaps equal to two Detroit bishops, his tactless flaunting of their authority earned him enmity which carried beyond his grave. Kolasiński was by nature given to rule and could not tolerate interference in his affairs, though in his twilight years he brought himself, at least outwardly, to accept authority. But, unlike many who purport to lead, Kolasiński never lost sight of his ultimate aim—which for much of his career in Detroit could be summed up by the word "vindication." Although he took rash and defiant measures, he never overstepped, so to speak, the point of no return. But perhaps Father Kolasiński's most characteristic feature was his deep attachment to traditional Polish religious practices and his intense Polish patriotism. It is these two features that most nearly explain the devotion of his followers. Seemingly no rational argument or evidence could budge their faith in him. It must be said, however, that Kolasiński was often a poor judge of character, especially in selecting his subordinates, though it is true that circumstances often limited his choices. Fr. Joseph Swastek has argued that few individuals "tantalized friend and foe, in life and death, as much as Rev. Dominic Kolasinski." He suggested that Kolasiński, perhaps unconsciously, showed "two faces," two personalities, "one to attract and charm his friends and followers, another to repel and affront enemies and opponents."[71] He posed an unspoken challenge to some of his fellow Polish clerics by his prodigious oratorical skills and especially by his innate ability to reach the innermost yearnings and anxieties of those recent Polish peasant immigrants (particularly from his native Galicia) who were bewildered and overwhelmed by the alien ways of urban America.

Kolasiński's vainglory and inflated self-image, no less than the sometimes petty jealousies of his rivals, accentuated divisions in the burgeoning Polish community of the 1880s and 1890s. It appears likely that at the onset of the troubles at St. Albertus's Church in late 1885, Kolasiński was the victim of malice (and here more blame must lie with the conniving Father Gutowski than with the unfortunate and much maligned Father Dąbrowski) as well as of shortsighted episcopal censure. But the suspended priest's own intransigence certainly contributed to the rapid escalation of a dispute among clerics into a full-blown crisis enveloping the entire Polish community. From 30 November 1885 to 18 April 1894, and even beyond, the Kolasiński Affair was essentially the story of one man's struggle to vindicate himself and triumph at all costs. Although there can be no doubt that Kolasiński cared deeply for the welfare of his congregation, circumstances made them pawns in the struggle between their stubborn pastor and two strong-willed bishops. Father Baart was perhaps closest to the truth when he noted that "too much personality, too much passion" and too little charity and concern over the fate of ten thousand humble souls had for a while consumed the diocese of Detroit.

The emotions and divisions that beset Detroit's Polish community in the last two decades of the nineteenth century did not fully subside with the ostensible reconciliation and untimely passing of Fr. Dominik Kolasiński. Almost a half-century after his death, a doctoral student, completing a dissertation on the stages of transition and adjustment of Polish peasant immigrants to urban Detroit, interviewed several persons who had known Kolasiński. He found that not only had the passions of those years not diminished, but that the intervening time had contributed to coloring events and intensifying partisanship. Frank Balicki, who as a youth had been Kolasiński's office boy, remembered the priest "first and foremost" as "a Polish patriot." He magnified the priest's prodigious achievements and ascribed the "source of his trouble" essentially to Gutowski, who had rewarded Kolasiński's "patriotic generosity" in bringing him to Detroit by "spying" on his benefactor and reporting to the bishop. Jadwiga Gibasiewicz, who recalled vividly the opinions of her Kolasińskiite parents, blamed the power and selfishness of the saloonkeepers who had comprised a strong political force in the early years of Detroit's Polish community. The priest's untiring efforts to improve and "refine" the social conditions and habits of the unsophisticated immigrants, Mrs. Gibasiewicz believed, had led him afoul of these profit-oriented elders of the Polish community.[72]

Memory, to be sure, has a way of coloring distant events and turning into one-sided exaggeration, but it usually retains an undercurrent of perceived reality. In this regard it is worth recalling Kolasiński's own words to Archbishop Elder of Cincinnati in a letter of 15 January 1886, written at the onset of the troubles. "By devoting my person strenuously and diligently to my duties, and by preaching the Word of God, I have eliminated completely the excessive drinking, thievery, and other evils which were rampant here among the Polish people."[73] The older, mostly Prussian-Polish leaders in the community, many of whom were engaged in the sale of groceries and alcohol, did feel threatened by Kolasiński's preaching against the avaricious ways of saloonkeepers—a message not uncommon among pastoral priests in Galicia, where most of the liquor trade was still in noble or foreign hands. (To be sure, Kolasiński's attack was motivated in part by his desire to see the money spent for drink on Sundays added to the collection plate.)

Kolasiński's charges of the lack of Polish patriotism of the Germanized Prussian Poles and Kashubs, many of whom had emigrated before the Kulturkampf, reflected heightened Polish national sentiments in Galicia in the wake of obtaining "autonomy" under Habsburg rule. Kolasiński's derision of first a "German" bishop and later of an "Americanizing" Irish bishop was partially a reflection of his own insularity; though capable of affability toward strangers, he was never really comfortable with persons outside the Polish community. Though he spoke fluent German as well as

Polish, in sixteen years in America he never learned more than a few broken phrases of English.

The charge has not infrequently been made that the Kolasiński Affair was in considerable measure the creation of American yellow journalism. It is true that the Detroit English-language press quickly saw the commercial value of printing the colorful affairs of the Polish community, but their appetites were more often than not whetted by Polish partisans who wished to have their viewpoints presented. And it must be conceded that the most inflammatory issues, in particular the allegations of moral turpitude against Kolasiński, were launched in the city's Polish papers.

But after nearly a century, the question of blame is no longer cardinal to understanding the significance of these years, just as an answer to the charges of moral failing is no longer germane to evaluating the tortuous public career of Fr. Dominik Kolasiński. The activities of Kolasiński and his contemporaries were symptomatic not only of the difficult adjustment confronting Polish immigrants in a new land but also of the attempts within the largely Irish-dominated Catholic church to define its posture toward the waves of immigrants from southern and eastern Europe and come to grips with the social and political ways of an America undergoing rapid change.

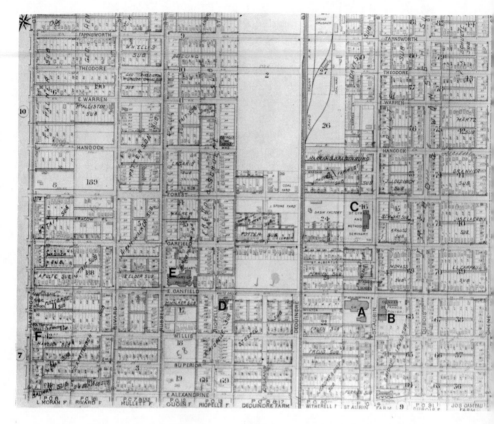

A portion of the east-side Polish quarter. A: *St. Albertus's Church and school;* B: *Felician Sisters' motherhouse and convent;* C: *SS. Cyril and Methodius Seminary;* D: *White Eagle Brewery;* E: *Sweetest Heart of Mary's Church;* F: *Żółtowski Hall.* Baist's Property Atlas of the City of Detroit *(1896). Courtesy of the Burton Historical Collection of the Detroit Public Library.*

⊂⟨◝⟩⌐CHAPTER 6 ⟨◝⟩⟨◝⟩◯
LIFE AND WORK IN POLISH DETROIT

Detroit's east-side immigrant neighborhoods in the latter part of the nineteenth century were a mosaic of ethnic diversity that seemed to fascinate, and on occasion trouble, "American" Detroiters. To be sure, many of them were but a generation or so removed from immigrant status themselves. In fact, the population of nineteenth-century Detroit was overwhelmingly "foreign." The census of 1890 indicated that 40 percent of Detroit's 205,876 recorded inhabitants were foreign-born, and an additional 37 percent were first-generation offspring of at least one foreign-born parent. Roman Catholics made up almost 50 percent of the city's population, and an estimated 70 percent of them lived and worshiped in the area east of Woodward Avenue. The transformation of Detroit in the second half of the nineteenth century from an essentially commercial city into a major manufacturing center was facilitated in large measure by the steady influx of immigrants and their families.[1] Ethnic neighborhoods, as a recent writer has noted, were "the benchmarks of late nineteenth-century Detroit." And traditionally it was on the city's near east side that successive waves of immigrants had first settled.[2]

Germans, who had begun to settle in Detroit in large numbers around midcentury, comprised the largest ethnic group, accounting by one estimate for over a third of the population in 1890. The social and commercial center of the German community was Gratiot Avenue, which a contemporary observer likened to a street in

Berlin. The Germans, especially the Protestants, tended to assimilate rapidly, and second-generation German Americans were found in large numbers in the city's administrative, commercial, and professional ranks.[3]

Detroit's Polish pioneers, as we have seen, first settled near the German Catholic churches. They gradually moved northward along Antoine, Hastings, Russell, Riopelle and St. Aubin during the 1870s, especially after the erection of St. Albertus's Church.[4] By the 1880s the Poles formed the most distinctive ethnic settlement on the city's then northeast side, characterized by the local press as the "Polack Quarter," "Polacktown," or "Little Poland" with increasing frequency, especially after the Kolasiński troubles began. From an estimated 300 Polish families in 1871, the community grew to about 22,000 persons by 1885.[5] In the next fifteen years that number would more than double; by the turn of the century the estimate was 48,000, a figure which, if accurate, encompassed over 16 percent of the city's population in 1900.[6] The figures cannot be positively confirmed, since many Poles indicated either Germany, Austria-Hungary, or Russia as their country of origin to the federal census takers. Furthermore, the church records usually recorded the number of families, not the individual members, of a given parish.

With the growth of the Polish community in the 1880s and 1890s, streets north and south of Canfield were laid out and lined with long rows of single and two-family dwellings. A reporter wandering through the east-side Polish neighborhood on a summer's day remarked:

> These districts are the hottest in the city. The sun beats relentlessly upon the low and poorly shaded cottages, yet the settlements are constantly astir with life. While other people are trying to make themselves comfortable in darkened rooms or under shade trees, Polish women and children are busy during the hottest hours of the day. They are digging and weeding in their gardens, or scattered all over the city with their pushcarts, gathering fuel for winter.

By the early 1890s the Polish quarter lay largely between Hastings in the west and Joseph Campau to the east, Illinois to the south, and Forest to the north.[7] As this area filled up, predominantly Polish settlements expanded north to Grand Boulevard and east to McDougall Avenue. This growth and extension coincided with the rapid expansion of the rest of the city. Between 1880 and 1890, the population of Detroit increased by 77 percent. The introduction of streetcars in 1892 stimulated expansion outside the city limits and enabled business enterprises to locate farther away from the central city. Factories in particular were situated along the rail lines that ringed the city and, like magnets, they attracted the immigrants, who built their makeshift homes nearby.

Such rapid expansion frequently led to land speculation and a sudden rise in real estate prices. The *Evening News* reported in May 1884, for example, that "lots on Farnsworth street, near Riopelle, which could have been bought last year for $300 have been sold during the past week at $500." Property bought five years earlier was being resold for more per lot than it had previously cost per acre.[8] A few Poles, notably Jan Lemke and Tomasz Żółtowski, were among those who profited. Nonetheless, evidence suggests that property values in the Polish neighborhoods rose more slowly than elsewhere in the city. A reporter for the *Detroit Journal* noted that whereas lots in the Polish quarter in the late 1890s rarely cost more than $1,000 (except for choice locations on St. Aubin or Canfield), comparable property, even within a mile of the Polish neighborhoods, went for from two to five times that amount. A Detroit realtor who frequently handled property transactions for the Poles attributed this imbalance to the fact that non-Poles were reluctant to buy into an area that was already substantially settled by Poles, thus limiting the market and depressing values.[9] By the first decade of the twentieth century Polish immigrants on the northeast side were paying approximately $1,250 for lots on which typical two-family cottages were built for about the same sum. Commonly, however, the buyer had to put down only $25 and could finance the balance at 7 percent interest, with monthly payments of $5.00.[10]

As the locus of the Polish quarter moved steadily outward and the Germans blended increasingly into the native population, the area originally settled by Poles and Germans between Gratiot and Illinois, along Antoine, Hastings, and Rivard, was gradually occupied by Negroes and East European Jews. This neighborhood was frequently referred to by Detroiters as "Kentucky," and a reporter in 1896 described Hastings Street as "without doubt" the most interesting of the thoroughfares dotting the city's near east side. Jewish shops on Hastings catered to blacks, Italians, and Poles, while Hassidic Jews were often seen on the street.[11] The main east-side artery, however, remained Gratiot Avenue. An enterprising *News* reporter ventured onto it early one summer's morning in 1891 to see how the inhabitants began their workday. By seven o'clock he found the avenue "fairly alive with people. A stream of humanity . . .

Jan Lemke. Reproduced by permission from the Sunday News-Tribune, *12 September 1897.*

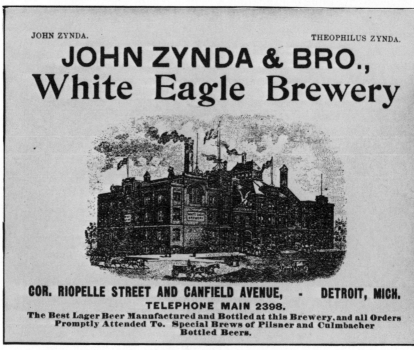

Advertisement, 1903.
Courtesy of the Burton Historical Collection of the Detroit Public Library.

The riot at Connor's Creek.
Reproduced by permission from the Detroit Free Press, *19 April 1894.*

Polish farmers in one of Mayor Hazen Pingree's "potato patches" in 1894.
By permission of the Archives of Labor and Urban Affairs, Wayne State University.

St. Josaphat's Church. Photo by the author.

Fr. Romuald Byzewski. Reproduced by permission from the Evening News, *15 April 1898.*

Fr. Józef F. Folta. Reproduced by permission from the Evening News, *24 July 1899.*

Nineteenth-century Polish newspapers published in Detroit.
Courtesy of the Burton Historical Collection of the Detroit Public Library.

surged along, stretching back [to the northeast] as far as the eye could reach." Many in the crowds were "stocky Polish girls, who appeared bright and cheerful, and jabbered to one another in their native tongue. . . . Nearly every one carried her midday lunch neatly wrapped in a newspaper." (Reports in Detroit's English-language press invariably referred to the "jabbering" of foreigners; Americans, of course, "talked" or "spoke" to one another.) The Polish men, "laboring men pure and simple," swinging their dinner pails, "lumbered along in big boots, overalls, and waistcoat." The crowds seemed to disperse to their various places to work upon reaching Monroe.[12]

Many of the Polish immigrants had been drawn to Detroit by reports of its expanding industries and of the availability of unskilled work stemming from municipal expansion and improvements. In good times the men had little difficulty finding jobs, but during periods of depression the Poles were often the first to be laid off. The other midwestern manufacturing centers—Chicago, Milwaukee, Buffalo—were also growing rapidly and also attracted large numbers of Poles. More often than not, the immigrant's choice of Detroit was determined by the presence of relatives, friends, or persons from his village in the old country.[13] The story of one of these immigrants (typical of many others) was relayed in the *Detroit Free Press*.

My godfather was in Detroit and wrote to me that he had paper on the wall, shoes, meat every day, fresh bread, milk, water in the house, beer on the corner, soup, and plenty of money. From that time, I was crazy to come. I had no money. I was a farm hand near the village of Jaroslaw, which is about 50 miles from Krakow, in Galicia. My godfather had big faith in me and sent me a steamer ticket, from Hamburg. . . . I had to make up the difference, about $28, by selling a cow and a cookstove, all I had in this world. I am 28 years old and have worked as long as I can remember; yes, since I was five years old; always in the fields, for nothing; first to help my father; then for wages, but my pay was never more than $5 a month and I had to sleep in the stable, with the cattle. Do they do that in America? They tell me not. I had to make my own shoes and my food was usually beans, onions, soup, sauerkraut, pork once in a long time, and lard for butter, with a pinch of salt.

When I came here, my godfather took me to the [railway] car shops to get me a job. I was put at handling iron on the yard, and the pay is more in a day than I could earn in two weeks at home. My godfather is a smart man. I will tell you how

he got me my job. You must not tell anyone. He gave the
foreman a pinch of snuff, which is equal to a fine treat. My
godfather does everything in that clever way.[14]

After 1900, with the emergence of the automobile plants, fewer
Poles arrived directly from Poland; increasingly they came from the
mining regions of Pennsylvania or other American cities where
employment opportunities were fewer.

The growth of the Polish population and the reconciliation of
Father Kolasiński and his flock with the Roman church caused
Detroiters to take a harder and in some ways more penetrating look
at the Polish community than had been the case earlier.[15] A striking
aspect of life in the nineteenth-century Polish community for native
Detroiters was the high birthrate among the Poles. In an article of
1896 John Greusel, an avid chronicler of Detroit's ethnic communities, noted that the number of children in a twenty-seven-block area
in the core of the Polish quarter was more than double that of the
area of comparable size in the fashionable Cass-Farm residential
district just west of Woodward. The Polish parish schools, he believed, provided a thorough and rigorous curriculum in both Polish
and English. The problem, however, as seen by the community
leaders who had formed a society to promote education and enlightenment among the Poles, was that Polish children left school too
young. As the society's president, Piotr J. Leszczyński, told Greusel,
"We want our people to learn more English. The trouble with the
Poles is that their children are not allowed to remain in school. The
boys are taken from their books often when only 11 years of age. Few
Polish boys go to school even up to 14, to say nothing of beyond that
age. They are placed in machine shops by their parents, who utilize
them to make money. Eighty cents a week is the average pay."[16]

By the 1890s, a growing number of Polish immigrants were
becoming naturalized citizens. Most Poles, however, at least until
1906, took out only so-called first papers which declared their intention of becoming citizens and which gave them the right to vote.
After that date, full naturalization (that is, "second papers") was
required. The taking out of first papers or even naturalization,
however, did not necessarily mean Americanization. As Sister Mary
R. Napolska wrote, "The Pole was not averse to the acquisition of
American ways but rather intent on retaining his own cultural heritage, deeply convinced that love for the land of his origin and its
culture is not inconsistent with loyalty to his adopted country."[17]
Students of ethnic Detroit in the late nineteenth century generally

agree that the Poles, perhaps more than any other major immigrant group, resisted assimilation and clung tenaciously to their native language and customs, and especially to their traditional religious practices. Nevertheless, there is evidence of accommodation, especially among the second generation of Polish Detroiters, or at least evidence of the influence of American material culture on the Poles. In 1894 a journalist observed that the children of Polish immigrants lacked the frugality and thrift of their parents. "The father never earned more than from $9 to $15 a week, and accumulated property. The son, on the same wages, is likely to keep nothing, besides his being in debt. He buys more things than did his father. He wants good clothes, entertainment and pleasures, and these eat up his money about as fast as he earns it."[18]

Nevertheless, traditional village attitudes, as well as ignorance and superstition, were still apparent among the more recent immigrants. They were particularly evident in the resistance of many Poles to smallpox vaccination and their reluctance to yield an infected member of their household to the city's health officials for quarantine. A widely publicized case occurred in December 1894, when a Józef Bilski armed himself with a shotgun and refused to allow the authorities to remove and isolate his eleven-year-old daughter, Marta. Melvin Holli has pointed out that the resistance to vaccination derived in part from the Poles' belief that it would prevent their being able to work, and he also notes their "strong strain of peasant fatalism."[19]

Although some Poles left their partitioned homeland to evade conscription in "foreign" armies or to escape governmental imposition of German or Russian ways, the principal impulse to emigration was a profound desire to improve their material well-being. In Detroit the immigrant's first and paramount concern was to find and keep a job. But, lacking a trade or skill other than farm labor, the mass of the immigrants could command only the most menial employment. For the most part they were forced to accept pick-and-shovel work on excavation and construction projects, and of course much of this work was seasonal or only for the duration of the project.[20] Even in good times there were frequently more job seekers than jobs available. An example can be seen in a newspaper report of late October 1888. A rumor had spread in the immigrant communities that ground was to be broken for a new central post office. Already by seven in the morning, the *Evening News* reported, a crowd of job seekers, estimated at one hundred and fifty men, 90 percent of them Poles, had gathered. As it turned out, on this day only the land was to be surveyed, but for the fraction who might be hired, the job would mean work through much of the winter at as much as $1.25 a day.[21]

On the other hand, Poles increasingly found unskilled work with the larger manufacturing firms in the 1880s and 1890s, especially with those making railway cars, such as the Michigan Car Company, American Car and Foundry Company, and Peninsular Car Company. Others found employment in the stove works, cigar-making shops, machine shops, and packing plants. Polish women and girls found jobs as domestics, as maids and washers in hotels and restaurants, and, as the century drew to a close, in the cigar industry. A few Poles were hired as field hands with the Ferry Seed Company and on the several farms that still dotted the outskirts of nineteenth-century Detroit. Wages for unskilled factory workers averaged $4.50 to $6.00 for a sixty-hour week, although more qualified workers might make up to $3.00 a day. The daily pay for construction and excavation work was $1.25 to $1.50 for ten hours' labor. For women, especially before the late 1890s, the wages were lower: 50 cents a day in factories and 25 cents for those doing housework or cleaning.[22]

Despite a great preponderance of laborers, a not insignificant number of Detroit's Poles were skilled mechanics, die-makers, tool-makers, and millwrights. Particularly among the Prussian Polish and Kashubian pioneers, some practiced crafts and trades, usually as individual entrepreneurs. The most popular trades were carpentry and construction, and work as butchers, tailors, bakers, masons, painters, and blacksmiths. Small Polish-owned enterprises flourished, including groceries, dry goods, hardware, boot-making and shoe repair shops, confectionaries and, to be sure, saloons. Canfield Avenue, on or near which many of these shops were located, became the main commercial artery within the Polish quarter. In 1895, it is reported, Stefan Rzeszotarski opened the first Polish restaurant at the corner of Rivard and Canfield. A much smaller number of immigrants had entered the professions, although there was a smattering of Polish lawyers, physicians, journalists, and musicians.[23]

By the turn of the century, several Polish entrepreneurs had amassed considerable wealth and influence. Foremost among these were Jan Lemke and his sons, who had a string of grocery and hardware stores as well as investments in real estate; Tomasz Żółtowski, who after starting as a grocer and saloonkeeper, had become a successful brewer, but who had also acquired wealth through real estate transactions; Jan Zynda, who had taken over the old Endriss brewery and reanimated it as the White Eagle Brewery; Ignacy Wolff, who in 1889 had started the White Eagle Tobacco Company on Grandy Avenue; Julian Piotrowski, who started the first Polish bookstore and print shop and also sold devotional items; Marcin Kulwicki, who opened the first Polish funeral parlor on St. Aubin; and Józef Sowiński, who in 1892 inaugurated a photography shop at Russell and Canfield. In 1903 a branch of the Central Savings Bank was opened at St. Aubin and Canfield. For thirty years it was managed by Bazyli Lemke, and to the Poles it was known simply as "Lemke's bank."[24] Indicative of the wealth of these few Poles were the gala weddings in 1898 and 1899 of Żółtowski's daughters Róża and Anna, which were described as the most elaborate social occasions ever staged in the Polish community.[25]

Yet the success of the few was overshadowed by the fact that the roughly decennial intervals of economic depressions that punctuated the late nineteenth century affected the unskilled Polish immigrants especially adversely. By early summer of 1874, the effect of the bank failures and worldwide depression that had begun the previous year was clearly evident in Detroit. Polish laborers, without work for some time, began searching out the sites where excavation work was still going on and attempting to force others to stop working. As the *Detroit Free Press* put it, "Wherever they found a man working they made him knock off, saying that if they couldn't work no one else should." Clashes occurred at several sites and a number of arrests were made.[26] The depression of 1883–85, though less severe and shorter, had, as I have noted, coincided with the concurrent efforts of Fathers Dąbrowski and Kolasiński to raise funds for their respective building projects, and thereby indirectly precipitated the factionalism among Detroit's Poles. Of unquestionably greater consequence for Polish Detroiters, however, was the financial panic and ensuing depression that spread across the nation in 1893 and lasted almost four years. It followed several years of sustained prosperity during which emigration, especially of Poles from Austrian- and Russian-held Polish lands reached new heights. By the early 1890s there were upwards of ten thousand unskilled Polish immigrants in Detroit.

By late summer 1893 the impact of the depression on Detroit's Poles was already severe. Day laborers, some of whom had been unemployed for several months, gathered daily, pick or shovel in hand, in front of Central Market, where work crews had been chosen in better times. On the morning of 24 August, when again no work was offered, a crowd of about one hundred and fifty, mostly Poles, moved over to City Hall to press their demand for public works jobs. They argued that if no new jobs were to be let, those who had worked through the summer should now give up their jobs to those who had had no recent work. Though not willing to consider this demand, city officials did take down the men's names, which led some of the laborers to believe that new jobs would be allotted. Thus, the next morning a much greater number—about four hundred—returned to City Hall. Learning that there was no new work and believing themselves deceived, many of them set off toward a paving site on Grand River Avenue where a large contingent of shovelers and teamsters were working. The angry, desperate men seemed determined to force the working crew to hand over their jobs. Soon violence erupted and the police were summoned. Several persons were injured and five rioters arrested. In court the next day, those arrested for disturbing the peace pleaded that their families were starving. Their wives and children added to the laments, and eventually the men were assessed only small fines and released.[27]

In an attempt to calm the desperate laborers and ease their plight, Dr. Walter J. Kwieciński, a respected leader in the Polish community, took it upon himself to organize the unemployed Poles and serve as a liaison with the city's Department of Public Works and with major private employers. Kwieciński himself represented one of the most remarkable success stories among nineteenth-century Polish Detroiters. His parents had emigrated from Prussian Poland in the 1860s, when Walter was still a youth. The child showed great promise in his studies, and, with support provided in part by a neighboring Irish family, he was able to attend college and later graduate from the Michigan College of Medicine. He returned to Detroit's Polish neighborhood, where he set up general practice and also served as physician to the Felician Sisters. In addition, he opened a drugstore at the corner of Rivard and Benton streets. In late 1891 he was appointed county physician, though he continued to live and practice in the Polish community.[28]

Kwieciński's task was hardly enviable. At a meeting of unemployed Polish laborers on 6 September 1893, he had to contend with the "radical" notion voiced by many of the five hundred persons present, which the press characterized as "society owes every man a living." Kwieciński listened to the workers' complaint that what few public works jobs there were were going primarily to Italians and Canadians. His own list of Poles seeking work contained eight hundred names.[29] His home was literally besieged every day from early to late by what the press described as "hungry looking" Poles, who apparently subsisted on "a diet of a mixture of flour and water." Each hoped to receive one of the approximately fifteen job tickets that the city officials had given him to allocate among the hundreds of supplicants. To make matters worse, the city's Polish priests, likewise unable to help their desperate parishioners, were telling them to seek aid from the doctor.[30]

During the last months of 1893 the crisis deepened. Few factories ran at capacity and those persons still working suffered wage reductions. On 2 December the *Evening News* announced, "25,000 men are out of work in Detroit," a figure that represented about one-third of the city's male labor force. The Poor Commission was overwhelmed and at most could offer some families a pauper's relief allotment. The city's foreign-born made up most of the Poor Commission's rolls, on which Polish families were far and away the largest group.[31] Unfortunately, the rivalry between pro- and anti-Kolasińskiites led to mutual accusations of fraudulent aid applications. Investigation invariably found the accusations to be unfounded, and these petty jealousies further stretched the commission's limited resources. The publicity surrounding such incidents also led some Detroiters to "believe that the Poles receive more than their share in the poor commission's distributions."[32]

The adverse economic conditions accentuated religious and ethnic tensions among Detroit's immigrant groups, which caused bitter recriminations and more than once led to bloody confrontations. At the 6 September 1893 meeting that Kwieciński had organized at Żółtowski Hall, a worker derided the Italians, whom he charged "get work all over the city." Raising charges that had not infrequently been directed at the Poles themselves, the man continued: "[The Italians] are not citizens, and they come here to get money and send it back to the old country. They do not spend it here in the city like we do."[33] On the other hand, the *Michigan Catholic*, which repeatedly had deprecated the Poles during the several outbreaks that punctuated the Kolasiński troubles, now, as economic conditions worsened, chastised the Polish laborers for their disruptive, un-American ways. At a time when anti-Catholic and anti-immigration sentiment was mounting throughout the country, Detroit's Catholic immigrant groups were seemingly embroiled in mutual recrimination and strife.[34]

The most tragic incident involving Polish laborers, and possibly the most celebrated labor clash in nineteenth-century Detroit, took place the following spring, on 18 April 1894, at an excavation site at

Connor's Creek, located just beyond the city's then eastern boundary. The Water Board planned to dig a trench for a new water main along Jefferson Avenue from the new pumping station to Connor's Creek, and had hired three hundred men, mostly Poles. Digging was to have begun on Monday, 16 April, but when the laborers were told that the city planned to split them into two six-hour shifts and pay them on a piece-rate, or job-work, scale, they refused to start digging. They reckoned that the rates offered, 11 cents per cubic yard of sand and 17 cents for clay, would not net much over 50 cents for six hours' labor, while the previous rate had been $1.50 for a ten-hour day. The change had been proposed by one Williams, the project engineer, and approved by the board on a trial basis. The board felt that the piece-rate system not only would save the city money but might benefit an enterprising worker. Though on 16 April a few men showed a willingness to work for any wages, they were quickly dissuaded from digging by the dissatisfied majority, and most of the laborers stayed at the site throughout the day to ensure that the Water Board did not try to bring in another crew willing to accept its terms.[35]

On the following day the stalemate continued; to break the impasse the board announced that it would seek the aid of the Wayne County Sheriff's Office the next day to ensure that anyone willing to work would be free from intimidation.[36] (Since the project site was located in Grosse Pointe Township, Detroit municipal police could not be dispatched, although the Water Board had employed privately a small number of officers.) As on the previous two days, the strikers arrived early on 18 April to occupy the site and prevent the Water Board from bringing in a substitute crew. A noisy exchange took place when Engineer Williams tried once more to get the men to begin work. Having failed, he returned to the board office for instructions. Later in the morning Sheriff C. P. Collins, together with Deputy Sheriff Bornman and Turnkey Matt Steyskal, arrived at the scene. Steyskal, a Bohemian who claimed to speak Polish, urged the men to try the piece-rate system, but they shouted him down. Not a popular figure among the city's lower social strata (he was seen as arrogant and a bully), Steyskal only further antagonized the men by his attempt at speaking Polish (it was likely closer to Czech, a tongue not fondly heard by most Poles). Steyskal's failure to convert the strikers prompted Collins to send in a call for reinforcements.

Shortly before noon, Engineer Williams returned with instructions from the Water Board to halt the project for the time being and collect the equipment. When the project foreman, George Cathey, entered the ditch to retrieve a pump hose, the strikers seemed to sense that they had been tricked, and a sudden rage spread among them. Steyskal began to speak again, this time reportedly in German, which only aggravated them further. Cries and shouts from the crowd to stop Cathey from dismantling the equipment were raised. An unidentified man jumped into the ditch and struck at Cathey's back with a shovel; other laborers joined him. Accounts vary as to who then actually fired the first shots. One eyewitness maintained that Cathey drew a revolver and fired directly at his attackers. Other reports say that Collins fired the first shots into the air. Whatever the truth, the shooting turned the men into a frenzied mob which surged forward with raised picks and shovels. The vastly outnumbered lawmen—the reinforcements had not yet arrived, and there were only seven present, including the four private officers—began to fire in earnest as they attempted to retreat before the onrushing mass of several hundred furious men. Both Cathey and Collins were felled by blows and beaten as they lay on the ground, and several other officers were injured. By one account the mob began to chase "any man in good clothes," which included an *Evening News* reporter and several bystanders. Within minutes the fury of the mob was spent and the bloody fracas was over. One Pole lay dead of gunshot wounds (early reports said two men died on the scene), and two would die soon after. A score of persons were seriously injured, including Cathey and Collins. Matt Steyskal had escaped unscathed, as did Williams.[37]

The immediate reaction of Detroiters was outrage at what the press characterized as a wanton attack on law and order. Sheriff Collins and Turnkey Steyskal were extolled for their courage in defending public order. Though the ranks of the laborers had included non-Poles, the *Free Press* called the mob "Polish-speaking cowards" and "human hyenas," while the *Michigan Catholic* characterized them as "howling Poles thirsting for blood."[38] Little sympathy was offered the laborers' point of view. Commenting editorially the next day, the Republican *Detroit Journal* could only offer the explanation that "it is an unhappy fact that the riotous Poles of yesterday are pitifully ignorant and not in sympathy with the American spirit." "A mistaken notion of their rights," the paper assumed, was what had "incited these poor, ignorant, misguided wretches to this furious and fatal rashness." The editorial closed by drawing a moral from the fate of the dead Poles: "Laws are made to be obeyed . . . ; when men do violence to these laws . . . they must suffer the consequences."[39] Yet the same issue contained an article pointing out that the cause of the tragedy lay not only in the foreigners' ignorance of the board's policy but also in the laboring men's deep opposition to the piece-rate system. When the change was first announced, "the objectors were not all Poles. . . . Those who were loudest in their denunciation of the board's scheme spoke fairly good English."[40] Kwieciński placed the principal blame on "that good-for-nothing Bohemian" Steyskal for "incensing the strikers with his insults." The doctor also alleged that the otherwise peaceful Poles had been incited to riot largely by anarchist agitators.[41]

The story of one of the dead Poles was not untypical of those of the other Polish laborers who struck for a decent wage at Connor's Creek. Andrzej Hernacki had boarded in a one-story shanty on Hastings Street, where he paid ten cents a day for bed and board. Since the railway car shops had shut down the previous fall, he had had almost no work. A *Tribune* reporter described Hernacki's last days.

It was this man's custom to walk every morning . . . from the house [on Hastings] to the brick yards, away out Michigan Avenue. He knew that the yards usually start up about the first of May, and he had hoped that by being one of the first applicants he might get work. After ten or twelve hours' walking he would return, and, eating some soup, would go out to the [Central] market, where he would idly hang around, waiting for the work that never was to come. This was the sort of black, bitter life that Andrew Hernacki, the Russian Pole, had undergone. He had a family of five children in the old country, and he was trying to save enough to bring them to America. That he could not do so worried him. He heard about the job at the water works, and started out with his pick and shovel. He left the house at 2 o'clock in the morning, and walked all the way out.

Hernacki had been shot, according to one report, in five places. Just before he died, he was heard to say, "I went to Grosse Pointe to obtain work. . . . I heard somebody yell something I did not understand; then a volley of pistol shots was fired at us."[42]

The authorities seemed bent on punishing the rioters. By late afternoon of 18 April the police had begun a sweep through the Polish quarter and around the city's hospitals, arresting anyone with gunshot wounds, as well as all men Steyskal and Deputy Sheriff Bornman identified as rioters. By evening twenty-one persons, mostly Poles, were under arrest. Bornman shot one Pole for allegedly resisting arrest. The day after the strike the police were claiming they had discovered the ringleaders who had exhorted their comrades and led the attacks on Cathey and the sheriff.[43] Mayor Hazen Pingree convened a special meeting of city officials at the Water Board office, and though he criticized the sudden switch to piece-rate pay scales, he went along with the consensus, forcibly expressed by Water Board Commissioner J. L. Hudson, that the work must proceed at Connor's Creek under the same conditions. To do otherwise would appear to be giving in to mob rule. "There is no question," Hudson maintained, "that a fair man can make as much by piece work as under the old system."[44]

Understandably, the Poles were shaken by the tragedy and the indiscriminate abuse they were receiving in the English-language press. In an attempt to smooth over the damage and halt the witch-hunt launched by the police and the sheriff's office, a self-appointed committee of prominent Poles called on Mayor Pingree on Saturday, 21 April. The group was headed by the realtor Antoni Conus and included Jan Zynda and Tomasz Żółtowski. The committee apologized on behalf of those Poles ("now truly repentant") who had taken part in the Connor's Creek affair. "All we would ask," the committee stated, "is that all prosecution of those who participated in the riot cease at once, except as to those against whom there is direct evidence of having committed a crime." Surely the Poles had already suffered enough for their mistaken behavior. In reply, the mayor made it clear that he could not influence the machinery of justice and that the guilty would have to be brought to account for their behavior.[45]

Among the Polish laborers there was more bitterness than repentance. In some quarters the feeling was strong that the Water Board and city authorities should be made to pay for the violence *they* had precipitated. But the prevailing attitude among the unemployed Poles was resignation and helplessness, well expressed by "an old Polander, who evidently had found the three score-mark long ago."

> What is the difference whether we are shot down like dogs or starve to death? I am told that the papers accuse us of having been kept all winter by the poor commission and that now we refuse to work when a chance is offered. I know that a great many of us, who have been out of work since last summer, have not asked anyone for charity nor received any, but we cannot, in justice to our families, accept a miserable pittance for a day's

work, especially when this offer comes from a rich corporation like the city of Detroit. Shame, I say, on a city board that offers starvation wages to any human being.[46]

Anxious for work though they were, the Polish laborers had kept their dignity and held together in the face of what they saw as an attempt to exploit their desperate economic situation. They were not entirely bereft of support. Two of the city's principal labor organizations called mass meetings on Sunday, 22 April, where speakers denounced both the accounts in the "capitalistic press" and the Water Board's switch to the piece-rate system. At Arbeiter Hall the Trades and Labor Union drew an estimated three thousand workingmen, and the largely German Central Labor Union held a similar gathering at Tinnette's Hall at Rivard and Catherine.[47]

The Water Board, however, was determined to proceed with the Connor's Creek project the next Monday, and the sheriff's office was already enlisting volunteers to help preserve order. The *Evening News* noted that "among them [were] many who had smelled powder in the army. Most of them were well dressed and quite a number were well-known business men, who offered their services free of charge for the sake of preserving the peace, and, if necessary, revenging the brutal treatment which had been bestowed upon Sheriff Collins and his assistants."[48] Detroit's middle classes seemed gripped by the specter of hordes of raging immigrants armed with picks and shovels or even peasants' scythes. The newspaper drawings of the Connor's Creek clash invariably depicted a mass of foreigners with insruments of wrath held threateningly above their heads.[49]

Polish leaders were aware that if the discontented laborers returned to Connor's Creek on Monday blood surely would be shed again. Hoping that their influence would prevent such an occurrence, all of the city's Polish priests at Sunday mass urged their parishioners to stay at home the next day. Father Kolasiński added, "You can go there to seek work, but if you riot it will only result to your disadvantage." It will create distrust of you and of the whole Polish community.[50] Of course many Polish laborers were worried that if they did not block the work their jobs would be given to other, non-Polish workers. In fact, that is what happened.

The city police and sheriff's office, meanwhile, seemed to be preparing for war on Monday. And lest anyone should forget the threat to public order, the morning *Free Press* reminded its readers that rage still swelled in "many a Sarmatian breast." The precautions taken seem excessive. One hundred policemen armed with Winchesters were to be stationed just inside the city limits, about seven hundred feet from the digging site. Another sixty-seven men, some with Winchesters, had been deputized by Under Sheriff Archer (and dubbed "Archer's army"). The men were taken to the site in wagons at four in the morning, presumably to take possession before any troublemakers arrived. Only a small number of Poles and Italians had showed up early to see what the Water Board planned to do. About 7:30 A.M., some thirty shovelers began work under a protective guard of close to two hundred armed men. The men working were said to be American, Irish, or German. Later, around 10:30 A.M., a large gang of Poles and some Italians approached; seeing the men working, they began to shout "Slaves! slaves!" at the diggers. But the demonstrators quickly scattered when the armed deputies threatened action.[51]

The next day a hundred men worked at the site, protected by the same armed cordon. Only a small number of outsiders, described as mostly intoxicated, came to jeer at those working. The forces of law and order and the Water Board had clearly won, as few doubted they would. The question of piece work was again taken up at a public meeting of the board on 27 April. Though spokesmen for the Trades' Council and the Central Labor Union sharply criticized the piece-rate system, it was again forcefully defended by Commissioner Hudson, who pointed out that under the new system a few men had made as much as $2.00 a day.[52] But, when the digging at Connor's Creek was completed and the security force withdrawn in early May, the board voted to return to its earlier policy of paying by the hour or day.[53]

The peaceful resumption of work at Connor's Creek did not end the abuse directed at the Poles or ease the plight of the men under arrest. For example, verses entitled "Wawski" appeared on the editorial page of the *Evening News*.

> He saw war at Warsaw, he
>   Saw the same at Connor's Creek;
> Wawski is a sight to see
>   With a musket or a pick.
>
> Wawski leaps ten feet or more;
>   Swings an awful shovel, he
> Roareth a most fiendish roar
>   At the foe that flyeth free.
>
> Wawski! man of many woes;
>   Wawski! ever doomed to fail;

> Partitioned off by Poland's foes;
> Partitioned in Wayne county jail.[54]

This example of contempt for Poland's historical misfortunes no less than for the plight of the laborers at Connor's Creek reflected the rising nativist sentiment fanned by the depression of 1893. John Higham has noted that as the crisis deepened, businessmen no longer saw the new immigrants as dollar assets but as "unemployed aliens [who] burdened the community and enlarged the stagnant pool of unused manpower." The Connor's Creek espisode unleashed the mounting anger and fear that Detroit's propertied elements felt toward the Poles, the most visible of the new immigrants in the city.[55]

In early May, those arrested in the aftermath of the riot were brought up for preliminary examination in Grosse Pointe; eight were bound over for arraignment and trial in Wayne Circuit Court.[56] In separate proceedings a coroner's inquest on 18 May determined that the three Poles—Jan Piłat, Andrzej Hernacki, and Józef Hodupske—killed at Connor's Creek had met their deaths "as a result of gun-shot wounds inflicted by officers while in the discharge of their duty."[57]

Ironically, just five days prior to the shootings, a group calling itself the Polish Laborers' Alliance had filed articles of association with the Wayne County clerk. Its objects were "to promote the interests of the members as laborers, and to provide for the sick, and the families of the deceased members."[58] Until this time, despite harsh working conditions and low wages, the Polish workers had shown little interest in organizing. The Polish clergy had traditionally preached against socialism and unions. The expense of dues and reluctance to join organizations run by "foreigners" militated against Polish participation in the union movement.[59] But after Connor's Creek, Poles increasingly affiliated with the Polish Laborer's Alliance and showed greater sympathy for the plight of other immigrant groups in the city and for the union movement in general.

Politically, the early Prussian-Polish and Kashubian settlers had tended to follow the lead of the Irish and German Catholics who preceded them in Detroit. This meant that those who had taken out their first papers tended to support Democratic candidates. Like other Catholic immigrants, the Poles associated the Republican party with Protestant, propertied Americanism, and detected strong nativist appeals and clear anti-Catholic, anti-immigration biases in it. In any case, not until the late 1880s, by which time the Polish community was sizable, did the political chieftains and ward bosses begin to show interest in the newcomers as a potentially significant electoral force.

The Democrats for the most part relied on Polish support without offering much in the way of the traditional spoils or patronage jobs that went with political victory. Nevertheless, the Poles' natural inclination to support Democratic candidates continued. According to an article published in the Polish Catholic weekly *Niedziela* on the eve of the 1893 election:

> [The Democratic Party's] interests are identical with our nationality. . . . [It] had always been favorably disposed toward the Poles, never slighted their nationality, never attacked Catholicism. . . . the Republican Party . . . in Detroit is under the influence of the Patriotic Sons of America whose aim is to prevent Catholics from holding public offices.[60]

However, the fact that the Democrats had offered Poles so little in return for their electoral support made Polish voters ripe for overtures in 1889 from the reform Republican mayoral candidate, Hazen Pingree. By eschewing the traditional Republican line on prohibiting drink, and by assiduously cultivating the Polish leaders, Pingree carried a number of precincts in Polish neighborhoods. Prominent among his early supporters were Tomasz Żółtowski and, it was said, Fr. Dominik Kolasiński. Pingree in 1889 was more successful in attracting Polish voters on the east side than in Fr. Paweł Gutowski's west-side parish. To consolidate his influence among Polish Detroiters, soon after his election Pingree nominated Franciszek J. Ducat to the post of city accountant. The Democratic majority on the Common Council, which had to pass on all major mayoral appointments, was determined to block all of Pingree's Republican nominations. But to oppose Ducat's confirmation meant risking further antagonism from Polish voters. The Democrats stalled for three months, meanwhile attracting considerable public attention, but finally saw no recourse but to confirm him in September 1890.[61]

Pingree's success among Polish voters in 1889 prompted the rival congressional candidates to devote special attention to wooing the Polish electorate during the campaign of 1890. The Republican candidate, Hibbard Baker, in addition to cultivating the Kolasiński-ites (whose strength was estimated at 1,000 votes), also worked hard to gain the support of the priest's opponents. Baker and his party spent lavishly in the Polish quarter and placed $150 in advertising with the anti-Kolasińskiite weekly *Gwiazda Detroicka*. Realizing that he was losing ground, Democratic incumbent J. L. Chipman staged a rally at Fredro Hall, but reliable reports stated that the principal attraction was not the candidate but the quantities of free drink.[62] Despite Baker's free spending and other efforts, he never attained Pingree's popularity among the Poles, and Chipman was returned to Congress in November. Two years later a new Republican congressional candidate also tried to parlay Polish votes into victory. Colonel Frank J. Hecker, president of the east-side Peninsular car works, which employed many Poles, counted heavily on Kolasiński's support and a record Republican turnout in Polish precincts.[63] Nevertheless, he was also unsuccessful.

The west-side Polish community remained solidly Democratic in the early 1890s, thanks largely to Father Gutowski of St. Casimir's, who used his influence to organize a Democratic Club among his congregation and made the parish school available for its meetings. Gutowski's political activities prompted Leonard F. Olszewski, publisher of the pro-Republican Polish weekly *Prawda*, to accuse the priest of taking unfair advantage of his position. Olszewski's so-called exposé of a "priest in politics" apparently did not appreciably diminish the Democratic hold on the west-side Polish parishes.[64]

Although the Polish Republican backing was generally limited to Pingree, some support did spill over to a couple of the mayor's close associates. In 1894 John B. Corliss, Kolasiński's long-time attorney, was elected to Congress as a Republican, and Pingree's secretary, Alex McLeod, was elected Wayne County treasurer, both with strong support in the Polish precincts of the east-side fifth, seventh, and ninth wards. In the 1890s there was clear evidence of ticket splitting in the Polish precincts. In 1896, for example, Polish voters supported Pingree in his successful campaign to move into the governor's seat, but they also backed by a large margin Democratic presidential candidate William Jennings Bryan.[65] Detroit's political professionals, the *Detroit Tribune* reported in 1895, were clearly finding the Polish voters enigmatic.

> The campaign in Polacktown is a subject which excites a great deal of curiosity before election in this city. There seems to be an opinion that the Polish American is governed in the exercise of his franchise by a complicated set of rules which only he and a few experts understand, and the motives which actuate others have little or no influence with him. For this reason many candidates have been lured repeatedly into spending money on men who professed to know all the intricacies neces-

sary to be explored in order to reach the well spring of Polish favor. Some very able politicians have considered the matter of such moment as to require their best personal attention, and they have devoted a great deal of study to it.[66]

Many Detroit politicians believed it was enough simply to cultivate the support of a few key Polish community leaders and hold out to them the promise of patronage; others, notably Pingree, came to realize that the Polish voter was more sophisticated, and that he responded more favorably to candidates and politicians who delivered on matters that affected his livelihood and respected his religious faith and national dignity. Pingree, for example, emerged from the Connor's Creek tragedy with his popularity among the Poles intact. One of his most successful measures, both economically and politically, was his "potato patches." As the depression of 1893 dragged on over the next three years, more than fifteen hundred families, mostly Polish, received a half-acre plot of undeveloped public or, in a few cases, private land on the city's outskirts, where they raised vegetables for their own use or to sell. Though the scheme encountered some opposition and ridicule from Pingree's former backers among Detroit's wealthy Republican families, the plan gained national attention. The program's success, even though it was implemented on a smaller scale than the mayor had hoped, was evident in a newspaper account of October 1896 on the harvesting of the crops at one of the principal sites, the fields lying beyond the terminus of the Warren Avenue streetcar line near Thirty-second Street on the city's northwest side. Corn, cabbage, carrots, and turnips were being harvested in addition to potatoes. The reporter marveled at how enthusiastically these recently transplanted European peasants seized the chance to do agricultural work.[67]

When Pingree moved to the governor's mansion in Lansing in 1897, Democrats saw an opportunity to recoup their losses among Polish Detroiters. One earlier supporter of the Republicans, the Kashub and anti-Kolasińskiite sewer contractor Jan Wagner, was so miffed at Pingree's failure to obtain his confirmation as a commissioner of public works that he publicly announced his endorsement of William Maybury, the Democratic mayoralty candidate, to succeed Pingree in a special election. Upon his victory in spring 1897, Maybury promptly nominated Wagner for parks commissioner. The Democratic-dominated Common Council, however, wanted appointments to go to party loyalists rather than to opportunistic patronage-seekers like the former Republican Wagner, and his nomination was rejected. As the end of 1897 Maybury tried again to get Wagner appointed to the Board of Public Works. But by this time other persons in the Polish community were ashamed of Wagner's efforts to buy himself a municipal appointment. Dr. Józef Iłowiecki, editor of the Polish paper *Swoboda*, informed the new mayor that Wagner had bought signatures for his purported petition of Polish supporters and that he did not represent the "Polish" community. At the same time, Bazyli Lemke announced that he too desired appointment to the Board of Public Works.[68]

It must be stated that the Poles had not taken effective advantage, at least in the 1890s, of the opportunities their electoral strength offered to obtain meaningful places in the city's administration. Both political parties had cultivated the Polish vote and played to the ambition and vanity of so-called community leaders such as Żółtowski and Wagner, but only a token number of Poles had in fact obtained electoral or appointive office by the end of the nineteenth century, and certainly far fewer than the Poles' 14–17 percent of the city's population merited.[69] Even in the first decades of the twentieth century, Detroit Poles would not acquire a share of political offices and power commensurate with their numbers. Though they gradually became more sophisticated in exercising the franchise, the Poles, with the exception of the Pingree years, essentially continued to support Democratic candidates and were especially pronounced in their opposition to Republicans who favored the restriction of free immigration into the United States.

In general, the typical Pole in nineteenth-century Detroit paid scant attention to American politics except, as I have noted, when politicians and their programs bore directly on his means of employment and the well-being of his nationality and religious faith. Outside his work and home, the Pole's principal interest was his church and the lay institutions it generated within his parish. As Stanislaus Blejwas has noted, "The parish became more than a religious association for the devout Roman Catholic Polish immigrant; it was the 'old primary community, reorganized and concentrated.' The parish, with all its organizations, became the community's center, fulfilling the immigrant's need for social recognition as well as for spiritual comfort. It was the chief instrument in the unification and organization of America's Polish communities."[70] As the century drew to a close, the immigrant became increasingly involved in one or more of the local groups affiliated with national Polish American fraternal organizations. As he acquired greater literacy he began to subscribe to one or more of Detroit's Polish newspapers, then usually published as weeklies.

Despite the publicity accorded Kolasiński's Sweetest Heart of Mary's Church, the core of the east-side Polish quarter remained St. Albertus's, the first Polish parish. Unfortunately, tranquility had not returned to the troubled parish with the reopening of this church in 1887. We have seen how Fr. Kazimierz Rohowski's pastorate was brought to an end, despite Bishop Foley's support of the embattled Silesian priest, by an irate congregation which believed, rightly or wrongly, that Rohowski lacked Polish sympathies. The three-year pastorate of his successor, Fr. Florian Chodniewicz, ended even more abruptly and ignominiously in July 1894, when charges against him of fathering the child of a domestic servant in the parish rectory became public. Acting on information provided by Marcin Kulwicki, an undertaker on St. Aubin and a prominent St. Albertus's parishioner, Foley first directed Chodniewicz not to officiate at St. Albertus's, and later, on 5 July 1894, he dismissed him as pastor.[71] Chodniewicz had not been unpopular, and there is no reason to assume that the charge was fabricated. Whether it was true or not, Chodniewicz was the third pastor of St. Albertus's within fifteen years to be removed primarily because of accusations of moral turpitude.

The ninth pastor of the church's first twenty-two years having departed, St. Albertus's was ready to welcome a priest who would guide the parish for the next two decades. Fr. Franciszek Mueller was only twenty-five when Bishop Foley appointed him pastor. He was born in Bytom (Beuthen) in Upper Silesia of mixed German-Polish parentage; his Polish mother was widowed when he was ten. She instilled in her son a deep pride in his Polish inheritance. His studies in Wrocław (Breslau) were interrupted when his mother decided to emigrate to Detroit. Young Mueller attended the Jesuit-sponsored Detroit College, and when the Polish seminary opened in 1886 he became a member of the charter class. He was ordained by Bishop Foley in St. Albertus's on 14 October 1891 and three days later was appointed assistant at the church. Prior to becoming pastor of St. Albertus's in July 1894, he had served as assistant at the city's German Sacred Heart Church. At the time Mueller took over at St. Albertus's, its congregation of fifteen hundred families was exceeded only by Kolasiński's newly legitimized parish.[72]

An event of particular significance and pride for Polish Detroiters occurred in 1897 when St. Albertus's celebrated its silver anniversary. The celebration began with a high mass on Wednesday, 14 July 1897, at which Fr. Szymon Wieczorek, the parish's founding pastor, officiated, and continued through Sunday, 18 July.[73] During its quarter-century of existence, St. Albertus's had seen considerable changes. Though many of the original east-side Prussian Polish and Kashubian immigrants remained, a large number had resettled to the north and east and would be instrumental in establishing several offshoot parishes in the late 1890s and early decades of the next century. Their former homes and pews were readily taken over by new waves of immigrants, especially from Russian Poland. Thus the parish continued to grow.

The Polish community on the west side remained relatively small until around 1890. But industrial expansion in that part of the city soon attracted a sizable share of the new Polish immigrants. Bishop Foley seemed to have special affection for the west-side parish, which had never caused any trouble to diocesan authority.[74] By the early 1890s the west-side Polish community was expanding more rapidly than the original east-side settlement. Soon after the new St. Casimir's was completed in 1891, construction began on a second west-side church, St. Francis of Assisi's (Św. Franciszek z Asyzu) at Buchanan Street and Wesson Avenue. St. Francis's first pastor was Fr. Romuald Byzewski, whom Foley in 1898 would call to succeed Kolasiński at Sweetest Heart of Mary's. By the turn of the century, especially after Kolasiński's death, the west-side parishes were drawing most of the Galician Polish immigrants, and in 1904 Foley dedicated a third west-side Polish church, St. Hedwig's (Św. Jadwiga), which was located on Junction Avenue near Michigan Avenue. Although this parish had a stormy beginning, complete with the temporary excommunication of a group of recalcitrant trustees, it soon became the most significant Polish parish on the west side and the stronghold of the Galician immigrants.[75]

Notwithstanding the rapid growth of the west-side community, the principal locus of Polish Detroit in the nineteenth century remained on the east side where it had begun. The original wooden structure of St. Josaphat's was replaced at the beginning of the twentieth century by the stone and brick church that stands today, perched forlornly atop the west bank of the Chrysler Freeway against a backdrop of urban renewal. A distinguishing feature of the new St. Josaphat's was a replica of the famous "Black Madonna" painting at the Jasna Góra monastery in Częstochowa, Poland. Three times a year—at Christmas, Easter, and Pentecost—a painting of Saint Josaphat behind the altar was raised to reveal the Madonna so revered in Polish religious tradition.[76]

Despite Bishop Foley's attention to the new St. Casimir's and St. Josaphat's, the most magnificent of Detroit's Polish churches continued to be Sweetest Heart of Mary's. When Kolasiński's sudden death in April 1898 left the parish without a pastor, the congregation's immediate choice was Byzewski of St. Francis's. Father Byzewski, described in the *News* as a "model priest"—"a man of great learning and a powerful pulpit orator"—showed no interest in succeeding Kolasiński. He remarked to reporters, "I shall resist with hands and feet a call to assume charge of the Sacred Heart of Mary Church. I shall beg and supplicate the bishop not to send me there." Even more candidly, he added, "That congregation is bankrupt. Its finances are hopelessly entangled."[77] Foley overcame his reluctance. By that time Byzewski had already ministered to Polish immigrants in America for almost a quarter-century, first at St. Stanisław's in Winona, Minnesota, for fifteen years, until ill health caused him to come to Detroit, where he served as Gutowski's assistant at St. Casimir's before moving to St. Francis's.

As fate would have it, Father Byzewski soon began to have difficulties with the volatile Sweetest Heart of Mary's congregation. Notwithstanding the parishioners' initial enthusiasm for him (roused largely by his moving sermon at Kolasiński's funeral), he was too reserved, reflective, and scholarly to follow in the footsteps of the dynamic and much-loved Kolasiński. Furthermore, his birth and upbringing in the Prussian-ruled German-Kashubian borderland did not endear him to his fanatically patriotic Polish congregation. His parishioners began to slight him in favor of his young assistant, Fr. Józef Fołta, whom Kolasiński had taken as his own assistant just two weeks before his death. Finally, on 16 July 1899, a little over a year after becoming pastor, Byzewski announced that he was leaving immediately to enter a monastery in Pulaski, Wisconsin, citing ill health and a need for peace and quiet.[78] A week later the congregation was overjoyed when Bishop Foley appointed the thirty-one-year-old Fołta to succeed Byzewski. Popular, energetic, and ambitious, Fołta appeared to the local press to be a second Kolasiński. For almost two decades he would guide the city's largest, and by reputation most unruly, Polish parish.[79]

To accommodate the outward migration of Poles living on the east side, the city's sixth nineteenth-century Polish parish, St. Stanisław's was founded in 1898. It was located about thirteen blocks north of Canfield and the three core Polish churches. A parish committee purchased from the German Lutherans "a modest frame building" at the corner of Dubois and Medbury streets to serve as a temporary home. (A permanent, Romanesque-style St. Stanisław's was dedicated fifteen years later, in 1913.) The new church was named for the most revered Polish saint, Stanisław, bishop of Kraków, and its first pastor was Fr. Franciszek Gzella. The parish began with about five hundred families, drawn principally from the three parishes on Canfield.[80] In the first decade of the new century, two additional Polish parishes would be established as the Polish community continued to spread north and east. In 1907 St. Hyacinth's (Św. Jacek) was founded at McDougall and Farnsworth avenues, and a year later St. Florian's, the first parish in Hamtramck Township, was established.

Although almost all Polish immigrants to Detroit in the nineteenth century were Roman Catholics or Jews, a handful of Protestants—some of whom had converted in America—were drawn in the early 1890s to weekly evangelical services conducted by the Reverend Władysław Lewandowski. Lewandowski had come to America in 1872 from Russian Poland and converted to Protestantism through the missionary activities of the Young Men's Christian Association in Cleveland. He held services at his residence at the corner of Beaubien Street and Willis Avenue and at the Tillman Avenue mission house not far from St. Casimir's. At first Lewandowski encountered some opposition to his ministry, but for the most part his followers were so few that the city's Polish Catholic prelates tolerated his activities. Most Poles in nineteenth-century Detroit regarded Polish Protestants primarily as objects of curiosity, not as threats to the Catholic faith.[81] By the early 1900s, however, there were enough of them to justify the establishment of a Polish Baptist mission by the Reverend Karol Strzelec, and in 1901 the first Polish Congregational church, at the corner of Hancock and Joseph Campau, was opened.

Another source of pride closely related to the religious sentiments of Detroit's Polish Catholics, including many Kolasińskiites, was the Polish seminary, which brought national attention to the city. The seminary's unique status, however, also made it the focus of controversy, since factional differences—especially the hostility between the Polish National Alliance (PNA) and the Polish Roman Catholic Union (PRCU)—increasingly divided Polish Americans in the 1890s. Although its founder, Father Dąbrowski, tried to steer a neutral course among the rival organizations and factions, when he accepted financial support from the PNA he was sharply criticized. To defend the seminary and to keep Polish Americans informed of its activities, Dąbrowski launched the Polish-language weekly *Niedziela* in 1891. *Niedziela* quickly gained a wide circulation and contributed much-needed revenue to the seminary. Notwithstanding the various difficulties, the faculty and the student enrollment, especially in the preparatory school, grew steadily. By 1896 Dąbrowski was able to stop teaching and devote more time to his position as chaplain to the Felician Sisters, whose number also was rising. Though he retained the presidency of the seminary, the administrative duties were handled increasingly by the vice-rectors, Fr. Witold Buhaczkowski and, after 1900, Fr. Jan Mueller.[82]

In early 1903 an incident occurred which many came to believe may have hastened Dąbrowski's death. On 23 January twenty-nine students submitted a petition to the rector which enumerated various grievances. Their main grievance was against the vice-rector and instructor in moral philosophy, Father Mueller. Dąbrowski, known as a firm disciplinarian, responded by ordering the students to apologize to Mueller; when they refused, he expelled all twenty-nine. The bishop supported his action, but the local press sided with the students. Brief though the incident was, its effect on the seminary's reputation lasted for several years. A few weeks later Dąbrowski was dead, presumably from a heart attack. His funeral mass was celebrated by Bishop Foley in St. Albertus's on 18 February 1903 and his remains were interred at Mount Elliott Cemetery.[83]

A few years after its founder's death, the seminary purchased several acres of land and buildings adjacent to Orchard Lake in Oakland County that had formerly housed the Michigan Military Academy, and in 1909 the seminary was moved to this rural site. Father Dąbrowski's dedication to the educational needs of Polish immigrants reached well beyond the diocese of Detroit. The seminary he founded and the work of the Felician Sisters he fostered are monuments to his tireless labors. Father Dąbrowski's achievements and contributions to American Polonia are better appreciated today than they were in the turbulent years of early Polish Detroit.[84]

Next to the parishes, the most important role in the coalescence of Detroit's Polish communities and the facilitating of the immigrants' adjustment to life in urban America was played by the Polish-language press. To be sure, at times—as during the heated moments of the Kolasiński Affair—the partisan Polish newspapers contributed to inflaming passions and accentuating divisiveness. But especially after the mid-1880s, the Polish papers served as a filter through which American life became more comprehensible to literate immigrants and their listeners; for the more educated Poles the papers provided a balance to the flow of information that otherwise would have come only from the city's German and English press.[85]

The first Detroit Polish-language newspaper was the *Gazeta Polska Katolicka* [Polish Catholic gazette], the paper originally intended to serve as the organ of Fr. Teodor Gieryk's newly formed PRCU that was published in the city for only a few months. Ten years later, in September 1884, Julian Piotrowski, in whose shop the *Gazeta Polska Katolicka* had been printed, launched a new weekly, the *Gazeta Narodowa* [National gazette]. This venture failed in less than a year, allegedly because the radical social and political posture of its editor, Józef Zawisza, offended the community's elders and priests. In 1885 a group of Polish community leaders, headed by Fr. Paweł Gutowski, started *Pielgrzym Polski* [The Polish pilgrim], which appeared weekly until 1888. Edited by Hieronim Derdowski, this paper staunchly opposed Father Kolasiński and was directly responsible for furthering the religious strife among Detroit Poles in the mid-1880s. At about the time *Pielgrzym Polski* ceased publication, another weekly, *Prawda* [Truth], was started by Leonard Olszewski; in 1893 he sold the paper to a former teacher at the Polish seminary, Dr. Karol Laskowski. Shortly thereafter the paper was again sold and moved to Bay City, Michigan. In 1889 another weekly, *Gwiazda (Detroicka)* [The (Detroit) star], founded a year earlier in Toledo, was brought to Detroit, where it was edited by Antoni Paryski and Józef Skupiński. This publication, also strongly anti-Kolasiński, survived only until 1891.[86]

These various weekly papers had only a modest circulation, but with the rapid expansion of the Polish community and the marked increase in literacy as the second generation grew up, the climate improved for the appearance of a successful daily Polish newspaper. The first to achieve wider circulation was the weekly *Niedziela* [Sunday], an illustrated popular journal of sixteen pages that began publication on 6 September 1891 at Father Dąbrowski's initiative. Although addressed to the broader Polish community in America, a regular feature was "Kronika Miejsowa" [Local chronicle], an overview of news of specific interest to Polish Detroiters. The journal, edited by a succession of teachers at the Polish seminary, reached a circulation of several thousand during its first year. It continued publication until 1904, and then briefly resumed with an altered format until 1907.[87] At about the same time a religious monthly successively titled *Niezapominajki* [Forget-me-nots] (1890), *Wiadomości misyjne* [Missionary news] (1891), and *Apostół* [The apostle] (1892), began publication. Its subscribers were far fewer than for *Niedziela*, and it did not attempt to report Detroit affairs per se.

The next attempt at a strictly lay newspaper was *Swoboda* [Liberty], founded in 1896 by Dr. Józef Iłowiecki, an ardent Republican and principal contributor to *Prawda* before it moved to Bay City. A native of Poznania, Iłowiecki, shortly after completing his medical studies, had emigrated to America and settled in Detroit around 1880. In addition to practicing medicine and his publishing ventures, Iłowiecki translated Lord Byron's poetry into Polish and composed his own verse. *Swoboda* was noted for its high editorial standards and for the caustic and satirical comments of its owner-editor, who quickly alienated most of the different factions.[88] In 1898 Iłowiecki began publishing *Swoboda* as a daily—the first such attempt in Detroit. The partisan newspaper failed to attract sufficient readership and folded within a year. Five years later, in 1904, a successful Polish daily would make its appearance. *Dziennik Polski* [Polish daily news], begun as a liberal and politically independent newspaper, is today in its seventy-sixth year of uninterrupted publication. *Rekord Codzienny* [Daily record], a second but more conservative daily, would appear in 1913. In the last years of the nineteenth century, two other weeklies were launched: *Polonia* (1898), the official organ of the Stowarzyszenie Polskie Ryzmsko-Katolickie (Polish Roman Catholic Association), a secessionist faction of the PRCU established in 1894, and *Robotnik Polski* [The Polish worker] (1899), which espoused socialist views.[89]

Although they initally eschewed participation in American cultural and social institutions, Detroit's Poles displayed among themselves a veritable passion for organizing parish, fraternal, cultural, and even paramilitary associations. Each parish spawned several societies, which, in addition to taking a leading part in various anniversary and dedication celebrations, provided fellowship and fostered benevolent and mutual aid work with the parishes. These societies facilitated the work of the usually overburdened Polish pastors and helped to tie the congregations still more closely to their parishes. The parish societies also played an active role in keeping alive such traditional Polish religious observances as the Christmas Eve celebration (*wigilia*) which was followed by the midnight or "shepherds' " mass (*pasterka*) that began Christmas Day. Charles D. Cameron, a chronicler of Detroit's ethnic populations, wrote: "When the Polish community was new, but scattered, they would gather from all parts of St. Albertus' Church, and on the way home through the long, dark streets, would be heard singing carols. Touching and intimate carols of the home life of Joseph and Mary were these, fragments from the Polish hymnology, which is the richest in the world."[90]

As the community expanded, however, Polish Detroiters began to associate increasingly in lay societies that were not associated with any particular parish. Among the Polish American national organizations, the strongest in Detroit was the PNA, or, in Polish, Związek Narodowy Polski. In 1885 the first Detroit group to affiliate with it called itself the Synowie Polski (Sons of Poland). A second affiliate was established in 1886, and a third in 1887. By September 1891 the Detroit affiliates numbered 615 members and hosted the organization's ninth national congress. In 1894, the seven PNA groups based on the east side joined in establishing a Gmina Detroicka (Detroit Commune) to coordinate their activities. The group on the city's west side did not join the Detroit Commune at this time; in 1913, a second Detroit Commune was created to include the west-side Poles. By 1906 the PNA counted twenty-five groups in Detroit, with a total membership of 1,500.[91] The first Detroit "nest" (*gniazdo*) of the Sokoli Polscy (Polish Falcons, or Turners), a gymnastic organization, was founded in 1892, and in 1901 an offshoot nest for women was established. In 1904 the Detroit nests formally affiliated with the national Związek Sokołów Polskich w Ameryce (Polish Falcons' Alliance of America). A nest on the city's west side was formed in 1906. A Detroit affiliate of another major national Polish American organization, the Związek Polek (Polish Women's Alliance) was set up in 1911.[92] Although founded in Detroit, the Polish Roman Catholic Union did not attract a following in the city comparable to that of the PNA. In the twentieth century, membership in these and other fraternal and sororial organizations expanded enormously, especially among second- and third-generation Polish Americans.

An early lay organization of Detroit Poles was the paramilitary Legion Strzelców Kościuszki (Kościuszko Guard), incorporated on 1 May 1877 for the purpose of keeping Polish martial traditions alive. Its articles of incorporation set forth its aims: to serve the Polish nation and, as Catholic Christians, to defend Holy Church. The guardists also pledged to help the poor and the sick. Members had to be at least seventeen and no older than thirty-five. With the proliferation of Polish parishes in the 1880s, and especially as a consequence of the Kolasiński Affair, separate factions of the guard were formed and loosely associated with the various parishes. Two decades after the original founding, the guards were reunited in an interparish society which called itself the Polish Military Battalion of Tadeusz Kościuszko. Throughout the nineteenth century, the Kościuszko Guards lent color and pomp to Polish-sponsored celebrations and parades.[93]

To provide a gathering place for lay organizations and accommodate the various meetings, lectures, and cultural events, two Polish halls were built to serve the community in the 1880s. Fredro Hall was erected in 1886 at the corner of Russell and Leland streets; in 1895 it was renamed Harmonia Hall and was used mostly for cultural events. Żółtowski Hall (later Polonia Hall) was built in 1889 at Hastings and Willis. Kudron Hall was constructed in 1898 on Junction Avenue to serve the west-side Poles and the city's first Dom Polski (Polish House) was completed in 1912 at Forest and Chene.

In the mid-1880s leading Polish Detroiters began actively to promote education within the Polish community. In 1887 a committee headed by the clothing dealer Piotr J. Leszczyński, son of the Polish pioneer Antoni Leszczyński and a founder of the first PNA group in Detroit, requested the Detroit Public Library to add Polish books to its collection. From an original 250 volumes the number of Polish books grew to 14,000 by 1901. A check of the use of foreign books at that time revealed that Polish books were circulating at four times the rate of works in French and twice that of those in German. Later Leszczyński promoted the establishment of a branch library in the Polish community, and in 1895 he helped to found and became the first president of the Towarzystwo Przyjaciół Oświaty im. Tadeusza Kościuszki (Kościuszko Society of the Friends of Learning), whose purpose was to promote adult education classes and provide scholarships for Polish students.[94]

The performing arts were dear to Poles and were nurtured in the immigrant community. A theatrical troupe, the Fredro Dramatical Society, was formed in the 1880s to perform plays in Polish. Beginning in 1891 the Harmonia Singing Society frequently entertained Polish audiences; in 1902 the Halka Choral Society—which took its name from the title of a popular opera by the nineteenth-century composer Stanisław Moniuszko—was formed, followed in 1903 by the Chopin Quartet. The number of performing groups increased greatly in the first decades of the twentieth century, and their performances became a major feature of Polish cultural life.

The first decades in Detroit were not easy for the Polish immigrants. Ignorance of American ways, periodic economic adversity, and religious division exacerbated by the uncomprehending and sometimes intolerant majority in the city posed severe hurdles to their adjustment. Yet these years were a time of remarkable achievement. The magnificent churches, no less than modest, privately owned homes, testified to the Poles' thrift as well as their dedication and perseverance. In 1907 Mayor William Thompson remarked in a public address that "Detroit is proud of its 70,000 Poles who helped its prosperity, built its most beautiful churches, maintained first class schools, paid their taxes, and obeyed the laws."[95]

The twentieth century brought great change to Detroit's Polish community. As in other cities, "both the native language and the traditional values and customs of a rural, agrarian society were modified by the novel environment of urban, industrial America, . . . the Polish immigrant was evolving into a Polish American."[96] The new automobile plants attracted ever larger numbrs of Poles to the city of the strait. The 1920 census shows the Poles to be the single largest European ethnic group in the city. The movement outward from the original east-side and west-side Polish neighborhoods, already discernible toward the close of the nineteenth century, continued at an accelerated pace. By the interwar years, the locus of Polish Detroit had become the municipal enclave of Hamtramck, still considered the most Polish city in America. After World War II Polish Americans on Detroit's east side increasingly relocated beyond Six Mile Road and in the suburban communities of Macomb County. Many of the original Polish homes on the east side passed on to new waves of migrants, especially blacks from the rural South. A similar pattern of out-migration occurred on the west side. As economic conditions improved, Poles moved in large numbers to Dearborn and the downriver suburban communities of Wayne County.[97] Only the three original Polish churches on Canfield remain as memorials to the vibrant immigrant community that had built them at such cost but with such love and pride in the late nineteenth century.

NOTES

CHAPTER ONE

1. Wacław Kruszka, *Historya polska w Ameryce* [Polish history in America], 13 vols. (Milwaukee, Wisc.: Spółka Wydawnicza Kuryer, 1905–8), 11:167–68. On the arrival of the Lemkes, Melins, and Mindak, see also Sr. Mary Remigia Napolska, *The Polish Immigrant in Detroit to 1914* (Chicago: Polish Catholic Union of America, 1946), pp. 28–29; John H. Greusel, "Detroit's Polish Pioneers and Their Remarkable Progress," *Detroit Free Press*, 3 June 1906, pt. 4, p. 7; *Sunday News-Tribune*, 12 Sept. 1897, p. 10; L. Gozdawa, "Polscy mieszkańcy Detroit w 1850–60 latach" [Detroit's Polish inhabitants in the 1850s], *Dziennik Polski* [Polish daily news], 17 Mar. 1951, p. 4; and "Pierwszy polski ślub w Detroit" [The first Polish wedding in Detroit], ibid., 20 Mar. 1951, p. 4. Copious but impressionistic information on these and other Polish pioneers in Detroit is contained in Wincenty Smołczyński, *Historya osady i parafii polskich w Detroit, Mich. oraz przewodnik adresowy* [History of Polish settlement and parishes in Detroit, Mich. and a guide to addresses] (Detroit: privately printed, 1907). These sources differ on the year of Stanisław Melin's arrival in Detroit: Kruszka says 1855; Napolska, Gozdawa, and Smołczyński, 1857; and Greusel, 1861.
2. Not until the late 1880s, however, did the distinction between "Pole" and "Kashub" become divisive. See Jan L. Perkowski, "The Kashubs— Origins and Emigration to the U.S.," *Polish American Studies* 23, no. 1 (1966):1–7; see also Joseph Swastek, *Detroit's Oldest Polish Parish: St. Albertus 1872–1973 Centennial* (hereafter *St. Albertus Centennial*) (Detroit: n.p., [1974]), pp. 34–35. Swastek, before his death in 1977, served for many years as archivist to the Detroit archdiocese.
3. *Detroit Free Press*, 11 July 1873, p. 1.

4. Greusel, "Detroit's Polish Pioneers," pt. 4, p. 7; see also Napolska, *Polish Immigrant in Detroit*, pp. 28–29; *Sunday News-Tribune*, 12 Sept. 1897, p. 10; L. Gozdawa, "Jan Lemke," *Dziennik Polski*, 29 Mar. 1951, p. 4; Allan R. Treppa, "Detroit's Polish Pioneers: John Lemke 1823–1914," *Polish Daily News* (Eng. ed.), 29–30 Dec. 1979, pp. 4, 6.

5. Greusel, "Detroit's Polish Pioneers," pt. 4, p. 7; L. Gozdawa, "Stanisław Melin," *Dziennik Polski*, 27 Mar. 1951, p. 4.

6. Napolska, *Polish Immigrant in Detroit*, p. 26; L. Gozdawa, "Polacy w Detroit przed 100 i 150 laty" [Poles in Detroit 100 and 150 years ago], *Dziennik Polski*, 6 Mar. 1951, p. 4. Cf. Józef Swastek, "Najdawniejszy Detroicki Dokument Polski" [Detroit's oldest Polish document], *Sodalis* 32, no. 4 (1951):19–22.

7. From data collected by Maria J. E. Copson-Niećko, "The Poles in America from the 1830's to 1870's," in *Poles in America: Bicentennial Essays*, ed. Frank Mocha (Stevens Point, Wisc.: Worzalla, 1978), pp. 173, 276n. Cf. L. Gozdawa, "Powstaniec Andrzej Kamiński—Pierwszy Polak, Który zamieszkał w Detroit" [The insurrectionary Andrzej Kamiński—the first Pole who settled in Detroit], *Dziennik Polski*, 8 Mar. 1951, p. 4, who maintains that Kamiński arrived in New York in 1834 (based on records of the United States Land Office) and was already settled in Detroit by 1837.

8. George Catlin, "First Pole to Settle Here was a True '100 Percenter,' " *Detroit News*, 21 Apr. 1925, p. 1; Napolska, *Polish Immigrant in Detroit*, pp. 26–27; Stephen Wloszczewski, "The Trail of the Polish Emigrants in Michigan," in *Poles in Michigan*, vol. 1 (all published) (Detroit: The Poles in Michigan Associated, 1953 [1955]), p. 26.

9. Catlin, "First Pole Was '100 Percenter,' " p. 1; L. Gozdawa, "Filip Jasnowski," *Dziennik Polski*, 15 Mar. 1951, p. 4.

10. Józef Swastek, "Pierwszy Kapłan Polski w Michigan" [The first Polish priest in Michigan], *Sodalis* 32, no. 2 (1951):21–24; and "Księża Polscy w Michigan Przed Wojną Domową" [Polish priests in Michigan before the civil war], ibid., no. 3, pp. 21–23; Kruszka, *Historya polska w Ameryce*, 11:167; L. Gozdawa, "Jak powstawała pierwsza polska parafia?" [How did the first Polish parish originate?], *Dziennik Polski*, 24 Mar. 1951, p. 4.

11. Kruszka, *Historya polska w Ameryce*, 11:167; Greusel, "Detroit's Polish Pioneers," pt. 4, p. 7; Napolska, *Polish Immigrant in Detroit*, pp. 27–28; L. Gozdawa, "Antoni Leszczyński," *Dziennik Polski*, 22 Mar. 1951, p. 4.

12. Swastek, *St. Albertus Centennial*, p. 35; Kruszka, *Historya polska w Ameryce*, 11:168. The close relationship between the early Prussian Polish immigrants and German-American settlements is examined in Victor Greene, *For God and Country: The Rise of Polish and Lithuanian Ethnic Consciousness in America 1860–1910* (Madison, Wisc.: State Historical Society of Wisconsin, 1975), pp. 31–34.

13. Kruszka, *Historya polska w Ameryce*, 11:169. Fr. Szymon Wieczorek expressed on several occasions the opinion that his work in Detroit was hampered by German intrigue and that even in his own Resurrectionist order he did not fully trust the "German hearts" (ibid., pp. 171–73).

14. Swastek, *St. Albertus Centennial*, pp. 34–36.

15. Ibid., 30–34; L. Gozdawa, "Ks. Szymon Wieczorek," *Dziennik Polski*, 3 Apr. 1951, p. 4.

16. Swastek, *St. Albertus Centennial*, pp. 34, 37–38; Kruszka, *Historya polska w Ameryce*, 11:170–72. On Wieczorek's brief career in Detroit, see also L. Gozdawa, "Detroicki etap życia Ks. Szymona Wieczorka" [The Detroit phase of Fr. Szymon Wieczorek's life], *Dziennik Polski*, 5 Apr. 1951, p. 4.

17. Swastek, *St. Albertus Centennial*, pp. 35–36, 40.

18. Ibid., p. 38; see also L. Gozdawa, "Początek budowy pierwszego kościoła polskiego" [The beginning of construction of the first Polish church], *Dziennik Polski*, 31 Mar. 1951, p. 4.

19. Swastek, *St. Albertus Centennial*, p. 39; Kruszka, *Historya polska w Ameryce*, 11:173–74.

20. Swastek, *St. Albertus Centennial*, p. 39. Kruszka points out that the principal Detroit newspapers—*Free Press, Tribune, Daily Post*, and German *Abend-Post*—in noting the dedication ceremonies mentioned only that a new Catholic church had opened and did not mention the words "Poles" or "Polish" (*Historya polska w Ameryce*, 11:175–76).

21. Swastek, *St. Albertus Centennial*, p. 39; Kruszka, *Historya polska w Ameryce*, 11:176–77.

22. Quoted in Swastek, *St. Albertus Centennial*, p. 41.

23. Ibid., pp. 41–42.

24. Ibid., pp. 42–44. Cf. Kruszka, *Historya polska w Ameryce*, 11:174–75, who argues that at this time the idea of ethnic parish schools was scorned not only by the "American" church hierarchy but even by General Superior Kajsiewicz. It was their opinion that Polish institutions in America were at the most temporary, and that the immigrants would soon be integrated into American schools and other native institutions.

25. Swastek, *St. Albertus Centennial*, p. 44. Borgess, however (perhaps to protect an already sizable investment), on 11 July 1873 did pay off the outstanding amount owed to Mary Moran, thereby acquiring the lot and partially completed school for $1,419.65 (ibid., p. 45).

26. See Kruszka, *Historya polska w Ameryce*, 11:177.

27. Swastek, *St. Albertus Centennial*, p. 46.

28. Ibid., pp. 47–48. On Gieryk's pastorate at St. Albertus's see also L. Gozdawa, "Ks. Teodor Gieryk," *Dziennik Polski*, 10 Apr. 1951, p. 4.

29. Swastek, *St. Albertus Centennial*, pp. 48–50; L. Gozdawa, "Pierwsza polska gazeta w Detroit" [The first Polish newspaper in Detroit], *Dziennik Polski*, 12 Apr. 1951, p. 4. See also Andrzej Brożek, *Polonia amerykańska 1854–1939* [American Polonia 1854–1939] (Warsaw: Interpress, 1977), pp. 59–61; Mieczysław Haiman, *Zjednoczenie Polskie Rzymsko-Katolickie w Ameryce* [The Polish Roman Catholic Union in America] (Chicago: Zjednoczenie, 1948). The exact dates of these first meetings remain a matter of conjecture.

30. Kruszka, *Historya polska w Ameryce*, 11:180.

31. Swastek, *St. Albertus Centennial*, pp. 50–52.

32. Ibid., p. 53.

33. Quoted ibid., pp. 53–55.

34. Ibid., pp. 57–58.

35. *Evening News*, 8 Sept. 1879, p. 4; 10 Sept. 1879, p. 4; 12 Sept. 1879, p. 4; 10 Oct. 1879, p. 4. See also Peter Andrew Ostafin, "The Polish Peasant in Transition: A Study of Group Integration as a Function of

Symbiosis and Common Definitions" (Ph.D. diss., University of Michigan, 1949), pp. 95–96.

36. *Detroit Free Press*, 11 Mar. 1873, p. 1; 8 Dec. 1874, p. 1; 24 Mar. 1875, p. 1.

37. *Detroit Free Press*, 15 Dec. 1874, p. 1; 13 July 1877, p. 1.

38. English translation in *Portrait of America: Letters of Henry Sienkiewicz*, ed. and trans. Charles Morley (New York: Columbia University Press, 1959), p. 45.

39. Swastek, *St. Albertus Centennial*, pp. 53, 56, 58–59, 61–63; see also Kruszka, *Historya polska w Ameryce*, 11:181.

40. Ostafin, "Polish Peasant in Transition," p. 96.

41. Swastek, *St. Albertus Centennial*, pp. 63, 65; L. Gozdawa, "Przyjazd Księdza Kolasińskiego" [The arrival of Father Kolasiński], *Dziennik Polski*, 14 Apr. 1951, p. 4.

42. Swastek, *St. Albertus Centennial*, p. 63; George Paré, *The Catholic Church in Detroit 1701–1888* (Detroit: Gabriel Richard Press, 1951), p. 556. On Kolasiński's arrival, see also *Missye Katolickie* [Catholic missions] 2, no. 6 (June 1883):167–68.

43. Eduard Adam Skendzel, who has probed Kolasiński's Polish background before he came to Detroit, notes that whereas the parish records in Mielec show that eleven children were born to Dominik's parents, Andrzej Kolasiński and Agnieszka Wydro, evidence suggests that only four sons and a daughter survived infancy. He also points out that documents at the Kraków archdiocesan archives provide conflicting information for the years of Kolasiński's birth and ordination (*The Kolasinski Story* [Grand Rapids, Mich.: Littleshield Press, 1979], pp. 4–5, 28n, 30n).

44. Quoted ibid., p. 5.

45. Ibid.

46. Quoted in Swastek, *St. Albertus Centennial*, p. 65.

47. Napolska, *Polish Immigrant in Detroit*, p. 30; Kruszka, *Historya polska w Ameryce*, p. 181; Ostafin, "Polish Peasant in Transition," pp. 96–97.

48. *Evening News*, 10 Sept. 1883, p. 4; 12 Sept. 1883, p. 1. See also Swastek, *St. Albertus Centennial*, pp. 70–71.

49. I believe Swastek exaggerates the significance of these reports, only two of which were sent to Poland (*St. Albertus Centennial*, p. 65).

50. *Missye Katolickie* 2, no. 6 (June 1883):167–68.

51. Ibid. 3, no. 8 (August 1884):232–35.

52. *Evening News*, 29 Nov. 1883, p. 3.

53. These infant gleaners were a particular source of curiosity to native Detroiters. Two years later the *Evening News* devoted a separate article to their ways (17 Aug. 1885, p. 2).

54. See *Detroit Tribune*, 6 Dec. 1885, p. 9, for a description of the Polish quarter shortly after the outbreak of the church troubles in early December 1885. For a latter-day Polish response to this article, see L. Gozdawa, "Polacktown w 1885 . . . ," *Dziennik Polski*, 3 May 1951, p. 5.

55. *Detroit Free Press*, 3 Mar. 1876, p. 1; 15 Apr. 1876, p. 1.

56. Kruszka, *Historya polska w Ameryce*, 11:189–90; John H. Greusel, "The Shepherds of the Polish Flock and Their Churches," *Detroit Free Press*, 17 June 1906, pt. 4, p. 5; Swastek, *St. Albertus Centennial*, p. 66. Cf. L.

Gozdawa, "Jak powstała druga polska parafia?" [How did the second Polish parish originate?], *Dziennik Polski*, 28 Apr. 1951, p. 4, who dates the founding of St. Casimir's amost a year earlier. Gutowski was formally appointed pastor to the new congregation on 1 December 1882, a post he would retain for over thirty-five years until his death in 1918. Other sources suggest that Gutowski actually came to America in 1875 with a group of Franciscan missionaries. See Skendzel, *Kolasinski Story*, pp. 82n–83n.

57. On Dąbrowski's background and his work in Wisconsin, see especially his biography, which contains extensive selections from his correspondence and writings (A. Syski, *Ks. Józef Dąbrowski 1842–1942* [Orchard Lake, Mich.: Nakład Seminarium Polskiego, 1942]). See also Joseph Swastek, "The Formative Years of the Polish Seminary in the United States," *Sacrum Poloniae Millennium* (Rome) 6 (1959): 47–55; Swastek, *St. Albertus Centennial*, pp. 59–60, 77; L. Gozdawa, "Ks. Józef Dąbrowski—ojciec polskiego duszpasterstwa i polskiego szkolnictwa w Ameryce" [Fr. Józef Dąbrowski—father of the Polish priesthood and Polish education in America], *Dziennik Polski*, 17 Apr. 1951, p. 4; 19 Apr. 1951, p. 4.

58. On the Felician Sisters' work in Detroit, see especially vol. 3 of the official history of the order: *Historja Zgromadzenia SS. Felicjanek na Podstawie Rękopisów* [History of the order of Felician Sisters based on manuscripts] (Kraków: Nakładem Zgromadzenia SS. Felicjanek, 1932); and several articles by Ludwik Gozdawa in *Dziennik Polski*: 5 May 1951, p. 4; 8 May 1951, p. 4; 10 May 1951, p. 4; 12 May 1951, p. 4; 19 May 1951, p. 4. See also *Missye Katolickie* 3, no. 11 (November 1884):336–37; *Detroit Free Press*, 5 Oct. 1880, p. 1.

59. Swastek, "Formative Years of the Polish Seminary," pp. 44, 46, 56.

60. Bishop's letter in *Michigan Catholic*, 27 Mar. 1884, p. 5; see also *Detroit Free Press*, 18 Mar. 1884, p. 3; *Detroit Post and Tribune*, 20 Apr. 1884, p. 2; Swastek, "Formative Years of the Polish Seminary," p. 59.

61. *Evening News*, 11 Apr. 1884, p. 3; Swastek, "Formative Years of the Polish Seminary," pp. 61–66. Swastek quotes a letter of 24 March 1884 to the bishops of America in which Dąbrowski wrote: "The Polish youth, being educated in the different American institutions [seminaries], cannot be well instructed in their native language, and on this account many are entirely unable to preach decently and to explain properly the truths of faith with benefit to the souls of their flocks" (p. 95).

62. *Detroit Free Press*, 20 May 1885, p. 3; 23 July 1885, p. 3; *Detroit Evening Journal*, 20 May 1885, p. 4; 23 July 1885, p. 6; *Detroit Post*, 23 July 1885, p. 5. See also Swastek, "Formative Years of the Polish Seminary," pp. 65–68; *Missye Katolickie* 3, no. 5 (May 1884):148.

63. *Detroit Free Press*, 23 July 1885, p. 3.

64. Swastek, *St. Albertus Centennial*, p. 66.

65. Ibid., p. 67.

66. Ibid., pp. 67, 69; *Evening News*, 19 Mar. 1884, p. 4. The masonry work was contracted to Patrick Dee and the carpentry and woodwork to Spitzley Brothers. The architect was H. Engelbert. The *Evening News* estimated the total cost at close to $75,000 when interior furnishings were added.

67. *Evening News*, 28 June 1884, p. 4.; *Michigan Catholic*, 3 July 1884, p. 5; *Missye Katolickie* 3, no. 8 (August 1884):232–35.
68. *Evening News*, 5 Dec. 1884, p. 3; see also Swastek, "Formative Years of the Polish Seminary," p. 64.
69. Swastek, *St. Albertus Centennial*, pp. 67–69; *Detroit Post*, 5 July 1885, p. 5; *Detroit Free Press*, 5 July 1885, p. 5; *Evening News*, 4 July 1885, p. 1; 5 July 1885, p. 4; *Michigan Catholic*, 9 July 1885, p. 5.
70. *Evening News*, 5 July 1885, p. 4.
71. Swastek, *St. Albertus Centennial*, pp. 72–73.
72. *Detroit Evening Journal*, 15 Oct. 1887, p. 7; Swastek, *St. Albertus Centennial*, p. 73; see also *Detroit Evening Journal*, 27 Nov. 1885, p. 1.
73. One set of charges was submitted to the bishop in early November by a Marcin Kopydłowski, who charged that Kolasiński condoned the taking of small doles from the collection by his old friend Józef Przybyłowski. Przybyłowski soon after filed a libel action for $10,000 damages against Kopydłowski (*Evening News*, 24 Nov. 1885, p. 4; *Detroit Free Press*, 25 Nov. 1885, p. 8). On charges against the pastor delivered to the bishop on 27 November 1885, by Tomasz Żółtowski, see *Detroit Evening Journal*, 27 Nov. 1885, p. 1.
74. See esp. *Detroit Evening Journal*, 30 Nov. 1885, p. 1; *Evening News*, 30 Nov. 1885, p. 4.
75. *Detroit Evening Journal*, 15 Oct. 1887, p. 7.
76. *Detroit Tribune*, 7 Feb. 1894, p. 2.
77. *Detroit Evening Journal*, 15 Oct. 1887, p. 7. The bishop's letter of suspension was apparently dated 28 November (that is, the day before Dempsey's first trip to the parish); this circumstance has led some later chroniclers of the crisis, notably Wacław Kruszka, to maintain that Kolasiński, already informed of his removal, had turned Sunday mass on 29 November into a passionate "farewell sermon" (*Historya polska w Ameryce*, 11:183). Swastek also states that Kolasiński was suspended on 28 November (*St. Albertus Centennial*, p. 73).

CHAPTER TWO

1. Paré, *Catholic Church in Detroit*, pp. 556–57; Swastek, *St. Albertus Centennial*, p. 73; *Detroit Free Press*, 1 Dec. 1885, p. 3.
2. Paré, *Catholic Church in Detroit*, p. 557; Swastek, "Formative Years of the Polish Seminary," p. 69; Gozdawa, "Przyjazd Księdza Kolasińskiego," *Dziennik Polski*, 14 Apr. 1951, p. 4.
3. *Detroit Free Press*, 31 Dec. 1885, p. 5. Kolasiński purportedly "advised the people to throw [Dąbrowski's] collectioners out by the collar."
4. *Evening News*, 1 Dec. 1885, p. 4; *Detroit Evening Journal*, 1 Dec. 1885, p. 1; *Detroit Tribune*, 2 Dec. 1885, p. 2.
5. *Detroit Free Press*, 2 Dec. 1885, p. 5.
6. *Detroit Evening Journal*, 2 Dec. 1885, p. 1; *Detroit Free Press*, 3 Dec. 1885, p. 5; *Detroit Tribune*, 3 Dec. 1885, p. 1. The newspaper accounts differ substantially from each other in the description of this and the previous day's riot.
7. *Detroit Evening Journal*, 2 Dec. 1885, p. 1; *Detroit Free Press*, 3 Dec. 1885, p. 5; *Detroit Tribune*, 3 Dec. 1885, p. 1.

8. *Detroit Free Press*, 3 Dec. 1885, p. 5.
9. Ibid.; see also *Michigan Catholic*, 3 Dec. 1885, p. 5.
10. *Detroit Free Press*, 4 Dec. 1885, p. 4.
11. Cited in Swastek, *St. Albertus Centennial*, p. 77.
12. *Evening News*, 3 Dec. 1885, p. 3; *Detroit Evening Journal*, 3 Dec. 1885, p. 4. The books were eventually delivered to Bishop Borgess's attorney, John Atkinson. Years later the lawyer stated that his careful examination of the records revealed no evidence of malfeasance by Kolasiński (*Evening News*, 16 Oct. 1893, p. 5).
13. *Evening News*, 3 Dec. 1885, p. 1.
14. Ibid. Żółtowski and Mrs. Danielska had earlier been identified as Kolasiński's accusers, but the sensational nature of the charges had not been made public. See *Detroit Evening Journal*, 27 Nov. 1885, p. 1.
15. *Evening News*, 4 Dec. 1885, p. 4; 5 Dec. 1885, p. 2.
16. *Detroit Evening Journal*, 4 Dec. 1885, p. 4; *Evening News*, 4 Dec. 1885, p. 4.
17. *Evening News*, 6 Dec. 1885, p. 4; Swastek, *St. Albertus Centennial*, p. 79.
18. *Evening News*, 5 Dec. 1885, p. 4.
19. *Detroit Free Press*, 7 Dec. 1885, p. 4; *Evening News*, 7 Dec. 1885, p. 2.
20. *Detroit Evening Journal*, 11 Dec. 1885, p. 4. In a second affidavit Mrs. Danielska withdrew her charge, saying that she had been paid twenty dollars to make her accusation by prominent parishioners who wished to be rid of Kolasiński (*Evening News*, 16 Oct. 1893, p. 5).
21. Swastek, *St. Albertus Centennial*, p. 75; *Detroit Evening Journal*, 14 Dec. 1885, p. 4.
22. *Detroit Tribune*, 2 Jan. 1886, p. 4.
23. *Evening News*, 10 Dec. 1885, p. 2.
24. *Evening News*, 21 Dec. 1885, p. 4; *Detroit Free Press*, 22 Dec. 1885, p. 5; *Detroit Evening Journal*, 22 Dec. 1885, p. 2; *Detroit Free Press*, 24 Dec. 1885, p. 5.
25. The following account of the "Polish Christmas riot" is drawn largely from the reports in the *Evening News*, 25 Dec. 1885, p. 1; 26 Dec. 1885, p. 1; *Detroit Free Press*, 26 Dec. 1885, pp. 1, 5; *Detroit Evening Journal*, 25 Dec. 1885, p. 1; 26 Dec. 1885, p. 1; *Detroit Tribune*, 26 Dec. 1885, p. 1; *New York Times*, 27 Dec. 1885, p. 1. Although there was general agreement among the major Detroit dailies on the actual sequence of events, the *Evening News* was inclined to sensationalize the occurrences and cast the Kolasińskiites in a particularly negative light.
26. *Evening News*, 27 Dec. 1885, p. 4.
27. *Detroit Evening Journal*, 26 Dec. 1885, p. 1; *Evening News*, 26 Dec. 1885, p. 1; *Detroit Tribune*, 27 Dec. 1885, p. 2; *New York Times*, 27 Dec. 1885, p. 1.
28. *Evening News*, 26 Dec. 1885, p. 1; *Detroit Evening Journal*, 28 Dec. 1885, p. 2; see also Kruszka, *Historya polska w Ameryce*, 11:184–85.
29. *Evening News*, 27 Dec. 1885, p. 1; *Detroit Free Press*, 28 Dec. 1885, p. 3; *Detroit Evening Journal*, 28 Dec. 1885, p. 4.
30. *New York Times*, 28 Dec. 1885, p. 1; see also *Detroit Free Press*, 5 Jan. 1886, p. 7.
31. *Evening News*, 27 Dec. 1885, p. 8. In another editorial on 28 Dec. 1885, p. 2, the paper defended the police's action toward the "unruly" Poles.
32. *Michigan Catholic*, 31 Dec. 1885, p. 4; 7 Jan. 1886, p. 4.

33. *Detroit Free Press*, 28 Dec. 1885, p. 3; *Detroit Evening Journal*, 28 Dec. 1885, p. 4; see also *New York Times*, 29 Dec. 1885, p. 2.
34. *Evening News*, 29 Dec. 1885, p. 4; 30 Dec. 1885, p. 4; *Detroit Free Press*, 30 Dec. 1885, p. 8; 31 Dec. 1885, p. 5; *Detroit Evening Journal*, 29 Dec. 1885, p. 1; 30 Dec. 1885, p. 4; *Detroit Tribune*, 30 Dec. 1885, p. 4; 31 Dec. 1885, p. 2. On the trial of the Lemke brothers and Stieber, see chap. 3.
35. *Evening News*, 30 Dec. 1885, p. 4; *Detroit Evening Journal*, 30 Dec. 1885, p. 4.
36. *Evening News*, 30 Dec. 1885, p. 1; *Detroit Tribune*, 31 Dec. 1885, p. 2; *Evening News*, 31 Dec. 1885, p. 5.
37. *Detroit Free Press*, 31 Dec. 1885, p. 3; see also *Evening News*, 31 Dec. 1885, p. 4; *Detroit Evening Journal*, 31 Dec. 1885, p. 2. While in Detroit, Domagalski was Father Dąbrowski's guest at the Felician convent.
38. *Evening News*, 15 Jan. 1886, p. 4; *Detroit Evening Journal*, 15 Jan. 1886, p. 2; *Detroit Tribune*, 16 Jan. 1886, p. 4. Cf. *Detroit Evening Journal*, 15 Oct. 1887, p. 7.
39. *Missye Katolickie* 2, no. 6 (June 1883):167–68.
40. *Detroit Tribune*, 16 Jan. 1886, p. 4; *Evening News*, 21 Jan. 1886, p. 1; *Detroit Free Press*, 22 Jan. 1886, p. 8.
41. *Detroit Tribune*, 6 Mar. 1886, p. 4; see also ibid., 15 Feb. 1886, p. 4; 23 Feb. 1886, p. 8; *Detroit Free Press*, 6 Mar. 1886, p. 5.
42. *Detroit Free Press*, 11 Mar. 1886, p. 5. On the background of Michigan law regarding the bishop's ownership of church property, see *Detroit Evening Journal*, 14 Jan. 1886, p. 4.
43. *Evening News*, 11 Mar. 1886, p. 1.
44. The following account of the trial is reconstructed from the *Evening News*, 19 Mar. 1886, p. 1; 20 Mar. 1886, p. 4; *Detroit Free Press*, 20 Mar. 1886, p. 5; *Michigan Catholic*, 25 Mar. 1886, p. 4.
45. *Evening News*, 24 Mar. 1886, p. 4; 25 Mar. 1886, p. 4; *Detroit Tribune*, 25 Mar. 1886, p. 2; *Detroit Free Press*, 26 Mar. 1886, p. 4.
46. On 15 January 1886, Kolasiński had addressed an appeal to Elder in which he denied all allegations raised against him and requested that he be reinstated as pastor of St. Albertus's pending a proper ecclesiastical investigation (Skendzel, *Kolasinski Story*, pp. 104D–104G).
47. *Detroit Free Press*, 29 Mar. 1886, p. 5; *Evening News*, 29 Mar. 1886, p. 4.
48. *Michigan Catholic*, 1 Apr. 1886, p. 5; see also *Evening News*, 31 Mar. 1886, p. 4; 1 Apr. 1886, p. 4; *Detroit Evening Journal*, 1 Apr. 1886, p. 4; *Detroit Free Press*, 1 Apr. 1886, p. 5; 2 Apr. 1886, p. 8.
49. *Detroit Free Press*, 5 Apr. 1886, p. 4.
50. Ibid.
51. *Evening News*, 3 Apr. 1886, p. 1; 5 Apr. 1886, p. 4.
52. Ibid., 9 Apr. 1886, p. 1; *Detroit Evening Journal*, 9 Apr. 1886, p. 4; *Detroit Free Press*, 6 May 1886, p. 8; *Evening News*, 20 Apr. 1886, p. 3.
53. Swastek, *St. Albertus Centennial*, p. 85.

CHAPTER THREE

1. *Evening News*, 3 July 1886, p. 3. Kolasiński had met Marty in 1884 at the dedication of the Capuchin monastery in Detroit (Skendzel, *Kolasinski Story*, p. 8).

2. The following account of the trial is drawn from reports in the *Evening News*, 8 July 1886, p. 4; 9 July 1886, p. 4; 10 July 1886, p. 4; 13 July 1886, p. 4; 14 July 1886, p. 4; *Detroit Free Press*, 9 July 1886, p. 5; 10 July 1886, p. 5; 11 July 1886, p. 10; 14 July 1886, p. 5; 15 July 1886, p. 5; *Detroit Evening Journal*, 8 July 1886, p. 4; 9 July 1886, p. 4; 10 July 1886, p. 4; 13 July 1886, p. 4; 14 July 1886, p. 4.

3. Cited in Swastek, *St. Albertus Centennial*, p. 86.

4. *Detroit Evening Journal*, 17 Aug. 1886, p. 4; 19 Aug. 1886, p. 4; *Historja Zgromadzenia SS. Felicjanek na podstawie rękopisów*, pt. 3, p. 192.

5. Swastek, *St. Albertus Centennial*, p. 86, where the draft of the bishop's order of excommunication is reprinted. According to Swastek the draft was dated 13 August 1886—that is, prior to the renewed outbreak of violence.

6. Cited in Swastek, "Formative Years of the Polish Seminary," p. 70.

7. Ibid., pp. 69, 71. Swastek cites *Wiarus* [The old warrior], a Polish-language weekly published in Winona, Minnesota, as his source. No record of this tragic incident could be found in the major Detroit papers.

8. Ibid., p. 71.

9. *Detroit Free Press*, 16 Sept. 1886, p. 3.

10. Ibid., 25 Sept. 1886, p. 8.

11. Ibid., 17 Dec. 1886, p. 8; *Detroit Evening Journal*, 17 Dec. 1886, p. 2; Swastek, "Formative Years of the Polish Seminary," pp. 72–74; *Missye Katolickie* 6, no. 2 (February 1887): 62.

12. The following paragraphs are drawn largely from Swastek, "Formative Years of the Polish Seminary," pp. 75–92. See also Kruszka, *Historya polska w Ameryce*, 11:147–48.

13. Swastek, *St. Albertus Centennial*, p. 87.

14. *Detroit Free Press*, 19 Mar. 1887, p. 8; *Evening News*, 19 Mar. 1887, p. 1.

15. This account of the events of 20 March is drawn largely from the reports in the *Detroit Free Press*, 21 Mar. 1887, p. 1; *Detroit Morning Tribune*, 21 Mar. 1887, p. 1; *Evening News*, 21 Mar. 1887, p. 4; *Detroit Evening Journal*, 21 Mar. 1887, p. 1.

16. On the change of pastors at St. Albertus's, see Swastek, "Formative Years of the Polish Seminary," pp. 76–77; *St. Albertus Centennial*, p. 88.

17. The *Tribune* first identified her as Barbara Manosk[a].

18. *Detroit Free Press*, 22 Mar. 1887, p. 8.

19. *Detroit Evening Journal*, 22 Mar. 1887, p. 1; see also *Evening News*, 23 Mar. 1887, p. 4.

20. *Detroit Morning Tribune*, 25 Mar. 1887, p. 1.

21. *Evening News*, 25 Mar. 1887, p. 1; *Detroit Morning Tribune*, 28 Mar. 1887, p. 2.

22. On this first day of testimony, see *Detroit Free Press*, 1 Apr. 1887, p. 5; *Detroit Morning Tribune*, 1 Apr. 1887, p. 4; *Evening News*, 1 Apr. 1887, p. 2.

23. *Detroit Free Press*, 2 Apr. 1887, p. 5; *Detroit Morning Tribune*, 2 Apr. 1887, p. 4; *Sunday News*, 2 Apr. 1887, p. 2.

24. *Detroit Free Press*, 6 Apr. 1887, p. 5; *Evening News*, 3 May 1887, p. 4; *Detroit Evening Journal*, 3 May 1887, p. 1.

25. Text in *Detroit Free Press*, 3 May 1887, p. 1; *Evening News*, 3 May 1887, p. 4. See also *Detroit Evening Journal*, 3 May 1887, p. 1.

26. Swastek, *St. Albertus Centennial*, p. 91.
27. Ibid., pp. 91–92.
28. *Evening News*, 3 May 1887, p. 4; *Detroit Free Press*, 3 May 1887, p. 1. James Cardinal Gibbons in an audience with Pope Leo XIII is alleged to have remarked; "This diocese is in a condition of demoralization on account of the bad management and unwise rule of Bishop Borgess" (*Evening News*, 16 Oct. 1893, p. 5). Swastek provides an eloquent, though to my mind somewhat forced, absolution of Borgess of anti-Polish sentiment and a share of responsibility for the outbreak of the church troubles in *St. Albertus Centennial*, pp. 36–37, 104–6. See also a lengthy positive review of Borgess's career in the *Detroit Evening Journal*, 8 and 15 Oct. 1887.
29. *Detroit Free Press*, 4 May 1887, p. 5.
30. *Evening News*, 20 May 1887, p. 4; *Detroit Tribune*, 20 May 1887, p. 5; 21 May 1887, p. 5; see also Swastek, *St. Albertus Centennial*, pp. 92–93.
31. See, for example, *Detroit Tribune*, 3 Jan. 1888, p. 4; *Evening News*, 3 Jan. 1888, p. 1.
32. *Evening News*, 24 June 1887, p. 1; see also Swastek, *St. Albertus Centennial*, p. 93; *Missye Katolickie* 3, no. 8 (August 1884): 241–44; 6, no. 6 (June 1887): 183.
33. *Detroit Free Press*, 24 June 1887, p. 5; see also *Detroit Tribune*, 24 June 1887, p. 3, which suggests that the police, prodded as always by Jan Wagner, still expected trouble from the Kolasińskiites at the reopening on 24 June.
34. On the reopening, see *Evening News*, 24 June 1887, p. 1; see also *Detroit Evening Journal*, 24 June 1887, p. 1; *Detroit Free Press*, 25 June 1887, p. 5; *Detroit Tribune*, 25 June 1887, p. 5. Cf. *New York Times*, 25 June 1887, p. 1, which emphasizes the Kolasińskiites' attempts to disrupt the proceedings.
35. *Missye Katolickie* 6, no. 9 (September 1887):286.
36. Swastek, *St. Albertus Centennial*, p. 90; Kruszka, *Historya polska w Ameryce*, 11:186.
37. *Evening News*, 25 June 1887, p. 1; *Detroit Evening Journal*, 25 June 1887, p. 4; see also Swastek, *St. Albertus Centennial*, p. 93. Joos's letter was published in English in the *Evening News*, 27 June 1887, p. 1.
38. *Evening News*, 25 June 1887, p. 2.
39. *Detroit Tribune*, 27 June 1887, p. 5; *Detroit Free Press*, 27 June 1887, p. 2.
40. *Evening News*, 4 July 1887, p. 4; *Michigan Catholic*, 7 July 1887, p. 4. The hapless Polish "convert" was identified as Rev. Józef Antoszewski.
41. Swastek, *St. Albertus Centennial*, p. 94.
42. *Evening News*, 14 Apr. 1888, p. 4; *Sunday News*, 15 Apr. 1888, p. 8.
43. *Evening News*, 7 June 1888, p. 1; 8 June 1888, p. 2; *Detroit Evening Journal*, 7 June 1888, p. 1; 8 June 1888, p. 4; 9 June 1888, p. 5.
44. *Detroit Free Press*, 11 June 1888, p. 2; see also *Detroit Evening Journal*, 11 June 1888, p. 4; *Evening News*, 9 June 1888, p. 4.
45. *Michigan Catholic*, 14 June 1888, p. 4.
46. *Detroit Tribune*, 8 Oct. 1888, p. 2.
47. *Sunday News*, 11 Nov. 1888, p. 8; see also Kruszka, *Historya polska w Ameryce*, 11:191. When later it was revealed that Kolasiński, after his June 1888 visit to Detroit, had journeyed to Baltimore to call on the

then soon-to-be Bishop Foley, the latter categorically denied having given him any assurances regarding his reinstatement (*Evening News*, 16 Oct. 1893, p. 5).

48. *Evening News*, 30 Nov. 1888, p. 1; see also *Detroit Journal*, 1 Dec. 1888, p. 5. Długi signed his writings "Longius." In Polish *długi* means "long."

49. Skendzel, *Kolasinski Story*, p. 86n; Kruszka, *Historya polska w Ameryce*, 11:186.

50. *Evening News*, 30 Nov. 1888, p. 1; Swastek, "Formative Years of the Polish Seminary," p. 89.

51. *Detroit Journal*, 24 Nov. 1888, p. 5; *Sunday News*, 25 Nov. 1888, p. 8. An earlier report, published in the *Detroit Journal*, 28 Sept. 1888, p. 1, had claimed that Bishop Marty had discharged Kolasiński on 1 September. The bishop's action allegedly was taken after Kolasiński had forcibly expelled two of the bishop's agents who had come to investigate charges made against him.

52. *Evening News*, 29 Nov. 1888, p. 1; *Detroit Journal*, 29 Nov. 1888, p. 1; see also Kruszka, *Historya polska w Ameryce*, 11:192.

53. *Evening News*, 1 Dec. 1888, p. 1.

54. *Michigan Catholic*, 22 Nov. 1888, p. 4. On 24 March 1887, in the aftermath of disturbances of St. Albertus's, this paper had chastized "the Polish people of the United States" for apparently being "content to live in shame and disgrace caused by the acts of their compatriots in Detroit" (p. 4).

55. *Detroit Free Press*, 2 Dec. 1888, p. 18; *Sunday News*, 2 Dec. 1888, p. 2.

56. *Detroit Free Press*, 3 Dec. 1888, p. 6.

57. *Sunday News*, 9 Dec. 1888, p. 2. A somewhat different and less sympathetic assessment of the Detroit press's coverage of the Kolasiński troubles is in Swastek, *St. Albertus Centennial*, p. 81. See also below, Bibliographic Essay.

58. *Detroit Journal*, 6 Dec. 1888, p. 4; *Evening News*, 7 Dec. 1888, p. 4; *Detroit Journal*, 7 Dec. 1888, p. 1.

59. *Detroit Free Press*, 9 Dec. 1888, p. 19; *Sunday News*, 9 Dec. 1888, p. 2. Kolasiński had informed Długi by telegram that he would arrive the previous evening to spend 8 December, the Feast of the Immaculate Conception, with his flock, but he was delayed in Chicago (*Detroit Journal*, 8 Dec. 1888, p. 5).

CHAPTER FOUR

1. *Detroit Tribune*, 10 Dec. 1888, p. 2; *Detroit Journal*, 10 Dec. 1888, p. 4.

2. *Detroit Free Press*, 10 Dec. 1888, p. 4; see also *Evening News*, 10 Dec. 1888, p. 2.

3. *Detroit Free Press*, 16 Dec. 1888, p. 20; see also *Detroit Journal*, 10 Dec. 1888, pp. 1, 4.

4. *Detroit Free Press*, 16 Dec. 1888, p. 20; see also *Sunday News*, 16 Dec. 1888, p. 1.

5. *Detroit Journal*, 15 Dec. 1888, p. 5; *Detroit Free Press*, 16 Dec. 1888, p. 20.

6. *Evening News*, 11 Dec. 1888, p. 1; *Detroit Journal*, 12 Dec. 1888, p. 1.

7. *Evening News*, 13 Dec. 1888, p. 4; *Detroit Journal*, 13 Dec. 1888, p. 1.

8. *Evening News*, 29 Dec. 1888, p. 1.
9. Ibid., 5 Jan. 1889, p. 4.
10. Ibid., 19 Jan. 1889, p. 1; *Sunday News*, 20 Jan. 1889, p. 8.
11. *Evening News*, 19 Jan. 1889, p. 1; *Sunday News*, 20 Jan. 1889, p. 8.
12. *Detroit Tribune*, 21 Jan. 1889, p. 2.
13. *Evening News*, 20 Feb. 1889, p. 1.
14. *Detroit Tribune*, 12 Mar. 1889, p. 5; *Detroit Journal*, 12 Mar. 1889, p. 3.
15. *Evening News*, 12 Mar. 1889, p. 4; see also *Detroit Tribune*, 13 Mar. 1889, p. 5; *Detroit Journal*, 12 Mar. 1889, p. 3.
16. *Evening News*, 3 Apr. 1889, p. 1.
17. *Detroit Tribune*, 13 Apr. 1889, p. 5; *Evening News*, 13 Apr. 1889, p. 2.
18. *Evening News*, 17 Apr. 1889, p. 4.
19. *Sunday News*, 12 May 1889, p. 2.
20. *Detroit Journal*, 23 Jan. 1889, p. 1; *Evening News*, 24 Jan. 1889, p. 1; Kruszka, *Historya polska w Ameryce*, 11:193.
21. Cited in *Evening News*, 25 Jan. 1889, p. 1.
22. Ibid., 26 Jan. 1889, p. 1. For the bishop's response to Raeder, see *Evening News*, 28 Jan. 1889, p. 4.
23. *Sunday News*, 27 Jan. 1889, p. 8.
24. *Evening News*, 20 Feb. 1889, p. 1.
25. *Sunday News*, 10 Mar. 1889, p. 2.
26. Ibid., 3 Feb. 1889, p. 11. The newspaper also carried an artist's sketch of Kolasiński's planned "chapel."
27. In English usage, the church, whose articles of incorporation were filed on 11 February 1889, was frequently referred to as "Sacred Heart of Mary."
28. *Detroit Tribune*, 10 June 1889, p. 3; *Detroit Journal*, 10 June 1889, p. 4.
29. *Evening News*, 10 June 1889, p. 4.
30. Ibid., 8 July 1889, p. 3.
31. Ibid., 25 Jan. 1889, p. 1; Swastek, *St. Albertus Centennial*, p. 94; Kruszka, *Historya polska w Ameryce*, 11:187, 191.
32. Swastek, *St. Albertus Centennial*, p. 95; *Detroit Tribune*, 12 Mar. 1889, p. 5. In 1892, after ministering for two years in Brooklyn, Bronikowski, through the influence of Mieczysław Cardinal Ledóchowski, the prefect of the Propaganda, became the first Polish monsignor in the United States.
33. *Detroit Tribune*, 12 Mar. 1889, p. 5; Swastek, *St. Albertus Centennial*, pp. 95–96.
34. Allan R. Treppa, "John A. Lemke: America's First Native-Born Polish American Priest?" *Polish American Studies* 35, nos. 1–2 (1978): 78–83; see also Swastek, *St. Albertus Centennial*, p. 98.
35. On the founding of St. Josaphat's, see L. Gozdawa, "Jak powstało 'Józefatowo'?" [How was St. Josaphat's established?], *Dziennik Polski*, 5 June 1951, p. 4; Swastek, *St. Albertus Centennial*, p. 97.
36. *Sunday News*, 7 Oct. 1889, p. 8; L. Gozdawa, "Ks. Jan Rzadkowolski," *Dziennik Polski*, 7 June 1951, p. 4; Kruszka, *Historya polska w Ameryce*, 11:200–202; Swastek, *St. Albertus Centennial*, p. 97.
37. The cornerstone laying was extensively covered in the Detroit papers: *Evening News*, 27 July 1889, p. 4; *Sunday News*, 28 July 1889, p. 8; *Evening News*, 29 July 1889, p. 4; *Detroit Free Press*, 29 July 1889, p. 4; *Detroit Tribune*, 29 July 1889, p. 2; *Detroit Journal*, 29 July 1889, p. 4.

38. *Detroit Free Press*, 22 Dec. 1890, p. 2; *Evening News*, 22 Dec. 1890, p. 1.
39. *Evening News*, 27 Feb. 1890, p. 1; 26 July 1890, p. 1. On 22 August the *Evening News* printed a sketch of "Kolasinski's Proposed Cathedral," on which preliminary foundation work had already begun (p. 2).
40. *Detroit Free Press*, 31 Oct. 1889, p. 5.
41. *Evening News*, 9 Nov. 1889, p. 4; *Detroit Journal*, 9 Nov. 1889, p. 1; see also *Sunday News*, 10 Nov. 1889, p. 2. Throughout the proceedings Raeder was referred to as Stefan Kamiński, presumably his new, more Polish and less German-sounding, legal name. On most other occasions, however, he was still identified as Raeder by the press. On the increasingly frequent use of the American courts by the Poles, see *Evening News*, 26 Dec. 1891, p. 5.
42. *Evening News*, 10 June 1890, p. 1.
43. Ibid.
44. Ibid., 12 June 1890, p. 2. Raeder printed several further circulars denouncing Kolasiński (Ibid., 2 July 1890, p. 1).
45. Ibid., 2 July 1890, p. 1; see also ibid., 27 Feb. 1890, p. 1. Swastek maintains that a second priest, Fr. J. Rodowicz, also defected from Kolasiński at this time ("Formative Years of the Polish Seminary," p. 91). The *Evening News*, however, indicated that Rodowicz was in fact Father Prowdzicki's real name, by which he was known in Buffalo before coming to Detroit (2 July 1890, p. 1).
46. *Evening News*, 27 Feb. 1890, p. 1.
47. On the emergence and spread of the independent movement at the end of the nineteenth century, see especially Hieronim Kubiak, *Polski Narodowy Kościół Katolicki w Stanach Zjednoczonych Ameryki w latach 1897–1965* [The Polish National Catholic church in the United States of America, 1897–1965] (Wrocław: Zakład Narodowy im. Ossolińskich, 1970), pp. 97–105; Brożek, *Polonia amerykańska 1854–1939*, pp. 95–108, passim; Greene, *For God and Country*, chap. 6, "The Rise of Independentism."
48. *Evening News*, 4 July 1890, p. 1.
49. Ibid., 24 July 1890, p. 1. Cardinal Ledóchowski became prefect of the Propaganda in 1892.
50. On the forgery of Simeoni's letter, ibid., 24 Sept. 1890, p. 1; 25 Sept. 1890, p. 1; *Detroit Tribune*, 25 Sept. 1890, p. 6; *Detroit Free Press*, 25 Sept. 1890, p. 5; *Detroit Journal*, 25 Sept. 1890, p. 4. Several weeks after Simeoni's letters (but before Rome could have learned of the forgery), Cardinal Ledóchowski sent a letter in Polish to Modlaff in which he reiterated Simeoni's points. A facsimile of this letter was later printed in the anti-Kolasińskiite weekly *Niedziela* [Sunday] (21 Feb. 1892, pp. 293–95).
51. *Evening News*, 27 Sept. 1890, p. 1.
52. Ibid., 29 Sept. 1890, p. 1.
53. Ibid., 26 Sept. 1890, p. 1; *Sunday News*, 28 Sept. 1890, p. 2.
54. *Evening News*, 29 Sept. 1890, p. 1.
55. Ibid.; see also Kruszka, *Historya polska w Ameryce*, 11:198–99; Greene, *For God and Country*, pp. 24–26.
56. *Sunday News*, 1 June 1890, p. 2.
57. *Evening News*, 12 Dec. 1890, p. 1.
58. Ibid., 13 Dec. 1890, p. 1; *Sunday News*, 14 Dec. 1890, p. 1.

59. *Evening News*, 29 Sept. 1890, p. 1. Unfortunately not all encounters between members of the opposing factions were peaceful. Early on Christmas morning 1891, for example, a young Pole named Józef Bołda was killed in a street clash between Kolasińskiites and Dąbrowskiites (ibid., 28 Dec. 1891, p. 5; Eduard A. Skendzel, "Two Christmas Tragedies," pt. 2, *Polish Daily News* [Eng. ed.], 22–23 Dec. 1979, p. 8).

60. *Evening News*, 4 May 1891, p. 1.

61. *Detroit Free Press*, 4 May 1891, p. 6.

62. On the 4 May celebrations, see *Evening News*, 4 May 1891, p. 1; *Detroit Free Press*, 5 May 1891, p. 8; *Detroit Tribune*, 5 May 1891, p. 6.

63. *Evening News*, 4 May 1891, p. 1.

64. Ibid., 5 May 1891, p. 1.

65. Ibid., 12 June 1891, p. 1.

66. Cf. Swastek, *St. Albertus Centennial*, pp. 98–100.

67. *Evening News*, 12 June 1891, p. 1.

68. Ibid., 13 June 1891, p. 1; see also *Detroit Journal*, 13 June 1891, p. 1.

69. *Evening News*, 13 June 1891, p. 1.

70. Ibid.; *Detroit Journal*, 15 June 1891, p. 1.

71. *Detroit Free Press*, 14 June 1891, p. 18; *Detroit Journal*, 15 June 1891, p. 4.

72. *Evening News*, 15 June 1891, p. 1; *Detroit Journal*, 15 June 1891, p. 4.

73. *Evening News*, 16 June 1891, pp. 1, 2; see also *Detroit Journal*, 17 June 1891, p. 4.

74. *Evening News*, 15 June 1891, p. 1; 20 June 1891, p. 1; see also *Detroit Journal*, 22 June 1891, p. 4.

75. *Evening News*, 18 June 1891, p. 1.

76. Ibid., 24 June 1891, p. 1.

77. Ibid., 13 July 1891, p. 1; 16 July 1891, p. 5; see also ibid., 18 July 1891, p. 1. Wałajtys later became pastor to the Polish community in Parisville.

78. *Sunday News*, 19 July 1891, p. 2; Swastek, *St. Albertus Centennial*, p. 88.

79. Swastek, *St. Albertus Centennial*, pp. 99–100.

80. *Evening News*, 16 July 1891, p. 5.

81. Ibid., 16 June 1891, p. 1.

82. Ibid., 16 July 1891, p. 5.

83. Ibid., 20 July 1891, p. 5.

84. Ibid., 12 Aug. 1891, p. 5. In 1888 Gibbons had personally recommended his friend, Fr. John S. Foley, to lead the Detroit diocese over objections in the Propaganda (J. T. Ellis, *The Life of James Cardinal Gibbons Archbishop of Baltimore 1834–1921*, 2 vols. [Milwaukee, Wisc.: Bruce, 1952], 2:456–57).

85. *Evening News*, 5 Sept. 1891, p. 1.

86. Ibid., 28 Oct. 1891, p. 1.

87. *Sunday News*, 5 June 1892, p. 1.

88. On the ceremony, see *Detroit Free Press*, 6 June 1892, p. 5; *Detroit Tribune*, 6 June 1892, p. 5; *Evening News*, 6 June 1892, p. 4; *Michigan Catholic*, 9 June 1892, p. 4. *Niedziela* denounced the day's proceedings as a disgrace and a fraud (12 June 1892, pp. 492–93).

89. *Evening News*, 6 June 1892, p. 4; *Detroit Free Press*, 6 June 1892, p. 5.

90. *Evening News*, 6 June 1892, p. 4.

91. Ibid.
92. Ibid., 4 July 1892, p. 1.
93. Ibid., 23 Jan. 1893, p. 1.
94. Ibid., 24 Jan. 1893, p. 1.
95. *Detroit Tribune*, 25 Jan. 1893, p. 1.
96. *Evening News*, 26 Jan. 1893, p. 1.
97. Ibid., 28 Jan. 1893, p. 5; *Detroit Free Press*, 28 Jan. 1893; *Michigan Catholic*, 2 Feb. 1893, p. 1. Later it was disclosed that Kolasiński filed a brief stipulating his conditions for reinstatement with the apostolic delegate on 19 January 1893 (*Evening News*, 5 Jan. 1894, p. 4).
98. *Evening News*, 26 Jan. 1893, p. 5.
99. The *Sunday News*, 12 Feb. 1893, p. 15, carried an extensive account of Satolli's activities in America. See also Ellis, *Life of Cardinal Gibbons*, 2:626–28 et passim.
100. *Detroit Journal*, 8 Sept. 1893, p. 3.
101. *Evening News*, 2 Dec. 1893, p. 6.
102. Ibid., 30 Dec. 1893, p. 5; *Detroit Tribune*, 31 Dec. 1893, p. 5; see also *Evening News*, 10 Jan. 1894, p. 1.
103. *Evening News*, 16 Dec. 1893, p. 8.
104. Ibid. The text of the petition appeared ibid., 23 Dec. 1893, p. 6; see also ibid., 30 Dec. 1893, p. 5; *Detroit Tribune*, 31 Dec. 1893, p. 5.
105. *Evening News*, 19 Dec. 1893, p. 1; *Detroit Free Press*, 23 Dec. 1893, p. 5.
106. *Evening News*, 22 Dec. 1893, p. 1.
107. Ibid., 23 Dec. 1893, p. 1.
108. Ibid., pp. 1, 6. On Vilatte's career, see esp. C. B. Moss, *The Old Catholic Movement, Its Origin and History*, 2d ed. (New York: Morehouse-Barlow, 1964), pp. 291–92; *Michigan Catholic*, 28 Dec. 1893, p. 5. See also Skendzel, *Kolasinski Story*, p. 87n.
109. *Sunday News-Tribune*, 24 Dec. 1893, p. 1.
110. On the 24 December ceremonies at Sweetest Heart of Mary's Church, see *Evening News*, 25 Dec. 1893, pp. 1, 6; *Detroit Free Press*, 25 Dec. 1893, pp. 1, 2; *Detroit Tribune*, 25 Dec. 1893, pp. 1, 4; *Detroit Journal*, 25 Dec. 1893, p. 1; *Niedziela*, 31 Dec. 1893, pp. 847–48.
111. *Evening News*, 25 Dec. 1893, p. 1.
112. Ibid., p. 6; see also *Michigan Catholic*, 28 Dec. 1893, p. 5; *Evening News*, 26 Dec. 1893, p. 5, for the speculation surrounding Vilatte. See also Kruszka, *Historya polska w Ameryce*, 11:194–95.

CHAPTER FIVE

1. See esp. Thomas T. McAvoy, *The Americanist Heresy in Roman Catholicism, 1895–1900*, 2d ed. (Notre Dame, Ind.: University of Notre Dame Press, 1963). See also "The 'Americanism' Crisis in the Catholic Church," in Sydney E. Ahlstrom, *A Religious History of the American People* (New Haven, Conn.: Yale University Press, 1972), pp. 825–41.
2. *Evening News*, 30 Dec. 1893, p. 5; *Detroit Tribune*, 31 Dec. 1893, p. 5.
3. *Evening News*, 3 Jan. 1894, p. 2; *Michigan Catholic*, 4 Jan. 1894, p. 5; *Angelus*, 7 Jan. 1894, cited in Ostafin, "Polish Peasant in Transition," pp. 122–23.
4. *Evening News*, 5 Jan. 1894, pp. 1, 4.

5. Ibid., 10 Jan, 1894, p. 1.
6. Ibid., 8 Jan. 1894, p. 2.
7. Ibid., p. 8.
8. Ibid., 10 Jan. 1894, p. 6.
9. Ibid., p. 1.
10. Ibid., p. 6.
11. *Detroit Tribune*, 5 Feb. 1894, p. 5; *Evening News*, 5 Feb. 1894, p. 5; *Detroit Journal*, 5 Feb. 1894, p. 8.
12. See esp. *Detroit Journal*, 10 Feb. 1894, p. 1; *Michigan Catholic*, 15 Feb. 1894, p. 4.
13. *Detroit Free Press*, 7 Feb. 1894, p. 4; *Detroit Tribune*, 7 Feb. 1894, pp. 1, 2; *Detroit Journal*, 7 Feb. 1894, p. 5.
14. *Detroit Tribune*, 7 Feb. 1894, p. 2.
15. *Detroit Free Press*, 8 Feb. 1894, p. 8; *Detroit Tribune*, 8 Feb. 1894, p. 5; *Detroit Journal*, 8 Feb. 1894, p. 8.
16. *Evening News*, 9 Feb. 1894, p. 7; see also *Detroit Journal*, 10 Feb. 1894, p. 1.
17. *Evening News*, 10 Feb. 1894, p. 1.
18. Ibid.
19. *Detroit Free Press*, 11 Feb. 1894, p. 6; *Sunday News-Tribune*, 11 Feb. 1894, p. 1; *Evening News*, 12 Feb. 1894, p. 6.
20. *Sunday News-Tribune*, 11 Feb. 1894, p. 1; *Evening News*, 12 Feb. 1894, p. 6.
21. *Evening News*, 12 Feb. 1894, p. 6; *Detroit Free Press*, 12 Feb. 1894, p. 6.
22. *Detroit Tribune*, 13 Feb. 1894, p. 5.
23. Ibid.; see also *Detroit Journal*, 7 Feb. 1894, p. 5.
24. *Detroit Free Press*, 13 Feb. 1894, p. 5.
25. Quoted in *Evening News*, 17 Feb. 1894, p. 1. The *Michigan Catholic*, on the other hand, reminded its readers, "All Catholics are bound to receive [the decision to reinstate Kolasiński] and it will be injudicious on their part to criticise it" (15 Feb. 1894, p. 4). Cf. *Niedziela*, 18 Feb. 1894, p. 112.
26. *Evening News*, 17 Feb. 1894, p. 1; *Detroit Free Press*, 18 Feb. 1894, p. 5; see also Kruszka, *Historya polska w Ameryce*, 11:196–97. Cf. *Detroit Journal*, 17 Feb. 1894, p. 2, which refuted the claim that Kolasiński was now to be made an "immovable" pastor of Sweetest Heart of Mary's. The official English text of the conditions of Kolasiński's reinstatement was published in the *Detroit Free Press*, 19 Feb. 1894, p. 3; a Polish version was printed in *Niedziela*, 25 Feb. 1894, p. 128.
27. *Sunday News-Tribune*, 18 Feb. 1894, p. 5.
28. On the reconciliation and reinstatement ceremonies, see *Detroit Free Press*, 19 Feb. 1894, pp. 1, 3; *Detroit Tribune*, 19 Feb. 1894, pp. 1, 3; *Evening News*, 19 Feb. 1894, p. 5; *Detroit Journal*, 19 Feb. 1894, p. 5; see also Kruszka, *Historya polska w Ameryce*, 11:195–96.
29. *Evening News*, 19 Feb. 1894, p. 5.
30. *Detroit Tribune*, 19 Feb. 1894, pp. 1, 3. A slightly different English translation of Kolasiński's sermon appeared in the *Evening News*, 19 Feb. 1894, p. 5.
31. *Evening News*, 19 Feb. 1894, p. 5. The full English text of Kolasiński's retraction was also published in the *Detroit Free Press*, 19 Feb. 1894, p. 3; *Detroit Tribune*, 19 Feb. 1894, p. 3; *Detroit Journal*, 19 Feb. 1894, p. 5.

The Polish text was printed in *Niedziela*, 25 Feb. 1894, p. 115. The diocesan authorities also distributed printed copies of it during the ceremonies.

32. *Detroit Free Press*, 19 Feb. 1894, p. 3.
33. *Evening News*, 19 Feb. 1894, p. 5; *Detroit Journal*, 19 Feb. 1894, p. 5. Several months elapsed before Foley visited Sweetest Heart of Mary's, and then he did so only after ordering a three-week mission among the congregation by a Polish Jesuit, Fr. Franciszek Szulak (Skendzel, *Kolasinski Story*, pp. 18, 40n).
34. *Michigan Catholic*, 22 Feb. 1894, p. 4; see also *Evening News*, 23 Feb. 1894, p. 5.
35. *Sunday News*, 19 Oct. 1890, p. 9.
36. *Detroit Tribune*, 13 Apr. 1894, p. 1; see also *Detroit Free Press*, 12 Apr. 1894, p. 7.
37. *Detroit Tribune*, 14 Apr. 1894, p. 1.
38. Ibid., 16 Apr. 1894, p. 1; *Detroit Free Press*, 22 Apr. 1894, p. 8; *Detroit Journal*, 23 Apr. 1894, p. 4.
39. The controversy dragged on for a couple of months. See *Sunday News-Tribune*, 20 May 1894, p. 5; *Evening News*, 18 May 1894, p. 7; 25 May 1894, p. 2; 20 June 1894, p. 5. Additional land was purchased for the cemetery in 1902 and 1910. See *Pamiętnik Złotego Jubileuszu Parafji Najsłodszego Serca Marii w Detroit, Michigan, 1890–1940* [Golden jubilee album of Sweetest Heart of Mary's Parish in Detroit, Michigan, 1890–1940] (Detroit, 1940), p. 35.
40. *Evening News*, 22 Aug. 1894, p. 1; see also *Detroit Journal*, 22 Aug. 1894, p. 1.
41. Ellis, *Life of James Cardinal Gibbons*, 1:362–63. Cf. Joseph A. Wytrwal, *Behold! The Polish-Americans* (Detroit: Endurance Press, 1977), pp. 183–84, who adds, "Gibbons—who reigned in Baltimore like a Czar—was annoyed with any nationality or individual if it differed from his Irish view."
42. *Evening News*, 23 Aug. 1894, p. 1; *Detroit Journal*, 23 Aug. 1894, p. 1.
43. *Detroit Tribune*, 24 Aug. 1894, p. 1; *Evening News*, 24 Aug. 1894, p. 6; *Detroit Journal*, 24 Aug. 1894, p. 2. To reporters, however, Foley intimated that no attention would be paid to the matter.
44. *Evening News*, 25 Aug. 1894, p. 1.
45. Brożek, *Polonia amerykańska 1854–1939*, pp. 102–5; Swastek, "Formative Years of the Polish Seminary," pp. 121–23; Greene, *For God and Country*, pp. 110–12.
46. *Sunday News-Tribune*, 14 June 1896, p. 10.
47. *Detroit Free Press*, 5 Mar. 1897, p. 5.
48. *Evening News*, 1 Feb. 1897, p. 6; 2 Feb. 1897, p. 6; *Detroit Free Press*, 3 Feb. 1897, p. 5. Cf. L. Gozdawa, "Katastrofa na 'Sercowie' " [Catastrophe at Sweetest Heart of Mary], *Dziennik Polski*, 22 May 1951, p. 4.
49. *Evening News*, 4 Mar. 1897, p. 5; *Detroit Journal*, 4 Mar. 1897, p. 6; *Detroit Free Press*, 5 Mar. 1897, p. 5.
50. *Evening News*, 5 Mar. 1897, p. 5; *Detroit Journal*, 5 Mar. 1897, p. 6; *Detroit Free Press*, 6 Mar. 1897, p. 10.
51. *Sunday News-Tribune*, 28 Mar. 1897, p. 2; *Evening News*, 29 Mar. 1897, p. 5; 12 Apr. 1897, p. 6; *Detroit Journal*, 12 Apr. 1897, p. 1.
52. *Evening News*, 20 Apr. 1897, p. 1; *Detroit Tribune*, 21 Apr. 1897, p. 5.

53. *Detroit Free Press*, 26 Nov. 1897, p. 5; *Evening News*, 26 Nov. 1897, p. 1.
54. *Evening News*, 27 Nov. 1897, p. 6; *Sunday News-Tribune*, 28 Nov. 1897, p. 16.
55. *Evening News*, 13 Dec. 1897, p. 1.
56. *Detroit Free Press*, 3 Jan. 1898, p. 5.
57. *Evening News*, 4 Jan. 1898, pp. 1, 6; *Detroit Tribune*, 4 Jan. 1898, p. 5. Curiously, the *Detroit Journal*, (4 Jan. 1898, p. 4) and the *Detroit Free Press*, (4 Jan. 1898, p. 6) initially interpreted the meeting as a triumph by Kolasiński, apparently because his backers, though a minority, applauded so loudly.
58. *Evening News*, 4 Jan. 1898, pp. 1, 6.
59. *Evening News*, 5 Jan. 1898, p. 6; 10 Jan. 1898, p. 6; *Detroit Journal*, 5 Jan. 1898, p. 6; 6 Jan. 1898, p. 1; *Detroit Tribune*, 5 Jan. 1898, p. 8; 6 Jan. 1898, p. 8.
60. On Kolasiński's fatal illness, see Kruszka, *Historya polska w Ameryce*, 11:197; *Evening News*, 9 Apr. 1898, p. 1; *Detroit Free Press*, 10 Apr. 1898, p. 10; *Sunday News-Tribune*, 10 Apr. 1898, p. 4; and esp. *Evening News*, 11 Apr. 1898, p. 5; *Detroit Tribune*, 12 Apr. 1898, p. 5; *Niedziela*, 14 Apr. 1898, p. 240.
61. *Evening News*, 11 Apr. 1898, p. 5.
62. Ibid., 11 Apr. 1898, p. 5; 12 Apr. 1898, p. 8; 13 Apr. 1898, p. 4; *Detroit Free Press*, 12 Apr. 1898, p. 10; *Detroit Journal*, 12 Apr. 1898, p. 8; *Detroit Tribune*, 13 Apr. 1898, p. 8.
63. Skendzel, *Kolasinski Story*, p. 21.
64. *Evening News*, 13 Apr. 1898, p. 6. On the requiem mass and funeral service, see esp. *Detroit Tribune*, 13 Apr. 1898, p. 6; *Detroit Tribune*, 14 Apr. 1898, p. 5; *Detroit Free Press*, 14 Apr. 1898, p. 10; *Niedziela*, 21 Apr. 1898, p. 256.
65. *Evening News*, 19 Dec. 1898, p. 5; see also ibid, 19 Jan. 1899, p. 1, where it is suggested that some irregularity may have occurred in the transfer of the remains.
66. Ibid., 14 Apr. 1898, p. 5; *Detroit Free Press*, 15 Apr. 1898, p. 5; *Detroit Journal*, 15 Apr. 1898, p. 5; see also *Sunday News*, 25 June 1893, p. 2. Father Nikodem had been pastor of St. Adalbert's in Berea, Ohio, from July 1884 to March 1889 and then of St. Anthony's Parish in Toledo until June 1893. Subsequently he served as a missionary priest among the Poles of rural Wisconsin until his death in 1903 (Skendzel, *Kolasinski Story*, pp. 14, 16).
67. *Evening News*, 15 Apr. 1898, p. 5; *Detroit Tribune*, 16 Apr. 1898, p. 8; *Detroit Free Press*, 16 Apr. 1898, p. 1; *Detroit Journal*, 18 Apr. 1898, p. 3; see also *Evening News*, 11 Apr. 1898, p. 5; *Detroit Journal*, 12 Apr. 1898, p. 8.
68. *Sunday News-Tribune*, 15 May 1898, p. 17.
69. *Evening News*, 12 Apr. 1898, p. 2; see also the assessments of Kolasiński's character in the *Sunday News-Tribune*, 10 Apr. 1898, p. 4; *Evening News*, 11 Apr. 1898, p. 5; *Der Herold* (Detroit), 15 Apr. 1898, p. 1.
70. *Detroit Tribune*, 12 Apr. 1898, p. 2; *Detroit Journal*, 11 Apr. 1898, p. 4; *Michigan Catholic*, 14 Apr. 1898, p. 4.
71. Swastek, *St. Albertus Centennial*, pp. 74–75.
72. Ostafin, "Polish Peasant in Transition," pp. 99–100, 102; see also L.

Gozdawa, " 'Wojna Domowa'—'Kolachów' z 'Dąbrochami' " ['Civil War'—'Kolasińskiites' with 'Dąbrowskiites'], *Dziennik Polski*, 24 Apr. 1951, p. 4, who records the impressions of another contemporary witness, Katarzyna Samarzewska, to the effect that Kolasiński's denunciation of the Polish "saloon-keepers" led the latter to bring the trumped-up charges against him to Bishop Borgess.

73. Skendzel, *Kolasinski Story*, p. 104E.

CHAPTER SIX

1. Napolska, *Polish Immigrant in Detroit*, p. 19. Twenty years later, the thirteenth census showed that persons of "foreign stock" still comprised 74 percent of Detroit's population. For a statistical analysis of Detroit's Catholic population in 1889, see *Sunday News*, 5 June 1892, p. 6.
2. David M. Katzman, *Before the Ghetto: Black Detroit in the Nineteenth Century* (Urbana, Ill.: University of Illinois Press, 1973), pp. 55–56.
3. Ibid., pp. 57–58; J. Oliver Curwood, "An Ethnographical Study of Detroit," *Detroit News-Tribune*, 21 Aug. 1904, Home Supplement, p. 4; Phyllis K. Metzler, "The People of Detroit: 1889," *Detroit Historical Society Bulletin*, Jan. 1964, pp. 10–11.
4. *Detroit Free Press*, 1 May 1872, p. 1.
5. See esp. Kruszka, *Historya polska w Ameryce*, 11:169, 185. The *News* in 1883 had written of 20,000 Poles in the city; however, the *Detroit Tribune*, 6 Dec. 1885, p. 9, stated that there were 14,000. Metzler also suggests a somewhat lower figure ("People of Detroit: 1889," pp. 10–11).
6. Kruszka, *Historya polska w Ameryce*, 1:116. The Polish weekly *Niedziela*, 23 Aug. 1900, p. 544, indicated 40,000. This figure for 1900 is also given in Curwood, "Ethnographical Study of Detroit," p. 4. A Polish visitor in 1892, Emil Dunikowski, wrote of 35,000 Polish Detroiters (*Wśród Polonii w Ameryce* [Lwów: P. Starzyk, 1893], p. 54). See also Józef Swastek, "Statystyka Polonii Detroickiej" [Statistics of Detroit's Polonia], *Sodalis* 32, no. 6 (1951):22–25.
7. Curwood, "Ethnographical Study of Detroit," p. 4; *Evening News*, 4 May 1891, p. 1; *Sunday News-Tribune*, 6 Sept. 1896, pp. 13, 18; *Detroit Journal*, 4 Feb. 1897, p. 8.
8. *Evening News*, 20 May 1884, p. 2.
9. *Detroit Journal*, 4 Feb. 1897, p. 8.
10. Greusel, "Detroit's Polish Pioneers," pt. 4, p. 7. Recent studies based on the 1900 federal census data and extensive sampling indicate that 69 percent of Detroit's Poles occupied multifamily dwellings (Olivier Zunz, "Detroit's Ethnic Neighborhoods at the End of the Nineteenth Century," Working Paper No. 161, Center for Research on Social Organization, University of Michigan, rev. ed. [February 1978], pp. 46, 56). This tendency is explained partly by the economies multifamily dwellings afforded, partly by the large number of single Polish immigrants who boarded with Polish families, and finally by the need of young Polish couples to continue to live with one of their parents.
11. *Sunday News-Tribune*, 6 Sept. 1896, p. 13; Curwood, "Ethnographical

Study of Detroit," p. 4; see also Katzman, *Before the Ghetto*, pp. 58–59, 73–74.

12. *Evening News*, 10 July 1891, p. 2.
13. Napolska, *Polish Immigrant in Detroit*, p. 25.
14. Quoted in Greusel, "Detroit's Polish Pioneers," p. 7.
15. For example, "Pole vs. Pole," *Sunday News-Tribune*, 22 Apr. 1894, pp. 1, 4.
16. John H. Greusel, "Human Hives," *Sunday News-Tribune*, 6 Sept. 1896, pp. 13, 18. In 1900 the Poles had the highest incidence of marital fertility among the city's major ethnic groups, as well as the most inhabitants per single-family dwelling (5.95 persons). The population density of a sample area within the east-side Polish quarter was 72.3 persons per acre—likewise the highest figure for Detroit residential areas. See Zunz, "Detroit's Ethnic Neighborhoods," p. 46; and his "Organization of the American City in the Late Nineteenth Century: Ethnic Structure and Spatial Arrangement in Detroit," *Journal of Urban History* 3, no. 4 (August 1977):457–59.
17. Napolska, *Polish Immigrant in Detroit*, p. 83.
18. *Sunday News-Tribune*, 22 Apr. 1894, pp. 1, 4.
19. Melvin G. Holli, *Reform in Detroit: Hazen S. Pingree and Urban Politics* (New York: Oxford University Press, 1969), pp. 186–87. On the Bilski case, see *Detroit Journal*, 11 Dec. 1894, p. 5; 12 Dec. 1894, p. 5; *Detroit Tribune*, 26 Dec. 1894, p. 5. Within two weeks, three more members of Bilski's household became infected.
20. Napolska, *Polish Immigrant in Detroit*, pp. 34–35; *Detroit Free Press*, 15 Dec. 1874, p. 1; see also L. Rankin, "Detroit Nationality Groups," *Michigan History Magazine* 23 (1939):177.
21. *Evening News*, 29 Oct. 1888, p. 4.
22. On the employment and wages of the unskilled Polish immigrants, see esp. Napolska, *Polish Immigrant in Detroit*, pp. 34–39.
23. Ibid., pp. 36–37, 45–48; Rankin, "Detroit Nationality Groups," p. 177; L. Gozdawa, "Po 50 latach—800 polskich przedsiębiorstw w Detroit" [After 50 years—800 Polish enterprises in Detroit], *Dziennik Polski*, 3 July 1951, p. 4.
24. On these successful nineteenth-century Polish entrepreneurs, see esp. the articles by L. Gozdawa in *Dziennik Polski*, 26 May 1951, p. 4; 29 May 1951, p. 4; 31 May 1951, p. 4; 14 June 1951, p. 4; 19 June 1951, p. 4. The *Sunday News-Tribune*, 12 Sept. 1897, p. 10, listed eight "wealthy Poles" whose combined worth the paper estimated at a half-million dollars.
25. *Niedziela*, 27 Oct. 1898, p. 688; *Evening News*, 12 July 1899, p. 10. Cf. *Sunday News-Tribune*, 15 Aug. 1897, p. 13.
26. *Detroit Free Press*, 2 June 1874, p. 1. On the fines levied on the "Polish rioters," see *Detroit Free Press*, 9 June 1874, p. 1.
27. *Evening News*, 24 Aug. 1893, p. 1; 25 Aug. 1893, p. 1; 26 Aug. 1893, p. 1; *Detroit Journal*, 25 Aug. 1893, p. 1; *Detroit Tribune*, 26 Aug. 1893, p. 1.
28. *Evening News*, 22 Dec. 1891, p. 3.
29. *Detroit Tribune*, 7 Sept. 1893, p. 8.
30. *Evening News*, 9 Sept. 1893, p. 1; 12 Sept. 1893, p. 1; *Detroit Tribune*, 12 Sept. 1893, p. 5.
31. *Evening News*, 2 Dec. 1893, p. 1; *Detroit Tribune*, 2 Jan. 1894, p. 5; Holli, *Reform in Detroit*, pp. 61–64.

32. *Detroit Journal*, 22 Dec. 1893, p. 1; *Detroit Free Press*, 7 Jan. 1894, p. 5.
33. *Detroit Tribune*, 7 Sept. 1893, p. 8.
34. Holli, *Reform in Detroit*, pp. 65–66.
35. *Detroit Tribune*, 17 Apr. 1894, p. 1. No comprehensive account of the Connor's Creek clash exists; for a brief survey see Holli, *Reform in Detroit*, pp. 66–67.
36. *Detroit Tribune*, 18 Apr. 1894, p. 5.
37. *Evening News*, 18 Apr. 1894, pp. 1, 6; *Detroit Journal*, 18 Apr. 1894, p. 1; *Detroit Free Press*, 19 Apr. 1894, pp. 1–3; *Detroit Tribune*, 19 Apr. 1894, pp. 1–2, 5, which provided the first accounts of the bloody clashes on 18 April. Numerous additional reports on the riot appeared in these papers in the days immediately following, and in reports of the testimony at the hearings and examinations of those arrested in the aftermath of the fighting. See also *New York Times*, 19 Apr. 1894, p. 1; *Niedziela*, 22 Apr. 1894, p. 255.
38. *Detroit Free Press*, 19 Apr. 1894, pp. 1–3; *Michigan Catholic*, 26 Apr. 1894, p. 4.
39. *Detroit Journal*, 19 Apr. 1894, p. 4.
40. Ibid., p. 5.
41. See *Detroit Tribune*, 19 Apr. 1894, pp. 1, 5. A group of Czechs subsequently publicly challenged what they deemed Kwieciński's slanderous characterization of their nationality.
42. Ibid., 20 Apr. 1894, p. 1; *Evening News*, 19 Apr. 1894, p. 1.
43. *Detroit Tribune*, 19 Apr. 1894, p. 1; 20 Apr. 1894, pp. 1, 5; *Detroit Free Press*, 20 Apr. 1894, pp. 1–2; 21 Apr. 1894, pp. 1–2; *Evening News*, 19 Apr. 1894, pp. 1, 5; 20 Apr. 1894, p. 1; *Detroit Journal*, 19 Apr. 1894, p. 1.
44. *Evening News*, 20 Apr. 1894, p. 1; *Detroit Journal*, 20 Apr. 1894, p. 1; *Detroit Tribune*, 21 Apr. 1894, p. 1; *Detroit Free Press*, 21 Apr. 1894, p. 1.
45. *Detroit Journal*, 21 Apr. 1894, p. 1; *Evening News*, 21 Apr. 1894, p. 1.
46. *Detroit Free Press*, 21 Apr. 1894, p. 2.
47. *Detroit Tribune*, 23 Apr. 1894, p. 1.
48. *Evening News*, 21 Apr. 1894, p. 1.
49. E.g., *Detroit Free Press*, 19 Apr. 1894, p. 1; *Detroit Journal*, 19 Apr. 1894, p. 5; *Detroit Tribune*, 19 Apr. 1894, p. 1.
50. *Detroit Tribune*, 23 Apr. 1894, p. 5; see also *Detroit Journal*, 23 Apr. 1894, p. 5.
51. On the police preparation and the resumption of work at Connor's Creek on Monday, 23 April, see *Detroit Free Press*, 23 Apr. 1894, p. 1; 24 Apr. 1894, p. 1; *Evening News*, 23 Apr. 1894, p. 1; *Detroit Journal*, 23 Apr. 1894, p. 5; *Detroit Tribune*, 23 Apr. 1894, p. 1; 24 Apr. 1894, p. 1.
52. *Evening News*, 24 Apr. 1894, p. 5; 28 Apr. 1894, p. 5; *Detroit Journal*, 24 Apr. 1894, p. 8; *Detroit Tribune*, 24 Apr. 1894, p. 1.
53. *Evening News*, 4 May 1894, p. 8.
54. *Evening News*, 25 Apr. 1894, p. 2. Despite the Connor's Creek tragedy and public abuse of them, the Poles went ahead with plans to celebrate on Memorial Day the hundredth anniversary of the Polish victory led by Tadeusz Kościuszko at Racławice on 4 April 1794 against tsarist Russia (*Detroit Free Press*, 27 May 1894, p. 5).
55. *Strangers in the Land: Patterns of American Nativism, 1860–1925* (New York: Atheneum, 1963), p. 70. Cf. Thaddeus C. Radzialowski (with Donald Binkowski), "Polish Americans in Detroit Politics," in *Ethnic*

Politics in Urban America: The Polish Experience in Four Cities, ed. Angela T. Pienkos (Chicago: Polish American Historical Association, 1978), pp. 62–63, who argue, "The Poles have been the victims of a strong and specific anti-Polish prejudice on the part of Detroit's establishment from the beginnings of large scale migration to the city." "Anti-Polish feeling in Detroit," they maintain, "derives from both anti-working class feeling and ethnic prejudice."

56. *Evening News*, 5 May 1894, p. 6; *Sunday News-Tribune*, 6 May 1894, p. 5; *Evening News*, 12 May 1894, p. 1; 5 June 1894, p. 1.

57. *Evening News*, 18 May 1894, p. 7.

58. *Detroit Free Press*, 14 Apr. 1894, p. 5; see also Holli, *Reform in Detroit*, p. 67.

59. Napolska, *Polish Immigrant in Detroit*, pp. 39–40; see also Richard Oestreicher, "Changing Patterns of Class Relations in Detroit, 1880–1900," *Detroit in Perspective* 3, no. 3 (Spring 1979):145–65, who argues that before 1900 the city's "ethnic, cultural, and economic diversity . . . interfered with union organization, and limited the possibilities of common action." He also notes, "Labor disputes . . . often involved as much conflict between workers of different nationalities as between workers and employers."

60. *Niedziela*, 5 Nov. 1893, p. 720, cited in Napolska, *Polish Immigrant in Detroit*, p. 52.

61. Holli, *Reform in Detroit*, pp. 11–13, 18, 20–21, 127–28; *Evening News*, 23 July 1890, p. 1; 24 Sept. 1890, p. 2; see also Radzialowski, "Polish Americans in Detroit Politics," pp. 41–43.

62. *Evening News*, 17 Oct. 1890, p. 4; 24 Oct. 1890, p. 1; 5 Nov. 1890, p. 1.

63. Ibid., 19 Oct. 1892, p. 1.

64. *Detroit Tribune*, 3 July 1892, p. 5; *Evening News*, 4 July 1892, p. 1.

65. Holli, *Reform in Detroit*, p. 145; Radzialowski, "Polish Americans in Detroit Politics," p. 42.

66. *Detroit Tribune*, 3 Nov. 1895, p. 5, cited in Napolska, *Polish Immigrant in Detroit*, pp. 53–54.

67. "The Harvest," *Sunday News-Tribune*, 4 Oct. 1896, p. 13; see also Holli, *Reform in Detroit*, pp. 69–73, 145; *Detroit Free Press*, 6 Nov. 1895, p. 1.

68. *Detroit Free Press*, 30 Mar. 1897, p. 3; *Evening News*, 27 May 1897, p. 5; 28 Dec. 1897, pp. 1, 6; *Detroit Tribune*, 29 Dec. 1897, p. 1. Lemke was later elected city alderman during the Democratic administrations of mayors Maybury and Thompson in the first decade of the twentieth century (Gozdawa, "Bazyli Lemke," p. 4).

69. One Pole who obtained state office in the nineteenth century was Adolf Jasnowski, son of the Polish pioneer of the 1850s, Filip Jasnowski, who was elected to the Michigan legislature for one term from 1889–90 (Napolska, *Polish Immigrant in Detroit*, p. 59).

70. "A Polish Community in Transition: The Origins and Evolution of Holy Cross Parish, New Britain, Connecticut," *Polish American Studies* 34, no. 1 (1977):29–30.

71. *Evening News*, 2 July 1894, p. 6. For a rather charitable assessment of Chodniewicz's pastorate, see Swastek, *St. Albertus Centennial*, pp. 100–104. Kulwicki had been identified as a prominent St. Albertus's parishioner in a feature article on the church in the *Sunday News*, 28 July 1889, p. 13.

72. Swastek, *St. Albertus Centennial*, pp. 106–9.
73. Ibid., pp. 114–15; *Sunday News-Tribune*, 11 July 1897, p. 9.
74. For example, Foley officiated when the new bells were installed at St. Casimir's in November 1893 (*Detroit Free Press*, 19 Nov. 1893, p. 7; 20 Nov. 1893, p. 5).
75. Greusel, "Shepherds of the Polish Flock," pp. 5, 8; see also L. Gozdawa, "Początki parafii Św. Franciszka" [The beginnings of St. Francis's Parish], *Dziennik Polski*, 16 June 1951, p. 4; Gozdawa, "Trzy nowe parafie w pierwszym dziesięcioleciu XX wieku" [Three new parishes in the first decade of the twentieth century], ibid., 31 July 1951, p. 4.
76. Greusel, "Shepherds of the Polish Flock," pp. 5, 8; L. Gozdawa, "Budowa nowego kościoła na 'Jozefatowie' " [The construction of the new St. Josaphat's Church], *Dziennik Polski*, 12 June 1951, p. 4.
77. *Evening News*, 15 Apr. 1898, p. 5; see also *Detroit Tribune*, 16 Apr. 1898, p. 8.
78. *Evening News*, 17 July 1899, p. 8; see also Kruszka, *Historya polska w Ameryce*, 11:199–200.
79. *Evening News*, 23 July 1899, p. 5. One curious consequence of the Kolasiński years was that the deed to the property of Sweetest Heart of Mary's Church remained in the name of the parish corporation, even after the outstanding debt was retired, and was not signed over until 1960 to the incumbent archbishop, John Deardon, although the diocesan hierarchy had made repeated attempts to acquire title. What had begun as a makeshift arrangement when Kolasiński was reinstated gave Sweetest Heart of Mary's Parish a unique legal status among Catholic churches in America for over half a century (Ostafin, "Polish Peasant in Transition," p. 127; *Detroit News*, 3 Mar. 1960, p. 6B).
80. Swastek, *St. Albertus Centennial*, pp. 109–10; four articles by L. Gozdawa on the founding of St. Stanisław's in *Dziennik Polski*, 23 June 1951, p. 4; 26 June 1951, p. 4; 28 June 1951, p. 4; 30 June 1951, p. 4.
81. *Evening News*, 1 July 1890, p. 2. The Poles had, however, as in July 1887, reacted sharply to proselytizing among them by Protestant converts. Another such incident occurred in March 1897, when the Reverend John Lewis, a Congregationalist, was threatened and attacked physically by several irate Poles when he called upon a Polish woman who had been attending his church (*Detroit Journal*, 30 Mar. 1897, p. 1).
82. See esp. Swastek, "Formative Years of the Polish Seminary," pp. 93–125, passim; see also *Sunday News-Tribune*, 29 May 1898, p. 17.
83. Swastek, "Formative Years of the Polish Seminary," pp. 139–45; *Detroit Free Press*, 15 Feb. 1903, pp. 1–2.
84. Swastek, *St. Albertus Centennial*, p. 88; Joseph Swastek, "Father Dąbrowski Reconsidered," *Polish American Studies* 26, no. 1 (1969): 30–40.
85. On the beginnings of the Polish press in nineteenth-century Detroit, see Charles D. Cameron, "Detroit's Foreign-Language Press," *Detroit Saturday Night*, 6 Mar. 1926, sec. 2, p. 10; Napolska, *Polish Immigrant in Detroit*, pp. 78–82; James Tye, "Polish Press in Detroit," *Polish Daily News* (Eng. ed.), 17–18 Nov. 1979, p. 6. For specific information on the actual runs of most of these newspapers and their respective publishers and editors, see Jan Wepsiec, *Polish American Serial Publications 1842–*

1966: An Annotated Bibliography (Chicago: privately printed, 1968).

86. On Detroit's Polish newspapers of the 1880s, see esp. L. Gozdawa, "Dzieje gazety polskiej w Detroit od zamknięcia 'Gazety Polskiej Katolickiej' aż do 1891" [History of the Polish newspaper in Detroit from the folding of the *Polish National Gazette* to 1891], *Dziennik Polski*, 24 May 1951, p. 4. Other sources suggest that *Gwiazda Detroicka* survived for almost a decade.

87. Swastek, "Formative Years of the Polish Seminary," p. 101; L. Gozdawa, "Pierwsze trwałe czasopismo polskie w Detroit" [The first lasting Polish periodical], *Dziennik Polski*, 2 June 1951, p. 4.

88. L. Gozdawa, "Dr. Józef Iłowiecki," *Dziennik Polski*, 1 May 1951, p. 4.

89. L. Gozdawa, "Prasa polska w Detroit w ostatnim dziesięcioleciu ubiegłego wieku" [The Polish press in Detroit in the last decade of the nineteenth century], ibid., 9 June 1951, p. 4.

90. C. D. Cameron, "Sant'el Claus and Sankt Niklaus," *Detroit Saturday Night*, 18 Dec. 1926, sec. 2, pp. 2, 11; see also "Midnight Mass in Fr. Kolasinski's Church," *Evening News*, 25 Dec. 1897, p. 5; Eduard A. Skendzel, "Christmas [and] Pioneer Detroit Poles," *Polish Daily News* (Eng. ed.), 23–24 Dec. 1978, p. 8; 30–31 Dec. 1978, pp. 1, 6.

91. L. Gozdawa, "Pierwsza Grupa Związkowa w Detroit w roku 1885" [The first PNA group in Detroit in 1885], *Dziennik Polski*, 4 Aug. 1951, p. 4; Gozdawa, "Druga Gmina Związkowa w Detroit" [The second PNA commune], ibid., 14 Aug. 1951, p. 4; Gozdawa, "Jak powstała 'Gmina Detroicka' " [How was the "Detroit Commune" established?], ibid., 18 Aug. 1951, p. 4; John H. Greusel, "Polish National Alliance in Detroit and Michigan," *Detroit Free Press*, 10 June 1906, pt. 3, p. 9; see also Napolska, *Polish Immigrant in Detroit*, p. 78.

92. L. Gozdawa, "Sokoli Polscy w Detroit" [Polish Falcons in Detroit], *Dziennik Polski*, 23 Aug. 1951, p. 4; "Związek Polek w Detroit . . ." [The Polish Women's Alliance in Detroit], ibid., 30 Aug. 1951, p. 4.

93. *Detroit Free Press*, 2 May 1877; Swastek, *St. Albertus Centennial*, pp. 113–14.

94. *Detroit Free Press*, 7 Oct. 1887, p. 5; *Detroit Journal*, 26 Oct. 1901, p. 8; *Sunday News-Tribune*, 6 Sept. 1896, pp. 13, 18; Napolska, *Polish Immigrant in Detroit*, p. 76; Gozdawa, "Piotr Leszczyński," p. 4.

95. Cited in Swastek, *St. Albertus Centennial*, p. 123.

96. Blejwas, "Polish Community in Transition," pp. 26–27.

97. See esp. Stanley Mackun, "The Changing Patterns of Polish Settlements in the Greater Detroit Area: Geographic Study of the Assimilation of an Ethnic Group" (Ph.D. diss., University of Michigan, 1964).

BIBLIOGRAPHIC ESSAY

The richest and most valuable, though not always the most consistently reliable, primary source for the study of Polish Detroit in the late nineteenth century is the city's contemporary press. Detroit's four major English-language dailies copiously reported the stages of the Kolasiński Affair and developments in the Polish community, though the most assiduous coverage is in the *Evening* and *Sunday News*. The inaccuracies or distortions that may have crept into some of the more than one thousand articles published on Kolasiński and Polish Detroiters in the 1880s and 1890s are, I hope, offset by comparing reports of specific occurrences in two or more different newspapers. Complete runs for this period of the *Free Press*, *News*, *Tribune*, and *Journal* are preserved on microfilm, as is the weekly *Michigan Catholic*, which commented frequently and usually caustically on events in the city's Polish quarter. Unfortunately, the most complete surviving run of the city's principal German-language daily, *Detroiter Abend-Post*, was not available for examination while this study was being prepared. The twice-weekly German *Michigan Volksblatt* featured little local news.

Of the several Polish papers published in nineteenth-century Detroit, only the weekly of the Polish seminary, *Niedziela* [Sunday], is extensively preserved in public repositories. The Archives of the Orchard Lake Schools have complete runs for the years 1891–94 and 1898–1903. The Burton Historical Collection of the Detroit Public Library possesses single copies of *Gazeta Narodowa* [National gazette] (30 Oct. 1884) and *Swoboda* [Liberty] (29 Oct. 1897). Scattered issues of *Pielgrzym Polski* [The Polish pilgrim] for 1885 and 1886 are in Kraków's Jagiellonian Library.

The first book to be devoted specifically to the history of Detroit's Polish community was published by Wincenty Smołczyński in 1907 (*Historya osady i parafii polskich w Detroit, Mich. oraz przewodnik adresowy* [History of Polish settlement and parishes and a guide to addresses] [Detroit, privately printed]). Like most local histories of its day, Smołczyński's work was largely a compendium of biographical vignettes of prominent citizens. At the time Smołczyński's work appeared, Fr. Wacław Kruszka was completing his

221

massive thirteen-volume history of Polish settlements in the United States (*Historya polska w Ameryce* [Polish history in America] [Milwaukee, Wisc.: Spółka Wydawnicza Kuryer, 1905–8]). Sections of his volume 11 succinctly describe the early Polish pioneers in Detroit and the establishment and history of the first Polish parishes in the city. In June 1906 John H. Greusel, a prominent Detroit journalist and avid observer of the city's ethnic communities, published a series of four retrospective articles on Polish Detroit in the *Free Press*.

Thirty years after Smolczyński's history appeared, F. W. Dziób, on the occasion of what he believed was the centennial of the arrival of Andrzej Kamiński, the first known Polish settler in Detroit, published a popular history of Detroit and its Polish community (*Sto lat historji polskiej w Detroit 1837–1937* [One hundred years of Polish history in Detroit 1837–1937] [Detroit: Polish Centennial Publications, 1937]). The first attempt in English to chronicle the history of Polish settlement in Detroit was by Sister Mary Remigia Napolska, *The Polish Immigrant in Detroit to 1914*, Annals of the Polish R.C. Union Archives and Museum, vol. 10 (Chicago: Polish Roman Catholic Union of America, 1946). Particularly useful are its sections on the Polish pioneers prior to 1860, the economic conditions of the newly arrived immigrants, and the religious, cultural, and fraternal organizations they founded in Detroit. Father Kolasiński and the Polish church troubles, however, are essentially passed over in Napolska's study. The tendency among these early historians of Polish Detroit, with the exception of Kruszka, was to minimize treatment of the controversial priest from Galicia and the church strife, which they viewed as embarrassing for Polish Detroiters. An example of this attitude toward Kolasiński is found in the third volume of the official history of the Felician Sisters, which contains a brief but scathing indictment of the "godless" Kolasiński (*Historja Zgromadzenia SS. Felicjanek na podstawie rękopisów* [History of the order of Felician Sisters based on manuscripts], vol. 3 [Kraków: Nakładem Zgromadzenia SS. Felicjanek, 1932]). In 1942 Fr. A. Syski published a semiofficial biography of Father Dąbrowski under the auspices of the Polish seminary to commemorate the centenary of the birth of the seminary's founder. Here too the church controversies of the 1880s are treated only marginally (*Ks. Józef Dąbrowski 1842–1942* [Orchard Lake, Mich.: Nakład i własność Seminarium Polskiego, 1942]).

Kolasiński and the church strife were largely sidestepped in the series of seventy brief articles by Ludwik Gozdawa that appeared under the general title of "Historia Polonii Detroickiej" [History of Detroit Polonia] in the Polish-language daily *Dziennik Polski* [Polish daily news] between 3 March and 30 August 1951, in conjunction with the 250th anniversary of the founding of Detroit. Gozdawa's articles, though occasionally factually inaccurate, nevertheless contain particularly valuable sections on the business enterprises and fraternal institutions established by Polish Detroiters before World War I.

At approximately the same time that Gozdawa's "History of Detroit Polonia" was being serialized, a Polish émigré, Stefan Włoszczewski, initiated publishing projects in Polish and later in English with the aim of providing a detailed survey of the evolution of Polish Detroit. Only a fragmentary beginning was made, however, and both projects soon ended (*Historja polska w Detroit*, pt. 1, *Do roku 1850* [Polish history in Detroit, pt. 1, To 1850] [Detroit: Nakładem Wiedzy o Polonii Amerykańskiej, 1951]; and *Poles in*

Michigan, vol. 1 [all published] [Detroit: The Poles in Michigan Associated, 1953 (1955)]). Two recent essays by Thaddeus C. Radzialowski on Detroit's Polish politics, though having scattered references to the Kolasiński years, deal essentially with twentieth-century developments: "The View from a Polish Ghetto: Some Observations on the First 100 Years in Detroit," *Ethnicity* 1, no. 2 (1974): 125–50; and "Polish Americans in Detroit Politics" (with Donald Binkowski), in *Ethnic Politics in Urban America: The Polish Experience in Four Cities,* ed. Angela T. Pienkos (Chicago: Polish American Historical Association, 1978), pp. 40–65.

In 1951 Fr. George Paré's *History of the Catholic Church in Detroit 1701–1888* (Detroit: Gabriel Richard Press) appeared. A two-page discussion of the beginnings of the Kolasiński Affair is included, but, since the work ends with the resignation of Bishop Borgess, the denouement of the church troubles is not mentioned.

Unquestionably the most scholarly treatment of the religious institutions of nineteenth-century Polish Detroit has been the work of the late Fr. Joseph Swastek. In 1959 his lengthy article, "The Formative Years of the Polish Seminary in the United States," covering the seminary's history before its move to Orchard Lake in 1909, appeared in volume 6 of *Sacrum Poloniae Millennium,* published in Rome (pp. 39–150). In 1974, Swastek wrote a comprehensive history of Detroit's first Polish parish for its centennial commemorative album (*Detroit's Oldest Polish Parish: St. Albertus 1872–1973 Centennial* [Detroit: n.p., (1974)]). Swastek's exacting, detailed, and lively account deals at some length with Kolasiński's troubled pastorate. He depicts Kolasiński as a "flawed" pastor who, notwithstanding his building of two magnificent churches, hindered the social adjustment of Polish immigrants in Detroit and brought disrepute on the community through his defiance of episcopal authority and his disruptive actions. In every way, however, Swastek's account of these years contrasts favorably with the meager historical information contained in several earlier parish jubilee books of Detroit's nineteenth-century Polish churches: St. Albertus's (fiftieth anniversary [1932]); St. Josaphat's (fiftieth anniversary [1939]); Sweetest Heart of Mary's (fiftieth anniversary [1940], and seventy-fifth anniversary [1965]); St. Casimir's (fiftieth anniversary [1932]); and St. Stanisław's (twenty-fifth anniversary [1923], and fiftieth anniversary [1948]).

Two unpublished dissertations have made useful contributions to the understanding of Polish Detroit in the nineteenth century: Stanley Mackun, "The Changing Patterns of Polish Settlements in the Greater Detroit Area: Geographical Study of the Assimilation of an Ethnic Group" (Ph.D. diss., University of Michigan, 1964); and Peter A. Ostafin, "The Polish Peasant in Transition: A Study of Group Integration as a Function of Symbiosis and Common Definitions" (Ph.D. diss., University of Michigan, 1949).

Most recently, interest in Kolasiński's career has been fostered by Eduard Adam Skendzel, whose several volumes of indexes to and photoduplicated copies of contemporary nineteenth-century newspaper articles on the controversial priest and his activities in Detroit have been deposited in the Burton Historical Collection. Although many of the reproductions are no longer legible and the articles he assembled provide only a partial record of the Kolasiński Affair, drawn especially from the *Evening News,* the volumes offer a convenient means by which interested persons can sample the contemporary public opinion of Kolasiński. In 1979 Skendzel published a chronological outline of the Kolasiński years, to which he added several documents illustrative of the controversy (*The Kolasinski Story* [Grand Rapids, Mich.: Littleshield Press]). His work is especially useful in unraveling the priest's troubled career in Poland and in tracing references to Kolasiński in nineteenth-century Polish-American newspapers published outside Detroit. Appended to the study are English translations of Kolasiński's two letters in 1883 and 1884 to the Kraków monthly *Missye Katolickie* [Catholic missions], and a letter of 15 January 1886 that the priest addressed to Archbishop Elder of Cincinnati. Skendzel also notes the basic impediment to lay scholars interested in probing fully Kolasiński's Detroit years—the unwillingness of the Detroit Archdiocesan Archives to open its files, should any still exist, on the controversial priest.

A journalist for the *Hamtramck Citizen*, Lawrence Chominski, relying largely on the English-language newspaper accounts, wrote a series of articles on aspects of the Kolasiński era and the history of Polish Detroit for that newspaper, beginning in January 1975. Two other amateur historians of Polish Detroit have made important contributions. A copy in typescript (1975) of James J. Tye's bibliography, "The Detroit Poles, a Comprehensive Bibliography and Compendium," is in the Burton Historical Collection. Allan R. Treppa has investigated facets of early Detroit Polonia, including the career of Andrzej Kamiński, and he recently published an article on Fr. John A. Lemke, the first American-born Polish Detroiter to be ordained in the Catholic priesthood. Treppa's article is available in *Polish American Studies* 35 (1978):78–83.

Unfortunately, the standard histories of Detroit by Clarence M. Burton, Silas Farmer, George B. Catlin, and George W. Stark, as well as more recent syntheses by Sidney Glazer, Robert Conot, Frank B. and Arthur M. Woodford and Don Lochbiler have paid scant attention to the early decades of Polish settlement in Detroit. Two excellent monographs, however, on aspects of late nineteenth-century Detroit by younger scholars have included passages on the city's Polish community. Melvin G. Holli's *Reform in Detroit: Hazen S. Pingree and Urban Politics* (New York: Oxford University Press, 1969) describes the efforts of Detroit politicians in the 1890s to cultivate the Polish vote and assesses briefly the impact of the 1893 depression on Polish laborers. David M. Katzman's *Before the Ghetto: Black Detroit in the Nineteenth Century* (Urbana, Ill.: University of Illinois Press, 1973) discusses the interaction of Detroit's Poles with the other ethnic groups in the city's near east side. Mention should also be made of the recent studies of Olivier Zunz, a French social scientist, which compare Detroit's ethnic communities in the late nineteenth century: "The Organization of the American City in the Late Nineteenth Century: Ethnic Structure and Spacial Arrangement in Detroit," *Journal of Urban History* 3 (August 1977):443–66; and "Detroit's Ethnic Neighborhoods at the End of the Nineteenth Century," Working Paper, No. 161, Center for Research on Social Organization, University of Michigan, rev. ed., February 1978. Richard Oestreicher has examined class consciousness in Detroit in the same period in his essay "Changing Patterns of Class Relations in Detroit, 1880–1900," *Detroit in Perspective* 3 (Spring 1979):145–65.

INDEX

American Car and Foundry Company, 27, 171
Angelus, 129, 139
Antoszewski, Rev. Józef, 206
Apostól, 191
Arbeiter Hall, 179
Assimilation of Polish immigrants in Detroit, 169–70
Atkinson, Col. John, 61, 203
Austrian Poland, immigrants from, 16, 27, 49–50, 55, 157, 168–69, 172, 187

Baart, Rev. Peter A., 128–30, 157
Bakanowski, Rev. Adolf, 19
Baker, Hibbard, 182–83
Balicki, Frank, 158
Barabasz, Rev. M., 68
Barański, Rev. Hipolit, 65, 69
Barszcz, Rev. Ignacy, 127, 146–47
Barzyński, Jan, 21
Bell, May, 83
Bilski, Józef, 170, 216
Blejwas, Stanislaus, 185
Bloom, Adam, 147–50
Bołda, Józef, 210
Borgess, Bishop Caspar H., 31–35, 74, 98, 129; attempts to reopen St. Albertus's, 64, 69–70; attitude of, toward Poles, 60, 124, 206; complicity of, in Christmas 1885 "Polish riot," 51, 53–54; and establishment of St. Albertus's, 17–26, 36; excommunicates Kolasińskiites, 65, 72–75; grants Kolasiński an exeat, 61–63, 132; and Polish seminary, 33, 65–66; resigns as bishop of Detroit, 72–74; secures Kolasiński's ejection from St. Albertus's rectory, 58–60; suspends Kolasiński as pastor of St. Albertus's, 36–42, 46, 48–49, 54, 56–58, 106
Bornman (deputy sheriff), 175, 177–78
Bronikowski, Rev. Wincenty, 65, 69; pastor of St. Albertus's, 71–72, 74–75, 77–79, 94, 97–98, 208
Buhaczkowski, Rev. Witold, 68, 140, 143, 190
Byzewski, Rev. Romuald, 113, 153–54, 187–88

Cameron, Charles D., 192
Cathey, George, 176, 178
Catholic Mutual Benefit Association Weekly, 128
Catholics in America: "Americanizing" tendencies among, 122, 158; apostolic delegation to, 122–23; Third Plenary Council of, 33, 128, 147
Central Labor Union, 179–80
Chipman, J. L., 183
Chodniewicz, Rev. Florian, 114, 186

225

Lawrence D. Orton is associate professor of history at Oakland University, Rochester, Michigan. He holds degrees from Stanford University (B.A., 1963; M.A., 1965) and Indiana University (Ph.D., 1971), and has also studied at the Free University of Berlin, Warsaw University, and Charles University, Prague. He has received International Research and Exchanges Board fellowships to Czechoslovakia and Poland, as well as a Fulbright fellowship to Poland and a senior research fellowship to the Institute on East Central Europe at Columbia University. In addition to this volume and several articles on various aspects of nineteenth-century Slavic history, Professor Orton is the author of *The Prague Slav Congress of 1848* (1978) and, with Robert C. Howes, has translated and annotated *The "Confession" of Mikhail Bakunin* (1977).

The manuscript was edited by Sherwyn T. Carr. The book was designed by Mary Primeau. The typeface for the text is Baskerville. The display face is University Roman.

The text is printed on 60 lb. International Paper Company's Book Mark text paper. The book is bound in Holliston Mills' Kingston Natural Finish Cloth over binder's boards. Manufactured in the United States of America.